Harriss

LONDON MARKETS

Cadogan Books plc
27-29 Berwick Street,
London W1V 3RF
e-mail: guides@cadogan.demon.co.uk

Distributed in the USA by
The Globe Pequot Press
6 Business Park Road,
PO Box 833, Old Saybrook,
Connecticut 06475–0833

Book and cover design by Animage

Maps reproduced by permission of Geographers' A-Z Map Co Ltd., based upon the Ordnance Survey maps with the permission of the Controller of Her Majesty's Stationery Office and drawn by Map Creation Ltd.

Reprinted 1997, 1998

Series Editor: Rachel Fielding
Editor: Dominique Shead
Copyediting: Chris Schiller
Proofreading: Fiona Clarkson Webb
Production: Book Production Services

Printed and bound in the UK by Redwood Books

ISBN 1 86011 040 1

A catalogue record for this book is available from the British Library

About the author

Phil Harriss was born in 1961, studied History at Birmingham University and first became addicted to street markets after a jostle down Dalston's Ridley Road. He has since mooched around markets in Asia, South America and Europe, and written about them for various publications including the *Independent* and *Time Out*. He reviews restaurants for the *Time Out Eating & Drinking Guide*, specializing in Indian and Chinese cuisines and Londoners' own delicacy, pie and mash. In the 1992 General Election he stood as an independent, calling for the protection of street trading and small enterprises against business, and attracting 148 votes. His ambition is to sell homemade soup on a street market.

Acknowledgements

Several have helped greatly in the preparation of this book. Special thanks go to the librarians and market officers of London's councils, most of whom gave information freely and promptly, as did staff at the Guildhall Library. Professor Neville Brown of Mansfield College Oxford suggested and supplied some useful articles, while my friend and fellow market moocher Ray Winch was invaluable in helping me mull over the work. Derek Cooper and BBC Radio 4's *Food Programme* provided inspiration via the air waves. Dominique Shead organized the project admirably and with patience, while Chris Schüler's desk-editing skills, coupled with his knowledge of London, immeasurably improved the book, as did Fiona Clarkson Webb of Cadogan. Thanks, too, to Rachel Fielding and Vicki Ingle, who gave me the commission and the freedom to express my views. I owe a great debt to my family, especially my mother and elder sister who had to endure many tales of woe on the telephone, and my father, without whose help I would be computerless. Above all, thanks to Ros Ballaster, whose support for this book, me and my addiction to street markets has been unstinting. I can almost forgive her shopping at Sainsbury's.

Please help us keep this guide up to date

We have done our best to ensure that the information in this guide is correct at the time of going to press. But markets and their environs are constantly changing: stalls come and go; standards and prices fluctuate; parking regulations change. We would be delighted to receive any comments concerning existing entries or omissions, as well as suggestions for new features. Significant contributions will be acknowledged in the next edition and authors of the best letters will receive a copy of the Cadogan Guide of their choice.

Markets are the essence of London, mirroring its best points: cosmopolitan, unpredictable, worldly wise, exciting. Through the two millennia of its existence, this great metropolis has been sculpted by trade. From the Docklands in the east, where the booty of empire was landed, to Heathrow in the west, where much modern-day cargo comes to ground, mercantile considerations have shaped the landscape. Even in the City, where high-tech finance and glassy new office blocks now hold sway, the streets bear witness to the spontaneity of medieval trading.

Introduction

No town planner could have dreamt up such higgledy-piggledy thoroughfares as Milk Street, Pudding Lane and Fish Street Hill.

There's a wealth of stories to be found around the capital's markets. Ask any old Londoners from a street-trading district about their past, and chances are the lines of barrows will figure large in their memories. Take Morrie, for instance, who remembers the prewar mayhem of the Caledonian market and, as a boy, being given a shilling to sprint and bag the best pitch for an old trader; or the two elderly women who sparkled like teenagers when reminiscing about a Saturday night on the razzle at the New Cut of the 1930s. And when, 50 years after VE day, costers put up a bit of bunting and had a knees-up, even the most ardent anti-jingoist couldn't blame them—there are still traders who remember clearing up the rubble during the Blitz to keep their markets going.

At the funeral of Bill Gallagher, a trader on Deptford market, the funeral procession passed along the street and stopped for a minute's silence in front of his old pitch. Apart from time spent serving in the Second World War, Mr Gallagher had run his stall from 1924 until his death, aged 84, in 1994. The *South London Press* remarked that 'He was a familiar sight to shoppers always wearing his brown trilby and smoking a cigar.'

George Jeffrey died just before Christmas 1994. With him the Farringdon Road book market ended, after 125 years. Mr Jeffrey had traded on this busy road for most of his life. His kindliness and patience were noted in a previous guide to London markets, published in 1936.

To George Jeffrey's and Bill Gallagher's memory, and to all independent traders who work on London's streets come rain, come shine, come snow, this book is dedicated.

Using This Book

Don't expect the 62 markets listed to be exactly as I describe them when you visit. The accounts should be seen as snapshots in the lives of constantly evolving organisms. I tried to visit all the markets listed when they were in full swing—usually on a Friday or Saturday. But from week to week markets change: that is part of their appeal. A few general rules can be made, however. January and February are the leanest months, when markets tend to finish early, and fewer stallholders turn up. Some private markets aren't even held at this time of year—if in doubt, phone the market organizers to check. Throughout the year, heavy rain has a similar effect.

Opening hours

Opening hours also vary. If you ask the council when the market is open, you'll get one answer; if you visit the market at different times in the week you'll get another. I've tried to give the times when traders are behind their stalls, but this varies through the year and depends on weather. If in doubt, don't go too late. There's nothing more dispiriting than arriving at a market when the stallholders have left and the rubbish is being cleared up. It's like being too late for a party.

Car parking

For every market, I have given details of nearby places to park. However, as any Londoner will know, it is often madness to look for a parking space in certain areas of the city. The two most difficult and expensive districts are the City and the West End. And any market in the area run by Westminster Council (including Church Street, Bell Street, Tachbrook Street, Berwick Street, Grays Antique Market and Strutton Ground) is best reached by public transport to avoid the notoriously rapacious car clampers.

Main wares/specifics

Under the heading 'main wares' I have listed the types of goods that are likely to be found at the market. 'Specifics' is a more subjective category, implying a recommendation. I have included commodities that seem particularly well-priced, unusual, of a high quality, or present in great variety. As food is my passion, there is an unashamed bias towards food stalls in this book.

Nearby cafés, pubs and shops

For every market, I have listed a few nearby places that serve inexpensive food, tea and coffee. As I have spent many years reviewing London's Indian, Chinese and pie and mash restaurants, these are likely to be over-represented. Fortunately, London is the best place in Europe for both Indian and Chinese cuisine, and in the case of pie and mash I make no apology; it is as much part of the market scene in east and southeast London as the traditional barrows. To absorb the full flavour of markets in these districts, a visit to a pie and mash shop is imperative. Very likely, you'll share a wooden bench with a costermonger wolfing down a plateful of mashed potato, minced beef pie, liquor (parsley sauce) and stewed eels.

The true companion of the street market is the small, independent shop. Despite occasional spats over the years, most street traders and small-shop owners now realize they have a symbiotic relationship, both helping to attract custom to an area. So it's no coincidence that some of London's best small shops operate in the same neighbourhood, often the same street, as a market. I've tried to list the pick of them.

How Markets Work

Wholesalers

Most fresh food traders on London's markets still buy their produce from the city's wholesale markets. Good fishmongers will travel to **Billingsgate** five days a week, from Tuesday to Saturday (don't buy fish on a Monday); butchers get their supplies from **Smithfield**. Fruit and vegetable costermongers have a choice of **Spitalfields** market in the east, **New Covent Garden** and **Borough** markets in the south, and the **Western International** market, near Heathrow in the west.

Antiques traders have a number of sources for their wares. **Bermondsey** (*see* p.146) is the most popular market, but there are also auctions around the city where goods from house clearances come under the hammer. **Academy Auctioneers** (Northcote House, Northcote Avenue, W5, © (0181) 579 7466), **Criterion Salerooms** (53 Essex Road, N1, © (0171) 359 5707), and **Moore's Auction Rooms** (217–219 Greenwich High Road, SE10, © (0181) 858 7848) all attract bidders from the trade. Antiquarian book traders tend to visit the **Bloomsbury Book Auctions**, held every other Thursday (3–4 Hardwick Street, WC1, © (0171) 833 2636).

Unfortunately, most clothes traders on London's markets seem to get their stock from a limited number of East End wholesalers who sell a near-identical range of low-cost women's wear, jeans and undergarments. However, the success of Camden market has led to more traders selling handmade garments from around the world; a few even bring their own designs to market. I have described the goods on sale on the stalls during my visits, but there are, of course, seasonal changes: summer frocks and short-sleeved shirts make way for jumpers, gloves and scarves in winter.

Renting a pitch

Most of the traditional street markets are still run by local councils; the rest are owned by private operators. They charge each trader a rent for the pitch. As this money often has to pay for street cleaning, rubbish disposal and health inspection, the small patches of land don't come cheap. A pitch at Berwick Street costs nearly £60 a week, while crafts and antiques markets in tourist areas charge upwards of £30 a day.

Rental of stalls/barrows

Many clothes traders now buy their own collapsible stalls, and can be seen erecting the metal-framed constructions first thing in the morning. But there are still costermongers who rent the traditional wooden barrows, just as they did in Victorian street markets. However, wheelwright firms, who rent out barrows and repair them, are a dying breed. There are only three small companies left: Tappy's of Lambeth, Hillier's of Bethnal Green, and Sullivan's of King's Cross. Tappy's charges £6 a week for a barrow. The firm has been trading since 1900, but these days few new barrows are made. As the current Mr Tappy told me, 'Markets aren't very good at the moment. Sunday trading, private markets and supermarkets are killing off the retail trade… If you're thinking of buying a barrow business, come and see me—you can buy mine.'

Movement of traders

At some markets such as Berwick Street, the operators expect traders to turn up every day the market is held; sub-letting of pitches is forbidden. But elsewhere, you might find stallholders popping up at different markets on different days of the week. Traders at Whitecross Street or Leather Lane during the week might appear at Chapel Market or Church Street on a Saturday and Brick Lane on a Sunday. The practice is particularly common with antiques traders. If you've been to Bermondsey market (*see* p.146) on a Friday, you're likely to see many familiar faces at Portobello Road (*see* p.64) on the Saturday.

Tips for cheap goods

Haggling is not common on London's street markets. If a costermonger tells you a pound of apples costs 30p and you offer 25p, some fruity language can be expected. But for certain goods, the practice of 'making an offer' has become widespread since the recession. Traders at antiques markets are often willing to drop their prices, so the usual rules of haggling apply: don't show too much desire to buy; pretend you're streetwise; hide any signs of wealth. Clothes and household goods sellers are more likely to let you have something off the cost if you buy several items from them.

Food traders are a different kettle of fish. Visit a fruit and vegetable market, or meat stall at 'knocking out' time (last thing in the evening, especially on Saturdays) and you'll be assailed by bargains. If you come from a large household, the savings can be enormous. The trick is to stroll along the full length of the market, to find the stalls with the best prices. Hold back until the last moment if you see the trader has a large surplus to shift. During the course of compiling this book, I have come away from London markets with 20 avocados for £1, a box of broccoli (about 30 stalks) for £1 and three pounds of mushrooms for £1. True, these goods needed to be used fairly rapidly (and I still have a gallon of broccoli soup in the freezer), but the prices beat the pants off those you'd find in a supermarket.

Some of the most memorable bargains can be found on the cheap packaged food stalls. Often their supplies come from bankrupt stock, and once in a while it is a luxury food store that has gone bust. On such occasions, you might find a trader selling tins of fancy French food for the same price as a can of beans, and the beans proving more popular among the market regulars. I still remember with relish the time I came across Roquefort being sold as Danish Blue for £1.50 per pound.

Warnings

You need to keep your wits about you when shopping at a London market. Pick-pockets can occasionally be a problem at places that attract large numbers of tourists (Camden, Petticoat Lane, Portobello), and are most likely to be active when a crowd's attention is diverted by, say, a street entertainer. And although, in my experience, traders are no more likely to short-change customers than are shop-keepers or bar staff, the practice of displaying the best fruit or vegetables while serving from an over-ripe batch is not unknown.

At several of the packaged food stalls, you're likely to encounter food that has passed its sell-by date. Again, few traders try to hide this fact from their regulars. The product costs half the shop price and, it could be argued, the markets are cutting the excessive waste of society by selling such commodities. It's worth checking sell-by dates and weighing the pros and cons before buying. I've always found this food perfectly acceptable—apart from a single unfortunate episode with some elderly cheese.

But most of the warnings you hear about buying goods on the street are merely the squealings of large companies feeling their profits being pinched. Markets are con-spiratorial places where the customers are enticed to join in the scam: 'Let's get one over on big business and the authorities,' is the gist of many street cries.

Thus if you see designer clothing or sunglasses being sold at less than a quarter of the shop price, the chances are they're fakes. Most customers are wise enough to know this, and buy them to fool those (sad) people to whom such things as designer labels are important. True these goods might sometimes be shoddily made and not last long, but as built-in obsolescence is the essence of the fashion industry, the street traders provide a means of cocking a snook at the big fashion houses.

Likewise, the video of a film that's still showing in Leicester Square will be a bootleg, and the quality might be less than perfect. But at half the retail price for a film that won't be out on video for six months, many people aren't disappointed. Yes, the practice infringes copyright laws, and the film company will be losing money (hence the ludicrous advertising campaigns which imply that every bootleg Disney film has been badly recorded over a video nasty), but many market punters aren't unduly worried. And few complain about the sale of bootleg cassettes or pirate computer software at knock-down prices. Go down to Brick Lane and you might find a trader yelling that everything is 'guaranteed stolen'. It isn't, but his shouts bring the crowds like flies to a hamburger, and the goods are a darned sight cheaper than you'd find in a chainstore.

The British are generally a painfully law-abiding nation. So it can come as a pleasure to find smuggled Gitane cigarettes surreptitiously for sale, next to bottles of dodgy whisky and gin. But goods stolen in car and house break-ins are another matter, and unfortunately London has markets where these goods are 'fenced'. It's worth noting that the ancient law of market overt gives legal entitlement to goods bought in an open market, provided that the transaction takes place in daylight hours, and the buyer does not know them to be stolen. But any stall full of second-hand video recorders and car radios should be viewed with suspicion.

It's easy to come a cropper at a market, particularly when buying secondhand goods (my white-noise telephone and my toaster that doesn't toast serve as warnings), but that's all part of the fun. There's a risk involved, but that makes the bargains, when you discover them, all the more enjoyable.

History

The Roman trading post

For more than four-fifths of its near 2000-year history, London was just the square mile on the northern bank of the Thames now known as the City. But from its outset as a Roman garrison and trading post, the town had a market. The Roman historian Tacitus describes Londinium in AD 60 as being full of traders and a celebrated centre of commerce. Olive oil, wine, pottery, glass and marble were among the goods that arrived from all over the empire, either unloaded from boats that had travelled up the Thames estuary, or via the newly-built bridge across the river near what is now London Bridge. Trading took place in London's forum, probably close to the present Leadenhall Market.

London remained within the Roman dominium until AD 410, when the emperor was unable to respond to a request for military assistance. Roman culture gradually disappeared from Britain. London's history during the Dark Ages is unclear, but though the town declined rapidly, it is likely that some people continued to live within the walls. Bede, writing of the 7th century, described London (or rather a settlement just outside the city walls) as a 'mart of many peoples'. But it was not until the late 9th century that Alfred the Great re-established London as a major town, rebuilding its defences and establishing new wharves at Billingsgate and Queenhithe.

Medieval markets

By the 12th century, London had become England's principal trading centre, with something between 14,000 and 18,000 inhabitants. The city had several markets, most of them based around Westcheap (now called Cheapside) and East Cheap, (*ceap* was the Saxon word for market). Many of London's citizens were craftsmen, engaged in highly specialized trades. Some catered for the expensive tastes of wealthy merchants or courtiers. Because of its large population, London had a high demand for a wide variety of goods. This enabled craftsmen to specialize in ever more esoteric goods. Unlike any other city in England, London had a large number of people who had moved off the land and were dependent on being able to buy food or raw materials, and to sell their wares.

Fairs were established at Smithfield in the 12th century (Bartholomew Fair) and Westminster in the 13th and 14th centuries. They attracted numerous French and Flemish merchants. In 1264–5 nearly a quarter of the royal court's purchases of cloth, furs and spices were made in London, and that share increased during the reign of Edward I (1272–1307).

The old chain of markets that stretched across the centre of the city was augmented by new trading areas. Each craft or trade was lodged in its respective street. Mercers, saddlers, haberdashers and goldsmiths were in Cheapside; grocers in Soper Lane; drapers and secondhand clothiers in Lombard Street and Cornhill; ironmongers in Old Jewry; butchers and cooks in Thames Street and Eastcheap; poulterers in the Poultry; horse-coursers and dealers in sheep and cattle at Smithfield; wine merchants in the Vintry by the river. Ready-cooked meals were prepared in the cookshops of Thames Street and Eastcheap. Foreign merchants also came to market. There was spice from Italy, gold from Arabia, jewellery from Egypt, furs from Russia and Norway, oil from Baghdad and wine from France. Today, the street names remain: Bread Street, Wood Street, Milk Street, Ironmonger Lane and Poultry are all off Cheapside; Garlick Hill, Fish Street Hill and Vintner's Place are closer to the river.

By 1300 London's population may have been as large as 100,000, and it was by far the biggest source of demand for agricultural produce in England. Supplies came from an increasingly wide area. Grain brought by road from the west side of the city was sold inside the walls by Grey Friars, Newgate. Grain from eastern parts was sold at Gracechurch. Londoners also bought grain and fish from the East Anglian coast and the Fenland regions of Norfolk and Cambridgeshire, using King's Lynn as the major collecting port. River trade along the Thames to London contributed to the growth of Henley and Maidenhead. The two main waterside markets were Queenhithe below London Bridge and Billingsgate above it. The River Lea was another means of access to London markets.

But what was it like to walk through London's markets in the Middle Ages? One of the earliest records is a sorrowful tale of impecuniousness written in verse by John Lydgate (1370–1449). His *London Likpenny* is worth quoting at length:

...Then went I forth by London stone,
Throughout all Canwyke streete;
Drapers mutch cloth me offered anone:
Then comes me one, cryde 'Hot shepes feete',
One cryde 'Makerell, Rushes greene', another gan greete,
One bade me by a hood to cover my head:
But for want of mony I myght not be sped.

Then I hyed me into Estcheape:
One cryes 'Rybbs of befe', and many a pye;
Pewter potts they clattered on a heape,
There was harpe, pype, and mynstrelsye:
'Yea by cock! Nay by cock!' some began crye,
Some songe of Jenken and Julyan for their mede;
But for lack of mony I myght not spede.

Then into Cornhill anon I rode,
Where was much stolen gere amonge;
I saw where honge myne owne hoode,
That I had lost amonge the thronge;
To by my own hood I thought it wronge,
I knew it well as I dyd my crede;
But for lack of mony I could not spede...

Having property stolen at one end of the street and being sold it at the other has been an apocryphal tale on London's markets ever since.

Much produce was sold directly to householders in the principal markets, but middlemen gained increasing power in the city, buying from producers and selling to consumers. Cornmongers, called blades, came to include some of the city's wealthiest men. It was during the Middle Ages that London's craftsmen and merchants first organized themselves into guilds or livery companies, and came to exert much power over the running of the city and its markets.

The livery companies did—and still do—help run the City of London Corporation. Throughout the centuries the Corporation fiercely protected its markets, often invoking charters that forbade a rival market to be set up within six and two-third miles of the City—the maximum distance deemed possible for a trader to walk to market, sell goods and walk home in a day. There are about 100 City livery companies in existence today. The Mercers' and Skinners' are two of the oldest companies (though few current members have much connection with the original trades), with charters granted in the 14th century.

As the markets grew, so fairs declined. In London, this happened in the 14th and 15th centuries—earlier than elsewhere—because the city's markets were able to provide on a weekly basis the luxury goods traditionally associated with annual or bi-annual fairs. St Edward's fair at Westminster, founded in 1245, had become a very restrained affair by the 15th century. Trade at St Bartholomew's cloth fair, held at Smithfield every August, became secondary to entertainment, which was so riotous that the fair was eventually suppressed by the City authorities in the 1850s.

The wholesale markets

The growth of London also caused an increase in wholesale trade. Three of the city's great wholesale markets date from the Middle Ages: Billingsgate, Borough and Smithfield. The oldest is probably Billingsgate, which for 900 years occupied a site in the City off present-day Lower Thames Street. It began as a general market, selling goods that arrived by river. By the 13th century it was used mainly by wholesalers trading in coal, corn and fish. By the mid-16th century, Billingsgate was devoted exclusively to fish, and gained a reputation for the colourful (and crude) language of its porters, dockers and fishwives.

Billingsgate remained on its ancient site until 1982, when archaic facilities, traffic on the newly-built Lower Thames Street, and the greed of prospective developers forced it out to West India Dock, near Poplar in east London. The low-crowned leather hats studded with brass nails (said to have descended directly from the helmets of bowmen at Agincourt) worn by porters to transport boxes of fish on their heads, have now gone. But Billingsgate still supplies nearly all of London's fishmongers, and most of the city's eel and pie shops.

It's possible that Borough market has a history almost as long as Billingsgate's. The ancestor of this small wholesale fruit and vegetable market is likely to have been the trading that spread onto London Bridge during the 13th century. The bridge, on which houses, shops and a chapel stood, was London's only river crossing. Its gates were closed at night, so travellers often had to stay in the Borough. Inns were built to accommodate them, and traders took advantage of this gathering. A map of 1542 shows the marketplace south of St Margaret's church in the High Street. The market's charter was granted by Edward VI in the mid-16th century, and confirmed by Charles II in 1671.

A growth in market gardening in Kent in the 17th and 18th centuries benefitted Borough, as it was the natural point of entry to London for the Kent farmers. By the 1750s, traffic had grown to such a volume that the market was moved to Rochester Yard, west of Borough High Street. It has remained there, still within a couple of hundred yards of London Bridge, ever since. Traditionally seen as the poor man's fruit and vegetable market, it continues to supply many costermongers with their produce.

From at least the 12th century there has been a market at Smithfield, or 'smooth field', a grassy area near Farringdon, just outside the city walls. In 1173 William FitzStephen, clerk to Thomas à Becket, wrote that 'every Friday there is a celebrated rendezvous of fine horses to be sold' on the site. Sheep, pigs and cattle were also traded there. The City of London was granted the tolls from the market by charter in 1400, and the Corporation of London still owns it. The procession of cattle herded through Islington on their way to market came to an end in 1852 with the Smithfield Market Removal Act. The site then became a wholesale meat market, which continues to be held five days a week.

An early morning trip to Smithfield, Europe's largest meat market, is essential for anyone interested in the history of London's markets. The large and elaborate building (designed in 1868 by Horace Jones, who also built Leadenhall Market) is full of activity through the night, as most carcasses are still unloaded by hand. Trading begins at 5am, and pubs in the area open at 7am. Smithfield is the last of the great medieval markets to remain on its original site, right by the City. Along with the equally ancient St Bartholomew's Hospital (now under threat from government cuts), it continues to bring life and vigour to this grey-suited district.

Rogue traders

Much of the documented material concerning markets of the Middle Ages describes the action taken against 'forestallers', who bought up all the stock at a market to sell it at a profit—capitalism was not regarded as a virtue in those days. Tradesmen who gave short measure, or sold food unfit to eat, were ridden round the town in a dung cart or on horseback, tied face to tail, with the offending commodity strung around their necks. Other transgressors had to ride from Newgate to the pillory in Cornhill, where they were left for a day, wearing paper mitres carrying the story of their misdeeds. In one case from 1319, a 'William Sperlyng of West Hamme' was caught by the City wardens selling beef that was 'putrid and poisonous' from 'bodies that have died of disease'. His punishment was to be placed in the pillory and have the two carcasses burnt beneath him. A couple of centuries later, the punishment for a woman who had caught fish that were too small was still more humiliating: she was condemned to ride about Cheapside with a garland of said fish around her head.

Some of the butchers' tricks were ingenious: washing old and festering meat with new blood, or selling elderly joints by candlelight. The City authorities appointed officials to patrol the markets and check for profiteering and malpractice. The carcass of a pig deemed unwholesome had its ears slit. Hygiene was a major problem in medieval London. Lack of it contributed to the worst catastrophe in the city's history: the Black Death of the mid-14th century, which killed over half of London's population.

The 17th- and 18th-century markets

The London markets in Shakespeare's time were described in detail by John Stow in his *Survey of London* published in 1598. He relates how trades had gradually moved from their original streets of the city:

> *But the brewers for the more part remain near to the friendly water of Thames; the butchers in Eastcheape, St Nicholas shambles, and the Stockes market; ...cooks, or pastelars, [remain] for the more part in Thames Street; ...poulters of late removed out of the Poultrie, betwixt the Stockes and the great Conduit in Cheape, into Grasse Street and St Nicholas shambles; pater noster makers of old time, or bead-makers, and text-writers, are gone out of Pater noster Row, and are called stationers of Paule's churchyard... horse-coursers and sellers of oxen, sheep, swine, and such like, remain in their old market of Smithfield...*

Stow also reports that a stock of freshwater fish was kept alive outside the city walls in the 'towne ditch'. But most fish on sale in London's markets were dried, salted or pickled.

By the turn of the 17th century, London markets displayed a quantity and variety of food that impressed visitors from abroad. As the century progressed, the markets went on growing as the city grew. London continued to attract ever more specialized goods from the provinces, and outstripped Antwerp as the great European market for exotic luxuries.

Market gardening only began to flourish in England in the 17th century, using techniques developed by the Dutch. Before then, a high proportion of fruit and vegetables were imported. Samuel Hartlib, writing in 1652 stated:

> *In Queen Elizabeth's time we had not onely our Gardiners ware from Holland, but also Cherries from Flaunders; Apples from France; Saffron, Licorish from Spain; Hopps from the Low-Countreys...wheras now...the Licorish, Saffron, Cherries, Apples, Peares, Hopps, Cabages of England are the best in the world.*

Vegetables began to form a larger part of the English diet, previously dominated by bread, fish, beer and a great deal of meat. Market gardens sprang up to the north and northeast of London, and the produce was sold, as it had been for centuries, in the market near St Paul's Cathedral.

The Great Fire of 1666 destroyed nearly 400 acres within London's city walls, and the subsequent rebuilding programme led to a major reorganization of the markets. Stalls were seen as a fire risk, so an Act of Parliament in 1674 banned street markets within the City. Cheapside, Lime Street and Gracechurch Street markets were closed. Newgate, Billingsgate, the Stocks market, Honey Lane and Leadenhall were rebuilt as covered markets. Spitalfields, the wholesale fruit and vegetable market, was granted its charter in 1682, and was held on its site to the east of the City until 1991 (*see* p.138). In the ensuing decades, markets developed outside the City at Whitecross Street, Leather Lane, Hoxton Street, Petticoat Lane and near Brick Lane.

The City authorities often invoked their charters to prevent markets setting up in competition with their own. As a result, several of London's early suburbs had shops before a market. Until well into the 18th century, however, markets were the normal place for Londoners to buy their food.

The property boom that followed the Great Fire soon covered much of the space between the City and Westminster with housing. Most of this land was owned by the nobility. As well as becoming housing developers, they were keen to earn revenues from their estates by running markets. One of the first such charters was granted to the Earl of Bedford in 1670 to run Covent Garden (*see* p.30). This was followed in 1680 by St James's market (near what is now Piccadilly Circus), built by Henry Jermyn; and Hungerford market (on the south side of the Strand), owned by Sir Edward Hungerford. Newport market (near Leicester Square), Carnaby market (near Carnaby Street), Brooke Market (near Leather Lane, *see* p.47) and Clare Market (the name still exists, near Aldwych) were all inaugurated in the late 17th century. The Haymarket (on the road of that name near Trafalgar Square) also dates from this period. All have now gone, cleared by road, housing, and office developments.

The trend continued into the 18th century. Grosvenor market (off South Molton Street), Mortimer market (off Tottenham Court Road) and Oxford market (held north of Oxford Circus; the name Market Place remains) all helped to feed London's burgeoning population. By the beginning of the 18th century, London was already the biggest city in western Europe, with about 600,000 inhabitants—10 per cent of the entire nation. In 1724, Daniel Defoe wrote of the 'general dependence of the whole country upon the city of London for the consumption of its produce'.

But as the 18th century continued, the city's population stopped rising so dramatically, as a result of the huge death rate in the slums. Overcrowding, open sewers, dirty drinking water and a widespread addiction to gin killed thousands who had recently migrated to London from the country. Two contemporary writers give a picture of the markets of the period. First, Ned Ward's description of Fleet market:

> *We mov'd on til we came to Fleet Bridge, where nuts, ginger-bread, oranges, and oysters lay pil'd up in moveable shops that run upon wheels, attended by ill-looking fellowes, some with but one eye and others without noses. Over against these stood a parcel of Trugmoldies [old former prostitutes], Straw-Hats or Flat-Caps, selling socks and furmity [wheat boiled in milk], night-caps, and plum-pudding.*

A still more unsavoury tale is related by Tobias Smollett in his 1771 novel *Humphry Clinker*:

> *It was but yesterday that I saw a dirty barrow-bunter in the street, cleaning her dusty fruit with her own spittle; and who knows but some fine lady of St James's parish might admit into her delicate mouth those very cherries which had been rolled and moistened between the filthy, and perhaps ulcerated, chops of a St Giles's huckster?*

The fact that market gardeners filled their carts with 'night soil' from the city to fertilize their crops did little to reassure nervous gentlefolk of the period.

Large supplies of fruit came from the Kent orchards, which expanded rapidly in the 18th century. More foreign fruits also reached London, with oranges and lemons from southern Europe becoming widely available for the first time. But Londoners were still great meat eaters. It has been estimated that during the first half of the 18th century nearly 80,000 head of cattle came to the city's market each year. Many had travelled long distances (from Wales, for instance), being sold from fair to fair, then fattened on the outskirts of the city before reaching the market. St James's market, Clare Market, Newgate and Leadenhall were all important meat markets. By the end of the century, city dwellers could also buy a variety of cheeses from traders, including Double Gloucester, Cheddar, Cheshire and Stilton.

The Victorian era

London and its markets were utterly transformed by the Industrial Revolution. The railways enabled people and produce to travel speedily into the city. Wholesale markets were started by rail companies near King's Cross, Stratford, Paddington and St Pancras stations, to sell fresh food from around the country. (The last of them, Stratford, closed in the early 1990s.) The population of what became known as Greater London soared from just over a million in 1801 to over six and a half million by the end of the century. As scores of suburbs sprang up near to rail, and later tube stations, traders moved in to cater for the new residents.

Henry Mayhew, in his magnificent work *London Labour and the London Poor*, described the markets of the 1850s in painstaking detail. Several of his discoveries are worth noting. He lists a total of 37 markets, 10 in south London, 27 north of the river. At these he counted 3911 traders. The largest markets were at Tottenham Court Road, which had 333 traders; New Cut (now Lower Marsh, *see* p.161), with 300 traders; and the Brill (near Chalton Street, *see* p.210), also with 300 traders.

Many stallholders sold what would now be called fast food. In the Victorian street market this included hot eels, fried fish, baked potatoes, ham sandwiches (an innovation from the 1840s), meat pies and, as in John Lydgate's time over 400 years before, hot sheep's trotters. Oysters (then cheap food) and whelks were also commonplace. Traders often described themselves in terms of the article they sold. A coster once enquired of Mayhew, 'Is the man you're asking about a pickled whelk, sir?'

Watercress, brought in by rail from Hampshire, was one of the cheapest and most plentiful foods. In winter most fruit stalls carried an old saucepan with a fire inside, to roast chestnuts and apples. Ginger beer stands and hot elder wine stalls could be seen across the city; coffee stalls, heated by charcoal, were also common; and fresh milk from the cow could still be had in St James's Park. But by the 1850s the number of traders selling 'eatables and drinkables' had already started to decline, partly as a result of the growth in the number of shopkeepers selling penny pies. London's eel and pie shops, which sprouted up towards the end of the century, soon finished off the hot eel sellers of the street.

Sellers of sheet music would sing their songs at the markets; boys would fire percussion caps at targets to win nuts; buskers joined in the melée—shopping and entertainment couldn't be separated. Mayhew describes one class of commodities being sold as 'pretended smuggled goods', a trick which is echoed in the 'guaranteed stolen goods' still occasionally advertised at Brick Lane. The largest Victorian markets were held on a Saturday night and Sunday morning, after the working men had received their week's pay. Trading on a Sunday was allowed to continue until church services began at 11am. Then 'the policemen in their clean gloves come round and drive the street-sellers before them.'

Costermongers were originally sellers of apples (the word 'coster' comes from a type of apple), but now the term applies to all market traders who sell fruit and vegetables. From Victorian times costermongers have been seen as the aristocrats of street trading. In some East End boroughs the costers elected leaders to protect their rights from competitors. These leaders became known as pearly kings and queens, after the tradition, started in the 1880s, of successful costermongers wearing pearl buttons sewn on to their dresses and suits. The Pearly Kings' and Queens' Association was founded in 1911 as a charity to help old and destitute costers. On the first Sunday of October at 2pm, London's remaining pearly kings and queens gather for a harvest festival thanksgiving service, now held at St Martin-in-the-Fields church, off Trafalgar Square.

The 20th century

Towards the end of the 19th century, several of London's markets were forced out of the main streets by traffic and the building of tramlines. During the 20th century, traders have continued to be shoved from pillar to post. Markets have changed streets or even districts, making it difficult to trace their lineage. Bermondsey market, for example, moved to its present site after the Second World War; before that it had been held near the Caledonian Road, in north London, since the mid-19th century; before that it had been an appendage to Smithfield market since the Middle Ages.

By 1900 it is estimated that London had about 60,000 street traders. After the First and Second World Wars many demobbed servicemen tried their hands at market trading, but like the more recently unemployed who have tried to switch to the job, few succeeded. There's a knack to selling on the streets, and the life is hard.

Many markets weren't officially recognized until 1927, when the London County Council (General Powers) Act gave the Metropolitan Borough Councils the authority to license street traders and pass hygiene legislation. During the Second World War several of London's market streets were badly damaged by bombing, and since the war redevelopment has forced many more traders off their pitches. Hydra-like, most markets have continued to survive, even on unpromising concrete sites. Some have thrived; the postwar influence of various immigrant communities has breathed new vigour into a number of traditional markets, especially Brixton (*see* p.172), Shepherd's Bush (*see* p.76), Ridley Road (*see* p.134) and Queen's Market (*see* p.132).

But several have closed, or are dying. On one Friday in 1995, there were only three traders at Lambeth Walk, SE11; in Mayhew's day there were 104. Broadway Market, E8, Burdett Road, E3, and Chatsworth Road, E5, are all Victorian markets on their last legs. Poignantly, an empty local shop on Chatsworth Road recently sported a poster calling to 'stop the hypermarkets on Hackney Downs'.

Save Our Markets

Street markets are under attack as never before in Britain. A combination of modern shopping habits, depopulation, gentrification and council indifference has hit street trading hard. Like small shops, whose numbers have fallen from more than 100,000 in the 1960s to only 34,000 in the mid-1990s, traditional markets are in crisis.

Superstores

Compared to many of England's towns, where 800-year-old markets are in danger of closing following the arrival of an out-of-town superstore, London has much to be grateful for. Relatively few superstores have been built in Inner London: there simply isn't room. Yet large shopping centres are taking trade away from the markets. Stallholders in Soho's Berwick Street, plum in the West End, believe that Brent Cross and Lakeside shopping centres, miles away on the outskirts of London, are damaging their businesses. A new threat is the growth of smaller supermarkets in central London, notably the Tesco Metro chain.

Food traders have fared worst. The supermarkets' share of the fruit and vegetable market has leapt alarmingly, from 24 per cent in 1983 to more than 50 per cent in 1995. Wholesale as well as retail markets are being badly hit, because most of the fresh produce sold by supermarkets is transported direct from growers to central depots, by-passing New Covent Garden and Spitalfields.

Producers are also suffering. Supermarkets require producers who can supply all their outlets through the year. Small suppliers who concentrate on regional foods and seasonally available produce aren't wanted. Neither are certain varieties of crop. Supermarkets want their fruit and vegetables to be uniform in appearance and to have a long shelf life. Some of the tastiest varieties of English apple are ignored because they don't take well to being kept in carbon dioxide for six months.

True, supermarkets offer convenience and thousands of goods on their shelves. In 1992, the chairman of Sainsbury's could state that 'the range of food and other goods we sell is four times as great as 20 years ago...' But such variety has been more than outweighed by a homogenizing process caused by the concentration of ownership. Increasingly, a half dozen or so firms are coming to dictate what we eat, and how much we pay for it. The social and environmental costs of supermarkets' policies are high. These include the use of prodigious amounts of packaging (according to the Consumers' Association, we pay about 10 per cent higher prices because of it, and supermarkets don't bear the cost of disposing of it); and excessive use of transport, leading to air and noise pollution, increased congestion, more accidents, and huge amounts of government money spent on road building. Superstores benefit some consumers, notably car-owners, at the expense of others without access to them: the old, the car-less, the poor.

In contrast, London's traditional street markets are concentrated in some of the most deprived parts of the city. Costermongers have always made a living by bringing food to the poorest sections of society. They usually buy their stock from the nearest wholesale market, and the most packaging you'll get is a plastic bag for your spuds. The seasons also make their presence felt more on the markets, though less so in London than in rural districts. Spring greens are followed by summer fruits; autumn marrows make way for the Kentish cobnuts and boiled beetroot sold near Christmas.

The domination of retailing by ever fewer companies affects not only the markets. The high streets of Britain's towns, and London's boroughs, are starting to look identical. Butchers' shops and bakeries are closing down apace; fishmongers and greengrocers are nearing extinction. Worthwhile and satisfying occupations are disappearing, as shopkeepers and stallholders are replaced by battalions of weary checkout assistants. Personal service is being lost. Above all, what we're in danger of losing is variety and a way of life.

Battles with government

With a few noteworthy exceptions, London councils rarely seem to value the markets in their care. Starved of funds, they are prone to look kindly on supermarkets who are prepared to build amenities in exchange for planning permission. Revenue raising often takes precedence over conservation. Many traders in central London believe that Westminster Council would rather have parking meters on its streets than markets, as the meters raise more cash. But more often, councils simply neglect their markets, taking them for granted, failing to respond when pitches are left empty, doing nothing until it is too late.

National government is little better. Its huge road-building programme in the 1980s helped subsidize out-of-town superstores. Market traders can't match the muscle of the supermarket companies, and so can expect no subsidies themselves when times are hard. The European parliament, too, seems to work in the interests of multinational companies, passing directives that are easy for large corporations to comply with, but crippling for small shops and market traders.

The flight from the city

After over 40 years of decline, the population of central London is slowly beginning to climb again, which is good news for the city's street markets. Less pleasing is the fact that businesses are continuing to relocate away from the centre, partly because of transport problems. This, together with the recession, has caused many of central London's lunchtime markets to decline in recent years. The American phenomenon of the 'doughnut effect' is a terrible warning of what can happen to the centre of cities if businesses and shops move out. Cities acquire holes in their centres, where those on low incomes live with few amenities, and where crime is rampant.

Gentrification and touristification

It is fast becoming a general rule that seekers after 'genuine' street culture, those wishing to see communities about their daily business (as opposed to play-actors performing for tourists) should shun the great sights, avoid all that is deemed quaint or beautiful. Rather they should search for the ugly and the unfashionable. Above all they should travel to districts not mentioned in guide books.

London is a big enough city to encompass both the worst of the synthetic self-parodies and the most lively of unspoilt street culture. Traditional street markets tend to be at the centre of the latter. Visit some of the markets listed in this book and you'll learn a great deal more about London's culture than you will from queuing with the hordes at the Tower.

But there is a danger that markets themselves could be repackaged for tourists and lose their *raison d'être* as providers of essentials for local people. The success of Camden market (now the fourth most popular tourist attraction in London) has caused a number of crafts markets to be set up, most notably at Greenwich, Merton Abbey Mills and St James's Piccadilly. These new markets, though mostly geared to tourists, have not displaced any existing traditional street trading. More worrying are the developments at Earlham Street and Rupert Street, where traditional markets are in danger of being taken over by stalls for tourists.

The gentrification of an area has a more ambivalent effect on street markets. Where the tastes of the new arrivals are represented on the stalls, as at Colombia Road and, to a lesser extent, Northcote Road, the market continues to be a success. When the market fails to respond to the changing population, as is the case at Exmouth Market, it is in danger of dying once its old constituency disappears.

Market predictions

The future for London's markets is not entirely gloomy. Go to Chapel Market, Brixton, Portobello, Wembley, Ridley Road, Camden or Brick Lane, and you will find entertainment and a sense of occasion that supermarkets couldn't hope to compete with. Within limits (perhaps exceeded at Camden, Petticoat Lane and Portobello), the crowds are an attraction in themselves; in a supermarket crowds are a mere nuisance. And in a market there is no sense of behind-the-scenes manipulation by middle managers, advertisers and corporate strategists. On the streets you are confronted by stallholders who usually own their business. They can be wily, but at least the transaction is on a human level, a kind of joust.

To survive, street markets, particularly those specializing in food, need to adapt. Over the past 30 years, a huge increase in the number of women working outside the home has led to a rapid growth in the consumption of convenience food, and to fewer people being able to shop during office hours. Supermarkets have responded by offering a wide range of ready meals, and by staying open later. Market traders rarely have the resources to provide chilled or frozen ready meals, but, with the notable exceptions of Camden and Merton Abbey Mills, they have also been slow to offer any takeaway food more imaginative than a hot dog or a burger. And it's rare that you'll find stallholders trading on London's streets after 6pm.

London, meanwhile, has become a city of food lovers. Restaurants have proliferated and the quality of cooking has soared. It is at this specialized level of food retailing that markets can compete. As is the case in France (and some rural areas of England, notably north Devon) small producers—organic farmers, cheese-makers, pie-, pudding- and jam-makers—must be encouraged to take stalls on London's markets once again. The Women's Institute markets of rural Britain, and the farmers' markets that are a relatively recent innovation in the United States, also show the way. Links between producers and consumers, cutting out supermarket middle agents, will benefit both.

The fledgling organic markets at Spitalfields, Portobello, Greenwich and Camden show there's a demand for food from small producers. With luck, their success will also encourage a move back towards seasonal and locally-grown food, reviving once again the glorious expectation of fresh asparagus in May, and strawberries in July. Such a shift in demand will cut the unnecessary transportation of goods halfway across the globe. But even if such organic and specialized food markets take off in London, they will cater mainly for more affluent consumers. Most of London's traditional markets have catered for low-income groups. Many are sited in areas of high unemployment, where locals aren't prepared to pay a premium for organic produce. If London's local markets are to survive, they have to appeal to their local population.

Councils often seem to think that all it takes to inject new life into a market is to pedestrianize it and install some street furniture. But too often it's a case of too little too late. Tachbrook Street and Exmouth Market are cases in point, where expensive repaving and/or pedestrianization have failed to regenerate markets. More fundamental measures need to be implemented urgently:

- Councils should inform local people about their markets, and the low prices to be found there. The multi-million pound advertising budgets of the supermarket chains obviously cannot be matched, but younger consumers especially need to know that there is an alternative. At present, Waltham Forest Council seems almost alone in widely promoting its traditional street market, Walthamstow.
- Councils should keep an eye on the markets they own. If food stalls are deserting them, traders should be enticed back with rent-free pitches to ensure the market remains balanced and attractive.
- Markets should be allowed and encouraged to stay open until late in the evening, as they did from Victorian times to the outbreak of the Second World War. This would allow people to shop locally after coming home from work. The benefits to the local community would be manifold. Not only would the market provide a meeting place and entertainment for those too young or without enough money to drink in a pub, so keeping them out of mischief; it would also ensure that more people were on the streets at a later hour, thus making the area safer, especially for women. Any outlay by the council would easily be counterbalanced by a decrease in local crime.

■ Local people from various ethnic groups should be encouraged to take pitches. The success of Brixton, Shepherd's Bush and Ridley Road points the way. There are still local markets in multi-ethnic areas of London that are dominated by a dwindling number of (occasionally xenophobic) old coster families. As a result, local people of Afro-Caribbean and Asian origin—many of whom come from cultures well used to street trading—shop elsewhere.

■ Cheap local parking should be provided where possible, to allow markets to compete with out-of-town superstores. The success of markets such as Wembley show the attraction of plenty of nearby parking.

Market-led recoveries

Councils too often see their markets as a liability, instead of a valuable resource capable of bringing prosperity to an area. In the 1990s, shopping is increasingly a leisure activity. Markets have always been an entertainment in themselves, so councils should capitalize on this. Camden Lock is the best-known example of a market reviving the fortunes of a declining area, but it is not the only one. Many chainstores left Peckham in the recession, but the low prices on its markets are helping to bring back the crowds; and Deptford's market, where new traders are being supported through a training programme, attracts people from miles around.

The danger is, of course, that successful markets in a previously run-down area can entice chainstores back into the district to compete for the crowds. However, when the market is flourishing, and the supermarkets are suitably near, both can thrive, as Ridley Road, Chapel Market and Walthamstow High Street show.

If this book is anything, it is a celebration of variety. The variety still to be found on London's markets is one of the joys of the city; each market district is distinctive—something that a street of chainstores will never be. Markets humanize their surroundings and, like street-corner pubs, act as a focus for the local community, providing a meeting place and free entertainment, as well as supplying daily essentials at a low price. If allowed to trade into the evening, they could also help create a safer environment. To avoid losing all this as we move into the 21st century, government, councils and stallholders need to take action, but so do consumers. Boycotts of specific goods or companies for ethical reasons have gained in popularity during the 1990s. Perhaps it is also time to switch patronage from the retail multiples to local markets and shops. We have nothing to lose but our chains. We have a world to gain.

Central London

Berwick Street, Soho

Berwick Street and Rupert Street

Address: Berwick Street, between Broadwick Street and Peter Street; Rupert Street, between Brewer Street and Archer Street, W1.

Public transport: ⊖ Piccadilly Circus, Tottenham Court Road, Oxford Circus; buses 3, 6, 7, 8, 10, 12, 13, 14, 15, 19, 23, 24, 25, 29, 38, 53, 55, 73, 88, 94, 98, 139, 159, 176, X53.

Opening hours: Mon–Sat 8am–6pm.

Best time to go: busiest at Thursday and Friday lunchtimes, best value fruit and veg after 4.30pm on Saturday.

Car parking: there's a limited number of parking meters on some Soho side streets (try Soho Square); otherwise, there's a multi-storey car park (expensive) on Brewer Street.

Main wares: **Berwick Street** fruit and vegetables, fabrics, clothes, herbs and spices, cheese, fish;
Rupert Street new and secondhand clothes, CDs and videos, watches, jewellery, greetings cards, fruit and vegetables.

Specifics: cheap and varied fruit and vegetables, inexpensive multi-national cheeses.

'They'll never get rid of the Berwick,' an old woman who had lived in Soho all her life told me five years ago, over a drink in the Blue Posts. Few would have disagreed then—Soho without Berwick Street's boisterous costermongers was unthinkable. Yet central London's best market is now facing the biggest threat in its history.

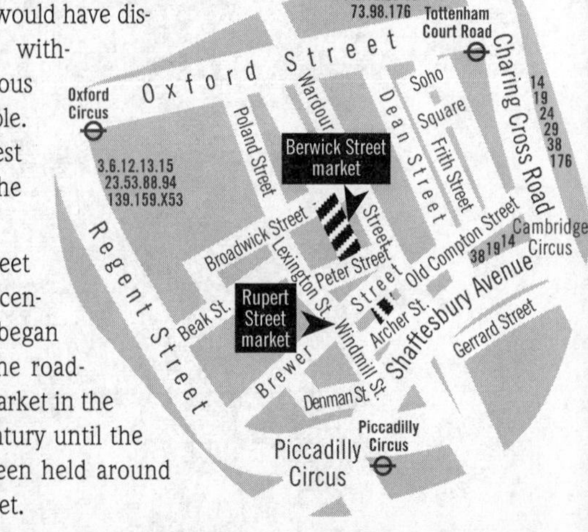

Street trading in Berwick Street probably started in the 19th century, when shopkeepers began displaying their goods on the roadside. But it wasn't the first market in the area. From the mid-17th century until the 1720s, a hay market had been held around the corner in Broadwick Street.

French Huguenots, Greeks, Italians, Jews—all helped populate this cosmopolitan but modest district. By the 1890s, several of these expatriates, or their descendants, had opened eating houses serving their native cuisines. As the market traders attempted to supply the ingredients, Berwick Street earned its reputation for selling a bewildering variety of fruit and vegetables. Tomatoes made their first appearance on a London street market here in 1880; grapefruit followed in 1890.

The spirit of Victorian Berwick Street survived into the 1930s. Teignmouth Shore, in his 1930 guide, called it 'one of the queerest sights in London', and describes 'barrows laden with fruits, vegetables, fish, meats, garments of all sorts, ironmongery; lit at night by flaring naphtha-lamps; an amusing and almost picturesque sight.'

In the late 19th century, Soho also became a centre for entertainment, as several theatres and music halls opened nearby. The area's reputation as a red light district also dates from this period. The potent mix of food and sex has been a feature of Soho ever since. In the 1980s, local pressure groups tried to curtail the number of Soho premises used by the sex industry. Largely as a result of their efforts, it dropped from 185 in 1982 to 30 in 1991. Recently, though, a butcher's and baker's on Peter Street have been replaced by outlets for pornographic magazines. The market continues outside unabashed.

With 80-odd stalls packed both sides of the narrow thoroughfare, Berwick Street used to be a scene of exuberant mayhem. Many a time I enjoyed a jostle along here, squeezed against a barrow as the rubbish cart edged its way through. In 1995, however, Westminster Council banned stalls from the eastern side of the street, halving the number of pitches to 41. Wanting congestion to be cleared, and eager to accept the larger pitches offered, the traders reluctantly went along with the plans. No one was forced out, but no new licences were granted until there were only enough traders to fill one side of the street.

This didn't take long. The older generation of costers called it a day, while, according to a council official, many of the younger traders only keep their pitch for a couple of years, seeing it as a stepping stone to getting a shop. No doubt the market is now more ordered and seemly, but it has been gravely wounded. 'The market is not what it was,' the official remarked, blaming its ill fortunes on the recession.

Yet the recession isn't the traders' only problem. 'In ten years' time, all you'll see is parking meters along here,' complains one coster. Meters, clamp-removal fees and parking fines net Westminster Council a sizeable income. Revenue raising appears to be the councillors' foremost concern, so the market is seen as little more than a drain on resources. Meanwhile customers arriving by car must pay hefty parking charges, and new stallholders aren't even provided with storage facilities for their barrows.

It's easy to understand why the traders feel despondent. They have presented the council with plans to improve the market. These include pedestrianizing the street, setting up more signposts to the market, improving the lighting, adding trees and street furniture, and creating parking and storage facilities. To these proposals should be added one more: allow the market to stay open later in the evening, as it did before the war. An entirely new crowd of people flocks into Soho at night, attracted by its restaurants, theatres and cinemas. The market would add to the nightlife, and local people returning from work would also be able to shop there. Were Berwick Street allowed to tap these markets, it might flourish again.

It is certainly worth saving. Although the bustle has diminished, dozens of stalwart traders still offer the cheapest fruit and veg in the West End. 'Fill yer boots with bananas, 19p a pound,' yells Paul outside the King of Corsica pub, while his mate Charlie, a Berwick Street star with a voice like a foghorn, sings the praises of 'sparragrass'. Charlie, known as Norman (after Norman Wisdom), is small and wiry. He never stands still, leaping around the stall, deftly tipping a scoop of 'avos' into a bag while foraging in his market trader's money-bag, a denim pouch with a zip-up pocket for notes. A passing group of schoolgirls goad him on as he explodes into action, hollering his heart out.

Some of the cheapest fruit and vegetables can be found at the Peter Street end of the market, while the stalls further north tend to concentrate on quality and variety. Watch out for over-ripe produce (those mushrooms at £1 for 3lb look a little brown), prowl the street checking price against price, and you'll usually get a bargain. Try finding prices like these in a supermarket: 25 oranges for £1; five avocados for 50p; 3lb of seedless grapes for £1.

Chinese, African, American and European chefs from local restaurants come to root around for ingredients: kaki fruit, sharon fruit, custard apples, sweet potatoes, dried chillies, Nashi pears from Japan, fresh figs, Italian plum tomatoes, oakleaf lettuces and golden passion fruit are just some of the varieties on offer.

Another Berwick Street regular who has survived the cut is the cheesemonger. Time was when you could buy three or even four antique cheeses for £1. EU legislation concerning refrigeration (often ignored by the unfettered French, by the way) stopped all that, but this is still the best cheese stall in London. Shropshire Blue, herb Brie, Swiss Appenzeller, American Monterey Jack, Danish Danbo and Samsoe and French Chaumes have all graced the counter. Prices are lower than in most shops (Stilton at £2.95 per pound; mature Cheddar at £2.25). Italian biscuits and salami are sold as sidelines.

The herb and spice trader is a relative newcomer, but no less welcome for that. Fresh herbs are sold growing in pots, while dozens of spices and dried herbs are kept in large glass containers. A solitary fish trader—whose catch might include prawns, coley, rainbow trout and lemon sole—and a purveyor of all sorts of nuts complete the food sellers.

It is the traders selling goods other than food who have been most severely affected by the reduction in the number of pitches, but you can still find a flower seller, and a trader with a mix of watch straps, batteries, bin-bags and cigarette lighters. Jewish refugees fleeing the pogroms of Eastern Europe settled in Soho towards the end of the 19th century. Several engaged in the rag trade. Mr Borovik keeps the tradition going from his shop (at No.16), though he has relinquished the two pitches he ran. But in the week there's occasionally a fabric stall still trading on the market.

Brian Berg now runs Berwick Street's only clothing stall. He has traded here for 25 years ('I'm one of the young ones'), having taken over the business from two uncles. His cousin runs a nearby fruit stall. Brian can remember when the costers collected their barrows at dawn each day from Seven Dials, stocked them up at Covent Garden wholesale market and wheeled them back through the streets to Soho.

From Berwick Street, head south through narrow, seedy Walker's Court to **Rupert Street**. A few years ago, Rupert Street was pedestrianized and cobbled. This, coupled with its position near the tourist hot-spot of Shaftesbury Avenue, has encouraged a rash of stalls sporting Union Jacks and selling football scarves. Most of the 20 or so traders sell clothes: their stock includes leopardskin leggings, suede or tapestry-fronted waistcoats, leather belts, woollen scarves from Italy, Aran jumpers, T-shirts printed with signs of the zodiac, checked shirts, silk ties and long flowing dresses. An army-surplus pitch is stocked with fatigues, rucksacks, and camouflage T-shirts. There's also a secondhand stall with vintage Levi's, and jackets in leather, suede and velvet (starting at £10).

The CD stall is worth inspection. A huge number are laid out in boxes; singles cost 50p, albums £3, and there are also a few secondhand video cassettes starting at £1.50. A knot of dedicated enthusiasts flicks through scores of records by little-known artistes. From here they will move on to **Cheapo Cheapo Records** (53 Rupert Street), thence to Berwick Street, London's prime quarter for independent record shops with stores at No.4, No.12, No.30, No.34 and No.94. There are only one or two fruit and veg traders left in Rupert Street. Their stalls are well stocked with high-quality produce, including fresh mint, coriander and basil, kaki fruit and dried apricots, but prices are high.

There's something tawdry about Rupert Street in comparison to Berwick Street. Traders rarely shout their wares; in the alleys by the market, you're more likely to hear the infamous Soho hiss, 'Show sir?', uttered by shivering young women in doorways.

I can't leave the market on this low note, so I return to Berwick Street and head for the King of Corsica. It's already dark, but several traders take their time packing up to catch the after-work crowds, including Charlie and his mate. Still they shout 'Mangoes to make you tango, kiwis to make you, er, wee wee.'

I sit drinking a pint and am astounded at Charlie's energy. Even when there are no customers, he races about, bellowing 'Aye aye, eh oh'—I can hear him now, above the juke box—and throwing empty boxes across the street. Over 12 hours before, at dawn, he had unloaded a lorry with the same vigour. He draws on a cigarette with gusto and polishes an apple. Berwick Street will survive as long as his like are here. Without the market Soho, and London, will be a greyer place.

Nearby cafés, pubs and shops

Soho has London's highest concentration of restaurants. Some suggestions: *dim sum* (Cantonese snacks and dumplings served from noon until 5pm) at **Harbour City**, 46 Gerrard Street; **Bar du Marché** (19 Berwick Street), a modish café-bar with French windows opening onto the market. The **King of Corsica** is the traders' pub, protected from gentrification by its postwar ugliness. More convivial and more crowded is the **White Horse**, a Victorian pub at the corner of Rupert Street and Archer Street. A superbly dingy 1950s caff, the **New Piccadilly**, can be found on Denham Street, towards Piccadilly Circus.

Two of London's best Italian delicatessens are near the market. **Fratelli Camisa** (1a Berwick Street) is a tiny place packed with Italian cheeses, breads and olive oils; **Lina Stores** (18 Brewer Street) is great for fresh pasta, sausages and balsamic vinegars. Brewer Street is fabulous for food shops; don't miss **Slater & Cooke & Bisney Jones** (a high-class butcher's at No.68) and **Richards** (wet fish, at No.11). Brewer Street also contains **Anything Left-handed** (No.57), a quirky shop providing left-handers with scissors, peelers and such like.

Charing Cross Collectors' Fair

Address: underground car park, beneath Charing Cross Arches (entrance on Northumberland Avenue, next to Playhouse Theatre), WC2, ✆ (01483) 281771.

Public transport: ⊖ Embankment, Charing Cross; buses 6, 9, 11, 13, 15, 23, 77A, 91, 176.

Opening hours: Sat 8.30am–3.30pm.

Best time to go: early.

Car parking: difficult; there's an (expensive) underground car park on Bedfordbury (*see* map, p.31).

Main wares: old coins, stamps, cigarette cards, postcards, phone cards.

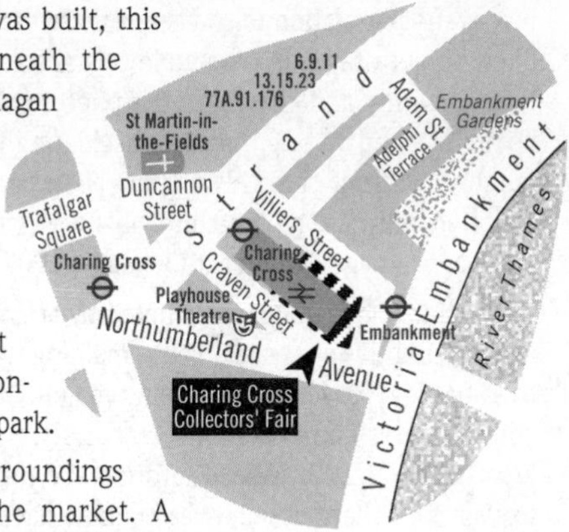

Until the Arches Shopping Centre was built, this captivating market was held underneath the very arches made famous by the Flanagan and Allen song. The spanking new postmodern redevelopment of Charing Cross station put paid to the stallholders' harmless fun. After a temporary exile to London Bridge station, they descended out of sight and you'll now find them down a concrete staircase in an underground car park.

In a strange way, the bunker-like surroundings suit the cabal-like atmosphere of the market. A pleasant hum of hushed conversation pervades the place, as traders enthuse about their stock. About 40 trestle tables are set up, with nearly half of them holding displays of old coins. An 1804 five shilling dollar now has a £45 price tag; a Greek coin from the 3rd century BC depicting Rhea, mother of Zeus, costs £28; a set of 1905 Maundy money, once presented by Edward VII, goes for £44. But to get more cash for your cash, head for the pile of old British pennies. These now seem unfeasibly large and heavy, yet only cost 10p each and include many well-worn Victorian coins. Otherwise, try the 'rummage trays' of assorted coins at 50p, £1, £2 etc. If you go early, before they have been thoroughly pillaged, you can pick up some bargains.

Foreign coins and banknotes are also up for sale or for swapping. Some traders keep their specimens in plastic sachets; the zealots file them meticulously. Watch out for the small emergency banknotes produced by many German cities around the end of the First World War. Often brightly coloured and beautifully designed, they are ludicrously cheap. There are also quite a few antiquities—Romano-British brooches, medieval pilgrim's badges and so on, found by metal-detectorists. Many of them come from the mud of the River Thames. One dealer, whose name is Dennis, calls his business 'Den of Antiquity' (boom, boom).

A decent distance away from the other traders is a single stall full of phone cards. The prices charged for these slices of modern technology are surprisingly high: £80 for four unused Irish cards emblazoned with an ad for Beamish stout. Quite a knot of devotees gathers round. Their excitement is feverish. Another trader who ploughs a lonely furrow deals in regimental cap badges, while nearby is a chap with hundreds of cigarette cards. My favourite set is of 1930s radio performers, including legendary stars like Stainless Stephen and Arthur Askey.

Just as the temptation to snigger at these careful collectors becomes urgent, you're likely to get drawn in. A couple of stalls specialize in old postcards arranged by British county and city. Both the photos and notes written on the back, often in beautiful handwriting, provide fascinating historical records. I now have my £3 purchase in front of me. The photo shows an old hall—long since demolished—of a Norfolk village. The note, probably written from the hall, tells the correspondent that harvest began that day, 23 August 1907.

My bucolic daydream is interrupted by an inadvertent elbow from the elderly gent scrutinizing the next stall. The remaining traders deal in stamps, and he is poring over first-day covers, deftly using magnifying glasses and tweezers. As with the coins, stamps come from all over the world, and prices start low—50p for an assortment of 100. Indeed, around the room, price-cuts seem common, which explains why hard-nosed investors now have little use for philately.

High finance is not unknown. Dealers have come here from all over the world to meet gents in wax jackets with Jiffy bags full of bronze-age spearheads. At such times, large wads of banknotes change hands. But for the most part, the market's habitués are genuine enthusiasts and gentle eccentrics. Browsing among them is a treat.

Nearby cafés and shops

There are a few sandwich bars along Villiers Street, running between Embankment and Charing Cross stations, but the best bet for a budget meal is the **Café in the Crypt**, below St Martin-in-the-Fields church off Trafalgar Square (*see* p.30). There is also a pleasant café in Embankment Gardens, and one in the booking office of Charing Cross tube station. **Stanley Gibbons International** (399 Strand) and **Strand Stamps** (79 Strand) should also be visited by earnest philatelists on a Saturday outing to the market, but numismatists will have to wait for a weekday to visit **A.H. Baldwin & Sons** (11 Adelphi Terrace) and peruse its collection of coins, tokens, medals and decorations.

The Courtyard, St Martin's

Address: Courtyard of St Martin-in-the-Fields Church, off Trafalgar Square, WC2, © (0171) 930 7821.

Public transport: ⊖/⇌ Charing Cross;
buses 3, 6, 9, 11, 12, 13, 15, 23, 24, 29, 53, 77A, 88, 91, 109, 159, 176, X53.

Opening hours: Mon–Sat 11am–5pm; Sun 12 noon–5pm.

Best time to go: Saturday, early afternoon.

Car parking: very difficult; there are a few parking meters on Chandos Place, or try the (expensive) underground car park on Bedfordbury.

Main wares: crafts, novelty goods, clothes, souvenirs.

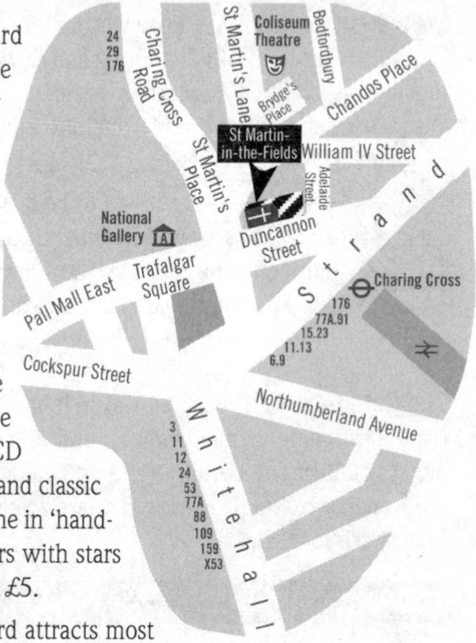

Try not to approach the Courtyard market from the Trafalgar Square entrance, for here it flaunts its tawdry side. While most of the 30 or so stall-holders deal in goods loosely described as 'ethnic', the first pitches are full of tosh for trippers—the Union Jack pinafore, the policeman's helmet, the London tea towel and the London T-shirt.

Things aren't so desperate near the Adelaide Street entrance, behind the church. Here you'll find quite a large CD stall with a fair choice of jazz, classical and classic rock music. The trader also has a sideline in 'hand-made' refillable lighters—cheap lighters with stars and glitter glued on to them. They cost £5.

Geared as it is to tourists, the Courtyard attracts most traders in mid-summer. In August you might encounter a couple of fast food stands to the rear of the church. One regular, the **Snack Shack**, dispenses jacket potatoes and breakfast fry-ups and entreats customers to 'stuff your boat-race'. I once encountered a chap who said he was from Belarus, selling Russian dolls and Soviet awards. A Mother's Glory Second Class medal cost £30.

There are usually plenty of African, Asian and Latin American crafts to be found here: Andean silver jewellery, batik printed cotton, African wooden carvings, and woven waistcoats. Attached to one stall is a collection of rainsticks. They are made from cactus plants found in the Atacama desert of northern Chile; the spines are pushed into the hollow stem, which is filled with small stones. When the stick is up-ended, the pebbles tinkle over the spines, making a sound like falling rain. No doubt this is reassuring in the Atacama desert.

More general crafts on view might include handmade jewellery boxes hewn from walnut, coloured glassware, and watches in the shapes of musical instruments. But several of the traders display the sort of goods that are commonplace at London's markets: leather jackets, hippyish clothes, pot pipes, aromatherapy goods, silk tops and mohair jumpers. Prices tend to be high.

The Courtyard market was inaugurated in the late 1980s, following in the footsteps of, but not quite managing to emulate, the Piccadilly market (*see* p.52) which is also held in a churchyard. It's a pity that there's little originality among the stalls, as the setting is sublime. A church has stood on the site for nearly 900 years, although the present neoclassical edifice was built by James Gibbs in 1722–6. Nell Gwynne (1687), Hogarth (1762) and Sir Joshua Reynolds (1762) are buried within. Young musicians give free lunchtime recitals in the church on Monday, Tuesday, Wednesday and Friday (from 1.05pm to 2pm), which can well be combined with a visit to the market.

How much better it would be if the stalls trading on the vast, venerable paving slabs around the church contained old books. The market would then echo the ethos of old Paternoster Row, by St Paul's Cathedral, which for centuries was a centre of book publishing.

Nearby cafés and pubs

The **Café in the Crypt** of St Martin-in-the-Fields (entrance on Duncannon Street) is the best value venue for meals and snacks in the area. It has a coffee bar and buffet counter. The **Lemon Tree** on Bedfordbury is a cosy backstreet pub adorned with opera posters (it is next to the rear entrance of the Coliseum, home to the English National Opera).

Covent Garden

Address: Covent Garden, WC2.

Public transport: ⊖ Covent Garden;
buses 6, 9, 11, 13, 14, 15, 19, 23, 24, 29, 38, 77A, 91, 176.

Car parking: very difficult; there are a very few parking meters along Chandos Place, otherwise try the expensive underground car park on Bedfordbury, or the equally expensive multi-storey on Upper St Martin's Lane.

Did London sell its soul when the great wholesale markets were banished from its centre? Were the moves a practical necessity, or did the prospect of lucrative redevelopment hold sway? The argument has continued since 1974, when the fruit, vegetable and flower wholesalers, who had traded at Covent Garden for 300 years, were relocated to Nine Elms in south London (*see* p.192).

The produce market began at Covent Garden (named after a medieval monastery's allotment) in the mid-1650s. About 15 years earlier, Inigo Jones had completed London's first square, a magnificent creation with Italianate arcades around its edges. (Only the much-altered St Paul's church remains of Jones's work.) Fashionable and wealthy folk were keen to bag a residence in the district. To cater for them, traders set up stalls in the gardens of Bedford House to the south of the square. The market received official status in 1670, when the owner of the land, the Earl of Bedford, was granted a licence. (The dukes of Bedford continued to own the market until 1918.)

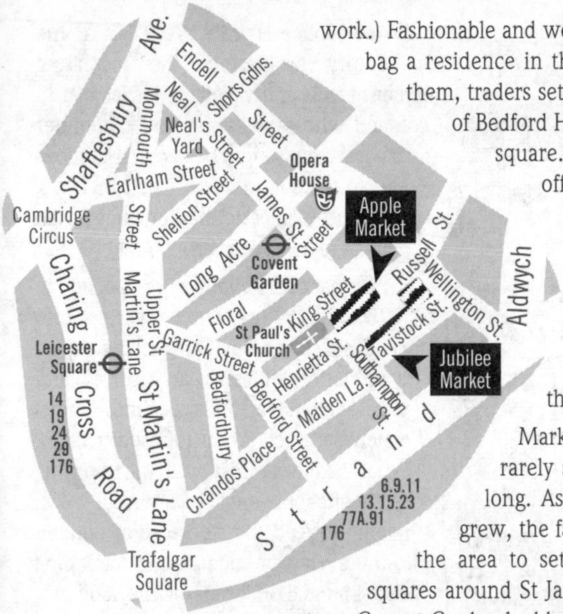

Markets and posh districts rarely survive side by side for long. As the number of traders grew, the fashionable residents left the area to settle in the newly built squares around St James's. By the mid-18th century, Covent Garden had become known for prostitutes, duels, gambling dens and gangs of aristocratic yobbos known as Mohocks. Coffee houses also flourished; Boswell, Pope, Fielding and Garrick frequented them. Though a row of permanent shops was built inside the square, much of the trading was still carried on in the open air, from temporary stalls and wooden huts.

In 1737, the closure of the Stocks market in the City increased Covent Garden's trade. About ten years later, £4000 was spent on new market buildings. Herbs, lavender and live hedgehogs, as well as fruit and vegetables, could be bought here—the hedgehogs were kept as pets to eat beetles. As London grew, so did the market, and after the Fleet market (near Fleet Street) closed in the 1820s, the trade increased still further.

By now, Covent Garden was the largest fruit and vegetable market in the country. Overcrowding continued to be a problem, so in the 1820s Charles Fowler was commissioned to design a new market building. The elegant results, though altered and enlarged, remain today. Tuscan colonnades and yellow stonework are topped by an expansive glass and iron roof which allows light through to the cobbled and paved thoroughfares below.

It's a beautiful place, but less than 30 years after its opening in 1831 it had reached capacity. And the market continued to grow. Other buildings were constructed during the late 19th century, and they were

Covent Garden

joined by the Jubilee Hall in 1904. But as the 20th century progressed, the increasing number of fruit and vegetable lorries had to contend with taxis, buses and commuter cars every morning. The decision to move out to the suburbs was taken in 1966, and the wholesale market came to an end here in November 1974.

The market buildings re-opened in 1980, their interiors converted into small shops and boutiques selling expensive clothes, 'lifestyle accessories' and gifts. The renovated Piazza almost immediately became a major tourist attraction. What had been lost was the morning bustle of people engaged in useful work, helping to feed the stomachs of London from the heart of London, and reminding office-bound Londoners of the food-production process. But there have also been benefits. Covent Garden has been in the vanguard of the movement to Europeanize London and re-introduce street life to the capital. The loosening of licensing laws has helped, and now, for most of the year, people dine and drink *al fresco* in London's oldest square, while street entertainers and buskers attract crowds onto the cobbles outside St Paul's Church.

And there are still markets in Covent Garden—of sorts. True, they are touristy, expensive and often naff, but at least they keep the streets vital. If you're looking for bargains, or wish to view Londoners about their daily business, steer clear. But if you want to see London at its most cosmopolitan, come and brave the crowds.

Apple Market

The Market, Covent Garden, WC2, © (0171) 836 9136. Open 9am–5pm daily. Crafts, clothes, novelty goods.

The Apple Market occupies the refurbished central building of Charles Fowler's old market. Along each side of the central space are shops selling crafts, designer clothes, posh toys and what not. These sorts of goods also dominate the stalls, where you'll find little pot pigs, models of penny-farthing bikes, Shetland jumpers and wooden puzzles. Some ornaments are moderately humorous—flying hippopotamuses to nail to the living-room wall in place of airborne ducks—but more often they are dull and twee (ghastly little mice dressed as Edwardian boys). And throughout the week, you'll never be deprived of designer jewellery.

At least clocks serve a purpose. Here you can buy them made from old 78rpm records, or shaped like a miniature Big Ben. Some of the clothes are also worth inspecting, especially the floppy hats and the dungarees and reversible jackets for children. Children are well provided for—provided they have rich parents or friends; the Apple Market usually has stocks of handmade teddy bears, porcelain dolls, dolls' houses and wooden toys.

At the time of writing, there are also about 50 similar stalls outside, at the northeast corner of the Piazza. Their future is uncertain, however, due to the imminent refurbishment of the nearby Opera House. A trader selling jazzy shorts and towelling dressing gowns is a regular. His stock may be vibrant, but the prices are no less astonishing—£25 for shorts. Wind chimes made from forks and spoons are also eye-catching, as are the collection of colourfully painted boomerangs. A higher percentage of crafts stalls fills the pitches at weekends. Draughts and chess sets, handmade in wood, are attractive, and there's always a selection of (expensive) leather handbags, crystal jewellery and T-shirts. A trader selling aromatherapy goods usually turns up at weekends, as does a charcoal artist who will knock out your cartoon in five minutes (£6) or produce a colour portrait (£30) in half an hour. Shona stone sculptures from Zimbabwe, curvaceous and pleasing, occasionally make an appearance. But you're more likely to encounter football scarves (why Juventus and Bayern Munich fans should want to buy their colours here, heaven knows), posters for blockbuster films, and novelty goods such as rubber monsters attached to bath plugs. Nice.

Jubilee Market

Jubilee Hall, south side of Piazza, off Southampton Street, WC2, © (0171) 836 2139. Open daily 9.30am–6pm (sometimes finishes earlier). Antiques, second-hand goods, bric-a-brac (Mon); general clothes, souvenirs, records (Tue–Fri); crafts, clothes (Sat, Sun).

Built in 1904 as a market for foreign flowers, the Jubilee Hall was extensively rebuilt in the mid-1980s using money raised by traders. It is now open on two sides; to the rear are cafés and sandwich bars, while a few permanent shops stocked with wooden furniture and various ornaments line the eastern side.

Market buffs should come here on a Monday. Few other London markets are at their best on this day of the week, and the antiques stalls that set up here on Mondays are far more enticing than the general and crafts traders you'll find here during the rest of the week.

Not all the pitches are always taken on a Monday, but the market's scope is wide, with stock ranging from cheap secondhand baubles and bric-a-brac to antiquities. Approach from Southampton Street and you are eased into the market by some undemanding junk: an old Thermos, a secondhand fishing reel. But at a neighbouring pitch is one of the highlights: a trader with a fine collection of Roman coins, medieval pilgrims' badges and thimbles from 1350 to 1800. A 14th-century bronze purse bar (from which once hung a leather purse) has a £75 tag, but prices for Roman coins can be as low as £3.

Traders seem to come from all over southern England. It's easy to imagine these respectable middle-aged folk running a quiet antiques shop in Winchester or Rye. Monday is their day out, and they make time for a chin-wag. The talk is of a dealer 'gone bad' and caught by the police. 'There's plenty more to be discovered in that case,' is the general opinion.

One woman is selling an ornate, silver-embossed pipe from 1829 (£140) and various cigarette cases. Nearby, scores of 19th-century prints of stately homes and churches are arranged by English county. Many stalls are devoted to crockery and jewellery. Among the others is an old record stall (artists range from Jim Reeves to the Beatles; most LPs cost £3), another full of elderly Gladstone bags and cricket bags, a third which has a Bakelite hairdryer in working condition for £20, and a fourth full of military medals and cap badges. Several customers are attracted to the postcard stall. Its huge stock is painstakingly ordered alphabetically, in categories such as film stars, pop stars, opera, and orchids. Most cost 50p. Victorian stirrup pumps, secondhand toys (including Dinky cars), old magazines, a collection of magnifying glasses, fountain pens, top hats, lace scarves and an old guitar amp might also grace Jubilee Hall on a Monday.

Two stalls display woodworking tools. At one, the trader is holding forth nineteen to the dozen: 'Some of these are a hundred years old. Look, you can see where the carpenter engraved his name.' At the other (full of well-weathered gouges, chisels and planes), a punter is inspecting the batch of old spirit levels. They are giving a wonky reading. 'Are you on the level here?' he asks. 'No, none of the dealers are,' is the quick-witted reply. By 2.30pm many of the traders call it a day.

From Tuesday to Friday a general market is held in the Hall. The wares are similar to those outside the Opera House, and there's little remarkable among the new clothes, handbags, watches and cheap jewellery. A bookstall has a fair collection of rock star biographies and children's books, and the record pitch has classical tapes for only £1.99 and dance CDs for £2.99, but the stalls that look out onto the Piazza are weighed down by the usual tourist tripe: busby-wearing dolls, London T-shirts and the like. The army surplus stall, with its sweat-soaked khaki, might be worth a sniff—if you like that sort of thing.

The weekend crafts market is moderately better. Look for the handmade walnut jewellery boxes, or the funny wooden windmills featuring a woman doing backstroke or a duck flying. But you need to be wary: a highly skilled craftsworker might occupy one stall, a dreadful charlatan the next. And prices everywhere are high.

One trader worth searching for is **Nicholas Crook**, a gifted calligrapher who sells handmade greetings cards (from 95p: a better deal than the usual mass-produced rubbish available from shops), and will write a message inside. He also accepts commissions to write notices on scrolls of parchment paper, and runs courses in calligraphy from his Sussex home.

But to find such gems, you must suffer the grotesquely mawkish: saucer-eyed cats and doleful dogs in china; cute lace pillows. With any luck, you'll be able to sluice this slush away with a visit to **Mervyn's Marvellous Marble** stall with its fabulous collection of bloods, crystal clears and multi-millionaires. Ah, to be seven again.

Nearby cafés and pubs

There are dozens of places to eat and drink within a couple of hundred yards; most are crowded and overpriced. For a drink, try **Bar Gritte** (1st floor, 46 The Piazza, open from 11.30am) a relaxed but trendy place that few manage to find (the entrance is in the market building, opposite Southampton Street), or the **Lamb and Flag**, an old and crowded boozer in an alley off Garrick Street. Vegetarians could do worse than a meal at **Cranks** (1 The Market), which has outdoor seating in the Piazza. But if you simply want to hang out and drink coffee, head for Neal's Yard, off Neal Street; as well as two vegetarian cafés, there's the **Neal's Yard Beach Café** with its wacky ice-creams. The best place for a budget meal is **Diana's Diner**, a five-minute walk away at 39 Endell Street.

Earlham Street

Address: Earlham Street, between Shaftesbury Avenue and Seven Dials, WC2.

Public transport: ⊖ Covent Garden, Leicester Square; buses 14, 19, 24, 29, 38, 176.

Opening hours: Mon–Sat 9am–5pm.

Best time to go: Friday lunchtime.

Car parking: very difficult; there's an (expensive) multi-storey car park on Upper St Martin's Lane.

Main wares: flowers, secondhand clothes.

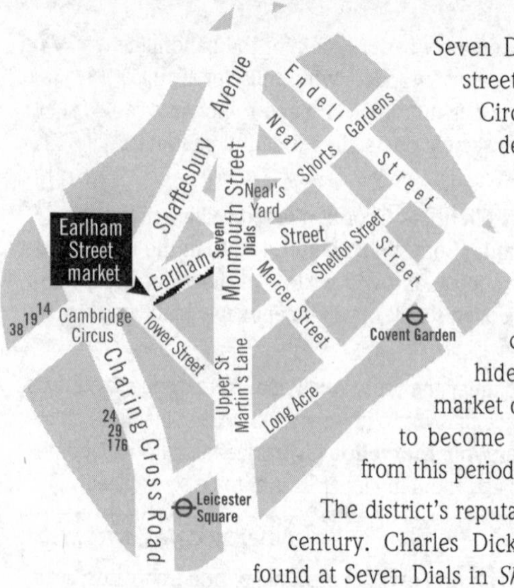

Seven Dials, that star-cluster of seven streets to the east of Cambridge Circus, was built by the property developer and Master of the Mint, Thomas Neale, between 1693 and 1710. It was intended to house fashionable Londoners near to Covent Garden and Soho, but by the late 18th century had become a notorious hide-out for thieves. The street market on Great Earl Street, which was to become Earlham Street, probably dates from this period.

The district's reputation didn't improve in the 19th century. Charles Dickens described the poverty he found at Seven Dials in *Sketches by Boz.* The building of Shaftesbury Avenue and Charing Cross Road in 1886 helped clear this impenetrable and squalid slumland, though in doing so it increased homelessness.

These days the area has been smartened up, and forms a backwater of the West End. The Seven Dials column, at the focus of the junction, supports six sundials; the pillar itself is the seventh. Removed in 1773 after (false) rumours circulated that a large stash of money was buried underneath, the column was replaced in the 1980s as part of the renovation of the area. Since then, many stylish new boutiques have opened in the old terraces, and the district is in danger of being absorbed into the Covent Garden tourist circus. But a few relics of another age—including a couple of old neighbourhood shops and a street market—still survive.

About a dozen traders set up stall on the west side of this short backstreet, away from the incessant traffic of Shaftesbury Avenue. Sadly the shellfish stand and the fruit and veg seller have gone, replaced by a mix of stalls that would seem more at home in Camden or the Apple Market of Covent Garden (*see* p.32). A large army-surplus stall takes up the first couple of pitches, displaying khaki shoulder bags, dungarees, belts and jumpers. The next trader sells Aran woollens and cotton sweatshirts; nearby, a chap flogs wooden toys, Russian dolls depicting leaders from Lenin to Yeltsin, pecking wooden chickens and metal hip-flasks with a hammer and sickle badge stuck to them.

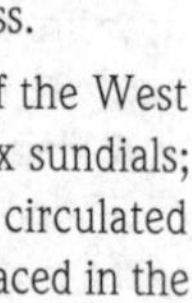

One of the most popular stalls is packed with CDs. There's a good choice of rock, pop, classical, dance and jazz (singles £1.50, albums £6). The secondhand clothes stall generates less interest among the punters—£10 is too much for an old jacket with flapping 1970s lapels, and the checked shirts, jeans and leather jackets are not as trendy as those you'd find at Camden. Still, the sales rail—everything for £5—is worth inspecting. A couple of jewellery traders turn up with their silver and glass dangly things; another pitch has a good choice of waistcoats. Nearest to the monument is a large flower stall that's been here for years. It stocks a wide variety of blooms, plus foliage for home decoration.

This small collection of stalls might not be worth travelling far to visit, but if you're in Covent Garden you should take the five minutes' stroll to Earlham Street if only to view two of its shops. The older, **Portwine** the butcher's (at No.24), dates back to at least 1760. Graham Portwine, the current family member at the helm, has steered the business towards supplying additive-free meat, free-range poultry and even vegetarian haggis. The pig's ear hanging in the window and the dark red hue of the well-hung beef (a rare sight in England) give some idea of the firm's celebration of meat.

F.W. Collins (at No.14) is a relative newcomer, having started trading only in 1835. It's an old-fashioned hardware shop, bursting with disparate bits and pieces—from nuts and bolts to a large tin bath.

During the property boom of the 1980s, rents and business rates in this area soared. Several shops selling essentials for local people (there's still a primary school and housing to the east of Seven Dials) closed down. It would be an abomination if businesses such as Collins and Portwine were forced out to make room for yet more ephemeral, exorbitantly priced boutiques.

Nearby cafés, pubs and shops

Belgo Centraal (50 Earlham Street) is an immensely popular and hip basement eating hall specializing in mussels, chips and Belgian beers. The nearest pub to the market is the **Marquis of Granby** (junction of Earlham Street with Tower Street). This welcoming Victorian boozer serves lunches such as lasagne, Cumberland sausages and fish and chips. The **Two Brewers** on Monmouth Street is a cosier place for a drink. The best place for coffee is the **Monmouth Coffee Company** (27 Monmouth Street). Good and low-priced vegetarian food can be had at **Food For Thought**, a café on nearby Neal Street (No.31). Neal Street and its environs have some of the best shops in Covent Garden. Foodies should make a pilgrimage to **Neal's Yard Dairy** (17 Shorts Gardens), with its unparalleled collection of British and Irish cheeses; and **Carluccio's** (28a Neal Street), one of the classiest (and most expensive) Italian foodshops around.

Exmouth Market

Address: Exmouth Market, near the junction of Farringdon Road and Rosebery Avenue, EC1.

Public transport: ⊖ Farringdon; buses 19, 38, 55, 63, 153, 171A, 243, 259, 505.

Opening hours: Mon–Sat 9.30am–4pm.

Best time to go: lunchtime on Tuesday and Friday.

Car parking: there are a few parking meters along Easton Street, northwest of the market. Otherwise, try the underground car park on Skinner Street, or the multi-storey car park on Bowling Green Lane—both are expensive.

Main wares: old books, secondhand clothes, bric-a-brac, shellfish, sweets.

Specifics: root around the secondhand stalls.

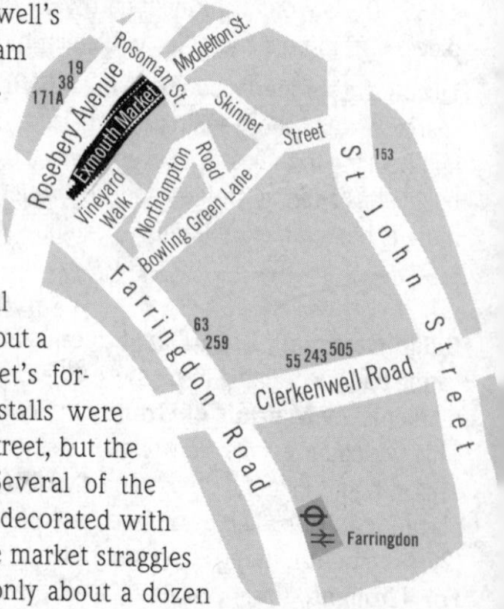

In many ways, the history of Clerkenwell's Exmouth Market mirrors that of Earlham Street in Covent Garden (*see* p.35). Both are old (this one is Victorian in origin) and occupy small streets; both fell on hard times when slum clearance reduced the local population; and both have been the object of rejuvenation attempts by their local councils. Islington managed to bring about a minor resurgence in Exmouth Market's fortunes in the late 1980s. Up to 50 stalls were attracted to the newly pedestrianized street, but the latest recession brought a relapse. Several of the street's shops are now boarded up or decorated with 'To Let' signs, and even on Fridays the market straggles along the short length of road, with only about a dozen pitches taken.

All the fruit and veg stalls have now gone, but most shops and stalls still cater for the local population. An ironmonger, an Asian grocer and a butcher have premises here, and some traders sell furniture and household appliances that no office workers could carry home. There's also a well-stocked news stand with a good choice of Irish titles (many Irish live in the locality), and a large sweet stall. An old-established seafood stand displays mussels, kippers, smoked haddock and Leigh-on-Sea cockles outside the Penny Black pub near the Farringdon Road. Both pub and stall are used by postal workers from the Mount Pleasant sorting office, opposite.

For years, Exmouth Market has been noted for old books. Traders unable to get licences for the Farringdon Road book market took up a pitch here. Several traders stock old books along with bric-a-brac and clothing. Sadly, most titles are pulp fiction written by little-known authors in the 1950s, or esoteric textbooks—but rummaging might uncover a gem.

On the first of the secondhand pitches, old jewellery shares space with a rail of women's clothes, a pair of skates (for £1), new bars of soap, a telephone of uncertain efficacy, a few postcards dating from the First World War (all £1) and a mottled collection of hardback books including the 1934 edition of *Who's Who of Women* (£1). The next trader has a new assortment of picture frames and children's jigsaws, while the following barrow contains a puzzling jumble of old stuff: clothes, an antique shaving set and some car manuals. Opposite, rails of army surplus clothes are displayed. This stall too has a small collection of books for sale (hardbacks, 50p each or five for £2). Further up the street, shoes and handbags are arranged on the pavement by traders unwilling to pay the price of a pitch.

Near the Exmouth Arms pub is one of the largest secondhand clothes stalls, with mock-fur coats, shirts for £2 and suits from £10. All the clothing is hung on rails in plastic bags to make garments look as though they've come straight from the dry-cleaner's. In addition, the trader has a baker's tray full of old books, some well-used saucepans, and a solitary pair of secondhand socks (for 20p). Mindful perhaps of Clerkenwell's history as a source of health-giving waters, he also tries to sell a 1970s electric foot spa of the type once advertised on afternoon TV by third-division celebrities. The small trickle of passers-by is unimpressed.

A hiatus in the market on the middle stretch of the street allows you to inspect the Church of the Holy Redeemer, an impressive late-Victorian structure built in Italianate style. There is another reminder of Clerkenwell's Italian community at 56 Exmouth Market; from 1818 to 1828 this was home to the famous clown Joseph Grimaldi.

A few more stalls cluster at the northeast end of the street. Most are extensions of shops. As well as the news stand, there's a household goods stall (which also has a stock of sweets), plus a collection of old cookers, chests of drawers and beds out on the street. Nearby is yet another barrow of old books.

Business isn't booming, but Exmouth Market remains an attractive street, with a collection of local shops rare in this office-dominated part of London. Yet if the market is to survive, it must go the way of Leather Lane and attract office workers at lunchtime. The opening of Al's Café-Bar (*see* below) has already drawn extra punters into the area. With luck, the street traders will benefit.

Nearby cafés and pubs

Clark's pie and mash shop (46 Exmouth Market) has an appealing new interior, though pies and eels have been served here since the 1930s. **Al's Café-Bar** (Nos.11–13) is a bright and invigorating new licensed café with great all-day breakfasts, warm focaccia bread and smashing coffee. **Carlo's Trattoria** (No.8) sells pizzas for about £4. The **Exmouth Arms**, on the corner of Exmouth Market and Spafield Street, is a friendly local. Nearby, at 159 Farringdon Road, is the **Eagle** pub, extremely popular for its expensive but classy lunchtime food.

Grays Antiques

Address: 58 Davies Street and 1–7 Davies Mews, W1, ✆ (0171) 629 7034.

Public transport: ⊖ Bond Street; buses 6, 7, 8, 10, 12, 13, 15, 16A, 23, 73, 94, 98, 113, 135, 137, 137A, 139, 159.

Opening hours: Mon–Fri 10am–6pm.

Best time to go: Thursday and Friday afternoons.

Car parking: there's an (expensive) underground car park at the London Marriott Hotel, entrance on Duke Street.

Main wares: antique silverware, jewellery, glassware, toys, ancient artefacts, commemorative china.

Specifics: Dinky toys, thimbles, old padlocks, Middle Eastern antiquities.

J. Bolding & Sons, Victorian manufacturers of sanitary appliances, brass founders and metal merchants, would likely flush their heads down their own toilets in surprise if they knew the use to which their factory off Oxford Street had been put. The ground floor and basement of this large 19th-century building is now given over to the antiques trade and, together with nearby premises on Davies Mews, houses up to 200 dealers. It's a peach of a place for browsing.

Grays is run by the firm Antiques Hypermarket, which also owns Alfie's Antiques Market (*see* 'Church Street', p.94). Situated on the edges of expensive Mayfair, it's perhaps not surprising that some of the jewellery stalls seem off-puttingly glamorous. On the whole, however, Gray's is not an intimidatingly pricey or pompous place. True, you won't find bargains, but many of the traders have high-quality

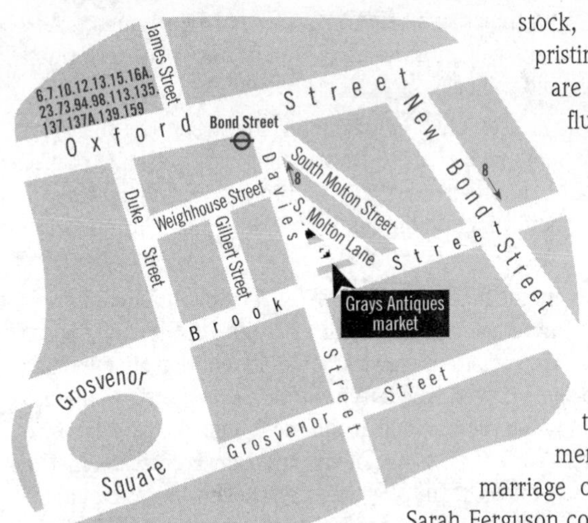

stock, and several display pristine, esoteric exhibits that are likely to get collectors flustered with pleasure.

The stalls are permanent structures, and many have glass counters. In the basement of 58 Davies Street, down a green-carpeted staircase, is a large floor full of traders. A mug commemorating the auspicious marriage of Prince Andrew and Sarah Ferguson costs £30 at the stall specializing in such things; a plate that celebrates Fred Archer's victories in classic horse races has a £295 price tag. As with many of the goods at Grays, the 'best price' is appreciably lower—just ask.

A huge variety of jewellery is kept down here, some of which was first sold 70 or 80 years ago at Mayfair shops (I spotted an Asprey's of Bond Street brooch). More interesting are the collections garnered by enthusiasts: the assortment of padlocks (impossibly cumbersome, but precision-made and lovingly restored and oiled) that evokes the workshops of Victorian Birmingham; the **Thimble Society of London**, with its array of bone bobbins and old thimbles commemorating historical events; and a fine collection of walking sticks, including a beautiful, well-worn example made from silver and partridge wood (£145).

Your eye might also be caught by the Eastern artefacts and ornaments at a stall called **Continuum** (bronze statues of the god Shiva; Buddhas from Thailand), or the Victorian policemen's truncheons, sold by a trader in militaria (ceremonial swords, cap badges and what have you). Other dealers specialize in glassware, including highly-prized Art Nouveau pieces by René Lalique; old lace; prints cadged from antiquarian books; silverware; vintage fountain pens (most costing £35); and Rolex watches. There's also a peaceful café down here, where you can stop for a cappuccino, sandwich, cake or hot meal (chicken in red wine, for instance), and gaze at yet more antiques.

More jewellery and silverware is displayed on the ground floor, where there's also a stall of old perfume bottles, and another with a display of pocket watches. One of the oddest collections is of antique hearing devices, including a tortoiseshell ear-trumpet, and painfully sharp dental instruments. Also worth perusing is Sean Arnold's stall (near the door) with its stock of old golf clubs, cricket bats, tennis rackets and golf balls.

The **Mews** section of Grays, scarcely 50 yards down the street, has still more stalls on both the ground floor and basement. Downstairs, there's also the chance to see the Tyburn, an old London stream that now runs entirely underground. Marshalled in a straight line through the room, it provides a home to a shoal of well-fed goldfish.

Toys and ancient artefacts are the highlights down here. The **Solaimani Gallery** is one of the poshest stalls (more a shop), and features tasteful displays of ancient Persian artefacts, Islamic art, pots from classical antiquity and Egyptian-looking ornaments. There's also some carved wooden furniture. Several other stalls also stock Middle Eastern antiquities. Persian and Islamic seals (much collected) are a strong point, but there's also ancient glass and pottery plus many Persian and Islamic silver coins. But even these exhibits (many of which surely belong in a museum) are outshone by the display of Dinky cars at a toy stall. All seem in mint condition, and come with their original boxes; a 1970 E-type Jaguar has a £120 price-tag. A couple of other dealers also specialize in old toys in tip-top condition. To many, the names Corgi, Chad Valley and Hornby will conjure up memories of childhood excitement. And for some sad individuals like myself, the sight of an old train set, or robot, or Thunderbirds contraption, still causes a *frisson*. Toy soldiers, cowboys and Indians, model aeroplanes, dinosaurs and circuses might also be on display.

The remaining stalls in the basement contain ceremonial swords and Oriental pots, the raw materials of interior design (cornices, fireplaces and the like), and wooden masks from Asia. There's also a bureau de change, and an attractive café with old pine tables, which serves vegetarian pasta and salmon fishcakes.

Upstairs at **Harrison's Antiquarian Books**, an elderly chap tells me the entire plot of a 1740s novel he has at home. Most of the small stock on display is leather-bound. A nearby dealer specializes in military stuff, including SS helmets, medals, suits of armour, uniforms from the First World War (including a German leather flight suit for £395) and a brief collection of war books. Coloured glassware, Chinese carvings and pottery, and more ancient artefacts including Roman and Byzantine coins and oil lamps, are also to be found on the ground floor.

The market is not held at weekends, which enables several of its traders to transport their wares to Portobello Road (*see* p.64) every Saturday. Many also attend Bermondsey market (*see* p.146) on Friday mornings, so if you're thinking of visiting on that day, best come in the afternoon.

A fair number of people, mostly European and American tourists, visits Grays, but it rarely gets unpleasantly crowded—odd when you consider that it is only a stone's throw from the turmoil of Oxford Street. Why London's most boring shopping street is also its busiest is one of the city's most mystifying conundrums. But if you find yourself struggling amid the chainstores and slow-moving, slow-thinking crowds, don't despair: there is an escape along Davies Street.

Nearby cafés, pubs and shops

Satay Stick (6 Dering Street, W1) is an inexpensive Malaysian restaurant with great satay. The **Hog in the Pound** pub, at Davies Street's junction with South Molton Street, is a touristy pub, but has outdoor seating, as does the **Red Rock Café** (40 South Molton Street), which sells pastries and sandwiches. Window-shopping at the designer fashion shops around South Molton Street or the millionaires' jewellery shops of Old and New Bond Street is a pastime pleasing to many.

Leadenhall

Address: Whittington Avenue, off Gracechurch Street and Leadenhall Street, EC3.

Public transport: ⊖ Monument;
⊖/DLR Bank;
buses 8, 15, 22A, 22B, 25, 26, 35, 40, 47, 48, 149, D1, D11.

Opening hours: shops vary, but most are open Mon–Fri 7am–4pm.

Best time to go: 11am, before it gets too busy.

Car parking: very difficult; try the (expensive) Vintry underground car park on Bell Wharf Lane (just east of Southwark Bridge).

Main wares: meat, fish, cheese, flowers, CDs, newspapers and magazines, tobacco, mobile phones.

Specifics: fish, shellfish, poultry, game birds.

Leadenhall is the oldest of London's surviving retail markets by centuries. The trouble is, it's scarcely a market any longer. The current structure is a grand Victorian arcade; it was built in 1881 by Sir Horace Jones, who also designed the market buildings at Smithfield and old Billingsgate. The businesses inside are divided into permanent premises—shops, in other words. But Leadenhall deserves to be included in this book for two reasons: its rich history, and its fresh food shops.

Before noon, the market can be a quiet place, but the peace is deceptive; listen carefully and you can hear the muffled roar of an immense city. London began here: when Sir Horace laid the foundations of his arcade, the remains of a Roman basilica and other administrative buildings were unearthed. In the Middle Ages, Leadenhall lay on the edge of the great markets of the City of London. Just examine the street names to the south and west of here: Cornhill, Poultry, Cheapside (*ceap* was a Saxon word for a market), Bread Street, Fish Street Hill, Milk Street.

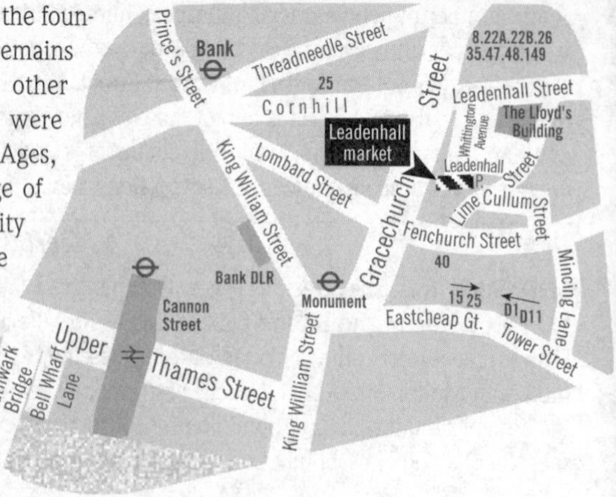

The name Leadenhall comes from the lead roof of a mansion on the site that belonged to the Neville family in the 14th century. According to John Stow's 1598 *Survey of London*, 'in 1408 Robert Rikeden of Essex and Margaret his wife confirmed to Richard Whittington [the Lord Mayor of pantomime fame] and other citizens of London, the manor of Leaden Hall. In 1411, Richard Whittington confirmed the same manor to the mayor and commonalty of London, whereby it came to the possession of the city.'

The market itself dates from the late 14th century, when a Hugh Neville was allowed to hold a market for his tenants. After the city came to run it, the trading area was reserved for outsiders—country people, provincials and even foreigners—to come and peddle their produce. From the first it was noted for poultry. Gradually other foodstuffs came to be sold here, and in 1444 the draper and one-time mayor Simon Eyre built a granary on the site. He also constructed a chapel on the east side of the building. Stow relates that every market day before noon, priests 'did celebrate Divine service there to such market-people as repaired to prayer...' This practice ended in 1484, when the market buildings were destroyed by fire.

By Elizabethan times, Leadenhall had been rebuilt. It was still the market for traders from outside London, but the poultry dealers were now joined in the street outside by traders in meat and dairy produce. They spilt out onto Gracechurch Street, almost joining up with the general market held there. Inside the market enclosure, hardware, leather and cloth were sold.

The market was destroyed once again in the Great Fire of 1666. It was soon rebuilt, and the new structure enclosed an open space divided into three. The beef market took up one section, poultry and fish another, while the third contained general shops. This system more or less continued until Sir Horace was commissioned to design the new building.

Structurally, the market has changed little since the 1880s. Four avenues, entered through tall, stone arches, meet in a central crossing. Ornate ironwork graces the interior, and glass roofing allows light onto the cobbled street below. At ground level, the building is divided into shops; no trading takes place on the street.

The best of the four avenues is approached from Gracechurch Street. By the entrance is **Nicholson and Griffin**, an old-fashioned barber's which now caters for women as well. In its basement premises you can view part of the Roman basilica on which Leadenhall is built. Inside the market, the first shop is occupied by **Butcher & Edmonds** (1, 2 & 3 Grand Avenue), a traditional butcher's with a superb choice of game birds in season. Sawdust is strewn on the floor, and a butcher in starched white tunic plucks a pheasant near the counter. Duck thighs (60p a pair), partridge legs (spindly things; 20p a pair), mallards (£3.95 each) and woodcock wrapped in bacon (£5.95) are presented for display. The turkeys are proud barrel-chested birds; the chickens are corn-fed.

Nearby, **H.S. Linwood & Son**, the fishmonger's (6–7 Grand Avenue), has a vivid, mouthwatering display outside its lock-up shop. Queen scallops, gurnard, tuna, sea bass and lobsters bask in the spotlight on crushed white ice. At the front of the shop, a chap tries to sell takeaway sushi to passers-by. **R.S. Ashby** (8 & 9 Leadenhall Market), is another butcher's, with big joints of Scotch beef, English and Welsh lamb, and calves' livers. There's another counter for cooked meats and pâté, and a fair choice of cheese, including Stilton and Shropshire Blue.

Around the corner, **Ashdown Oysters** (23 Leadenhall Market) sells rock oysters for 50p each, in season, fresh from the Duchy of Cornwall. Smoked cod's roe isn't badly priced at £6.70 per lb; oven-

Leadenhall

ready pheasants cost £3.50; and there's also fresh lobster, tuna, skate and swordfish. Feathered fowl are hung on hooks at the back. Like most fresh food shops at Leadenhall, Ashdown's has had to appeal to lunchtime snackers and diners, so outside the lock-up is a huge frying pan in which Cajun jambalaya is kept warm. The firm also owns **Beauchamp's**, a rather starchy seafood bar and restaurant next door.

There's only one fruit and veg merchant at Leadenhall, **John Kent**, who operates from No.39. The solitary florist's, **A. Booth**, sells pot plants, wicker baskets and cut flowers from No.16. Several snack bars trade in the market: **Croissant Express** appears the most popular; **Hamilton's cocktail bar** and restaurant seems one of the poshest; the tiny **Regis Snack Bar** on Leadenhall Place is one of the oldest.

Two other old-school businesses at Leadenhall are **Kandies** (No.58), a 'tobacco blender and cigar importer' according to the sign over the tiny kiosk; and **Leadenhall News**, its miniature premises bursting with magazines.

By 12.30pm the market is crowded. There's a high suit-count as stockbrokers, insurance dealers from the nearby Lloyd's Building, merchant bankers and their ilk spill out of the offices and into the snack bars, or come for a whisky and cigar at the **Lamb Tavern** or the **New Moon** (a pleasantly murky, wood-lined pub). Several drink out on the avenue, where the smell of beer mixes with that of meat.

Leadenhall remains an Epicurean oasis amid the humming air-conditioning of the finance factories. But it may not stay this way for long. New businesses coming into the market are acutely aware of the customers they can attract within this most wealthy square mile in Britain, and few want to sell food. Already one of the units has become a mobile phone showroom, and a butcher's has applied for planning permission to turn its first floor into offices. **Gieves & Hawkes**, the Savile Row tailors, have a branch nearby (18 Lime Street), as does the women's fashion chain **Jigsaw**. **Thornton's** chocolates and a greetings card place are on hand to provide office gifts. There's also a CD shop called **Farringdon's**, a sleek and roomy place that doesn't dirty its hands with pop and rock, though the classical and jazz sections are impressive.

But while poultry is still sold at Leadenhall, and reeking water from the fishmonger's flows onto the cobbles, the vestiges of the ancient market remain.

Nearby cafés

Should you not find anything you want to eat at Leadenhall, the **Seashell** fish and chip restaurant (Gutter Lane, off Gresham Street) is worth the ten minutes' walk for value and quality. Also a walk away is **Noto Ramen House** (Bow Bells House, 7 Bread Street), an inexpensive Japanese noodle bar. Good coffee can be found at **Lococo** (9a Cullum Street), a tiny coffee bar with a few stools.

Leather Lane

Address: Leather Lane, between Greville Street and Clerkenwell Road, EC1.

Public transport: ⊖ Chancery Lane, Farringdon; buses 8, 17, 22B, 25, 45, 46, 55, 63, 171A, 243, 259, 501, 505, 521.

Opening hours: Mon–Fri 10.30am–2.30pm.

Best time to go: 11.30am, before it gets too busy.

Car parking: difficult; there's a multi-storey car park (expensive) on Saffron Hill.

Main wares: women's clothes, pot plants, jewellery, handbags, children's clothes, menswear, books, fruit and vegetables, electrical goods, magazines.

Specifics: women's office wear, old magazines, bicycle spare parts.

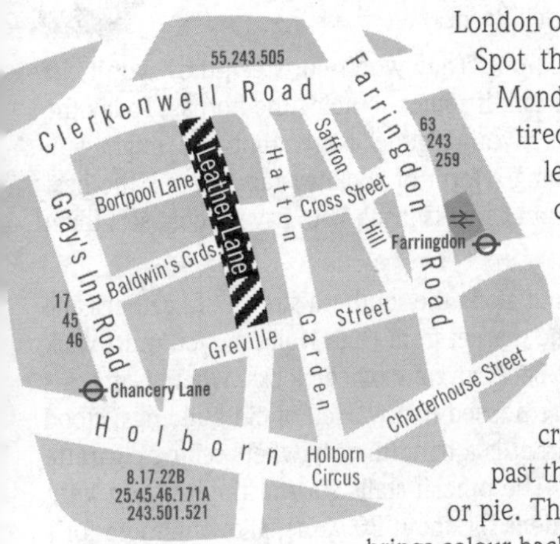

London office workers are a strange species. Spot them on the tube first thing on a Monday morning and their grey faces and tired, melancholic expressions would lead you to believe that these corporate foot-soldiers were being overworked and used up in the cause of the company. Catch sight of them at Leather Lane market at lunchtime, however, and they present a very different picture as they cram into the narrow street, shuffling past the stalls while devouring a sandwich or pie. The bustle is invigorating; the market brings colour back to their faces.

Leather Lane attracts office staff (mostly from finance institutions and the nearby Inns of Court) like worker-bees to a honey pot. This ancient street has played host to a market for well over 300 years. There are several explanations for its name. Maybe it derives from *leveroun*, French for 'greyhound', perhaps the name of a local inn; on the other hand its etymological grandparent could be *le vrune*, Flemish for 'district'; in the late 13th century, the street demarcated two districts, forming the western boundary of the Bishop of Ely's garden. Most historians agree that the derivation has nothing to do with leather, even though leather sellers have long been a feature of the market, and you can still buy leather shoes, handbags and even mini-skirts here today.

Like Whitecross Street, Leather Lane was never a major thoroughfare, so stalls have never been forced off the street by traffic or trams. In 1692 it was joined by a meat market opened by Lord Brooke. This survived until the late 19th century, when it succumbed to competition from the new deadstock market at Smithfield. Today only the name remains; Brooke's Market is a small square off Dorrington Street to the west of Leather Lane.

Mary Benedetta, in her *Street Markets of London*, describes the Leather Lane of 1936. Surprisingly little seems to have changed, though less food is now sold on the stalls. Office clerks already made up many of the punters. In those days the majority of them were men, so the clothes stalls were full of braces, belts and men's suspenders, rather than today's skirts, tights and women's suits. The electrical goods traders then sold wireless sets; now they sell Walkmans. A few toby men, whose job it was to set up traders' stalls, remained, and at that time traffic still used the street as a short cut between High Holborn and Clerkenwell Road.

In 1936, the razor blade seller called out 'They won't cut steel, they won't cut corns, they might cut off a bullock's tail, if someone holds the horns.' Today the poetry may have changed and the rhyming gone askew, but you might still encounter a gravel-voiced trader doing a form of cockney rap: 'Here's the best material, the best made, the boxer *shorts.* Marks insult you, have a look, sort them out today, *c'mon!*'

A great deal of building was carried out along the southern stretch of Leather Lane in the 1970s and 1980s. To reach the market from High Holborn, you must walk down a wide pedestrianized passage between new office blocks, where Gamage's (a famous Victorian department store housed in a warren of old buildings) stood until 1972. The first sign of the market is a handful of hawkers selling cigarette lighters, silk ties and pirate videos. The official stalls start at the junction with Greville Street, where the street widens for about 30 yards, allowing room for a few rows of semi-permanent stalls with corrugated roofs. There's a well-stocked household goods pitch with many useful bits and pieces such as household cleaners, razors and Superglue. A video stall majors in old blockbusters, most of them priced between £5 and £8. Children's clothes are sold nearby, while another trader has a large supply of leather moccasins. Woollen suits for women, tights and underwear can also be bought here. Leather Lane has the best choice of women's clothes to be found at any of London's lunchtime markets, with several unusual lines among the mass-produced stuff. Styles range from the vaguely prim to the almost saucy. Women's suits are sold at a number of stalls, and there's also a good selection of mohair jumpers, mini-skirts, smart Cashmere woollen coats, jeans, jackets (from only £15), and lingerie. The one secondhand clothes pitch has 'vintage' jeans starting at £7. The range of men's clothes is smaller but there are always plenty of ties, socks and underwear, and occasionally some jogging suits for pre-office workouts.

As you continue northwards, the street narrows and the crowd thickens. Much of Leather Lane is lined with Victorian terraces, interspersed with more recent buildings including some 1970s blocks. Back at street level, women's shoes and jewellery are much in evidence on the stalls. Among the more everyday items you might find something out of the ordinary, such as amber brooches, Andean earrings and pendants depicting signs of the zodiac. Perfumes, hair accessories and handbags are also snapped up, and there's a stall of bestseller paperbacks for office juniors to read surreptitiously under the desk.

Over the years, the amount of food available on the market has declined, but there's still a fruit stall which sells single bananas to lunchers. Near the Clerkenwell Road end, a traditional fruit and veg pitch and a trader in cheap packaged food (soup noodles 25p, sweets, peanuts 40p for 170g) still cater for locals from the neighbouring Peabody Estate.

Greetings cards, cheap tapes and CDs, towels in football colours, natty pyjamas, watches, glassware, puppets on a string and car speakers are also sold at the market, and a couple of stalls have pot plants and flower bulbs. One business that's been trading here for years sells spare parts for bicycles, including tyres, wheels and reflective strips. It also has a stock of basketballs.

Another of Leather Lane's oddities is the magazine stand. Scores of titles are kept, many of them back issues sold cheaply. Stock includes foreign-language titles, stock-car racing magazines, *Marvel* comics, *True Detective* magazine and a two-month-old copy of *Yours* with a cover picture of nice newsreader Martin Lewis wearing a nice cardigan. You can even buy old copies of *Time Out*, London's listings magazine, to remind you of all the events you've missed.

Nearby cafés, pubs and shops

There's a plentiful supply of takeaway food shops along Leather Lane, such as the **Bagel Bakery** (No.91), a strangely cross-cultural place which, along with filled bagels and saltbeef sandwiches, also stocks chocolate croissants, Turkish breads, Lebanese hot snacks and Eccles cakes. Fish and chips can be had at No.83, the **Traditional Plaice**; there's seating in the basement. The smart new **Gallery Café and Bar**, at the market's southern end, has marble-topped tables, walls decorated with film posters and a deli counter full of sandwich fillings. It also serves fry-up breakfasts and good pasta. The northern end of Leather Lane enters Clerkenwell, long a home to London's Italian population. At 138–140 Clerkenwell Road is England's oldest Italian deli, **L. Terroni & Son's**, which has a great choice of foodstuffs and alcoholic drinks. **James Gubb** the butcher's (No.85), **Brett's Provisions** (No.87) and, opposite them, **Ferraro Continental Stores** (No.90) form a clutch of Leather Lane's best food shops.

There's a couple of new pubs at the Holborn end of Leather Lane, but probably the best in the immediate vicinity is the **Melton Mowbray** (18 Holborn), a new Fuller's Ale & Pie house.

St James's and Piccadilly

Address: St James's Churchyard, Piccadilly, W1, ✆ (0171) 734 4511; south side of Piccadilly, between Hyde Park Corner and Queen's Walk, W1.

Public transport: ⊖ Piccadilly Circus, Green Park; buses 8, 9, 14, 19, 22, 38.

Opening hours: **St James's** Thur–Sat 10am–5pm; **Piccadilly** Sun 9.30am–4pm.

Car parking: difficult; try the (expensive) underground car park at Arlington House, on Arlington Street.

Main wares: crafts, paintings.

To view Christopher Wren's St James's church is reason enough to flee the Piccadilly maelstrom for the relative tranquillity of this walled courtyard. But on three days a week there is the added draw of a crafts market. The church—famed for its liberal leanings—was considered something of a ground-breaker when it allowed the market to be established here in the early 1980s. Indeed, St Martin-in-the-Fields (*see* p.28) followed suit a few years later. But the authorities were simply reviving a custom common in the Middle Ages, when traders would gather outside (or sometimes inside) a church porch each Sunday to wait for the congregation to emerge.

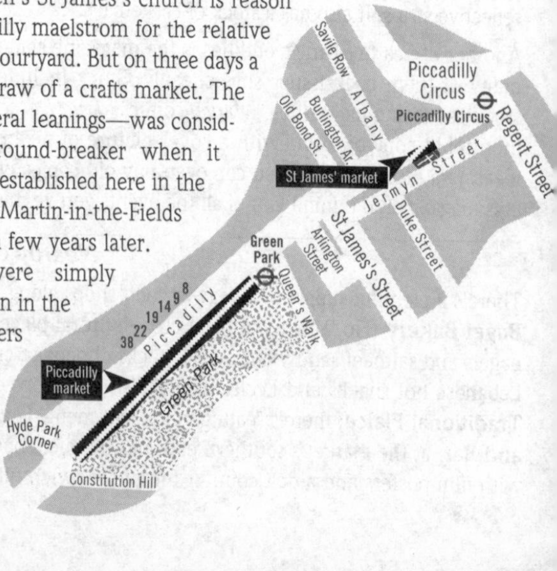

About 30 dealers set up stall outside St James's, selling a fair mix of imported goods from Third World countries, own-made artefacts and antiques. There is relatively little tourist junk, and the variety and quality of the goods is higher than you'll find at St Martin's. Most of the punters are, of course, tourists.

St James Piccadilly from Southwood Gardens

A man from Tibet sometimes turns up to sell small rucksacks with tapestry fronts, thick woollen socks and 'Free Tibet' car stickers. Nearer the courtyard wall, Fred Segal regularly takes a pitch. He stocks jewellery made from coins, and collections of stamps, but is mainly concerned with selling his own paintings. Most of these cost between £40 and £60 and feature London scenes or semi-clad women.

Wood carvings from Africa and printers' wooden blocks seem to be obligatory at this type of market, and St James's doesn't disappoint. You might also find silver jewellery from Indonesia and carved wooden boxes from India. British-made crafts include jade, wooden and Celtic jewellery, chunky woollen jumpers, pens made from wood, ornaments made from horseshoe nails, pottery, sculptures made in Devon from Alpine marble, and Egyptian-style paintings on papyrus. One long-established business specializes in wooden pipes; prices start at about £10.

The Camdenesque New Age factor can be found at one stall displaying fossils and crystals, and another with hippyish new clothes. Among the goods more obviously aimed at the general tourist market are miniature painted pub signs and nondescript brass ornaments. A trader selling prints of E.H. Shepherd's sketches from A.A. Milne's *Winnie the Pooh* books attracts a fair amount of interest.

There are always a few antiques stalls. One regular sells cutlery and silverware, including silver snuff boxes; a nearby stall has old opera glasses and crockery. Lovers of antique pottery dogs (are there any?) might also find a visit here rewarding, and there are usually some 19th-century prints to be had. Occasionally a secondhand clothes dealer turns up. His suede jackets (from £10) are cheaper than many you'd find in Camden, but as a rule prices at the market—sited in one of London's most expensive districts—are high.

Wren built St James's, the only London church he constructed on an entirely new site, between 1676 and 1684. Though the church was badly damaged in the Second World War, it is still a fine building, with a modest and well-proportioned exterior and restrained classicism within. Don't miss the reredos (altar screen) carved in limewood by Grinling Gibbons. To the west of the building, a garden of remembrance commemorates the Londoners who died during the Blitz.

Further west on **Piccadilly** every Sunday, another market of sorts takes place when traders hang their wares and paintings onto the railings of Green Park. This is really an extension of the Bayswater Road market (*see* p.60), which takes place at the same time. Overpriced trinkets and pictures of bright-eyed beefeaters are the norm, though there might also be a few traders from the previous day's market at St James's.

Nearby cafés and shops

The **Wren at St James's**, a vegetarian café built on to the church, is a bright space decorated with paintings for sale. It's open all day, has good coffee, and much of the food (wholesome soups, casseroles, snacks and cakes) is organic. A posh but not too expensive alternative is to take tea (or breakfast, lunch, a snack or one of the fine choice of ice-creams and sundaes) at the Fountain restaurant on the ground floor of **Fortnum & Mason** (181 Piccadilly). Shops around here are unfeasibly expensive, but it can be fun to window shop along the Burlington and Piccadilly Arcades (both off Piccadilly) or down Savile Row. Watch out for old buffers straight out of a P.G. Wodehouse novel.

Strutton Ground

Address: Strutton Ground, off Victoria Street, SW1.

Public transport: ⊖ St James's Park;
buses 11, 24, 88, 211, 507.

Opening hours: Mon–Fri 11.30am–3pm.

Best time to go: midday Friday.

Car parking: difficult; try the (expensive) car park near the junction of Tufton Street with Great Peter Street.

Main wares: clothes, umbrellas, fruit, household goods, electrical accessories, flowers, greetings cards.

There is an evocative—but most likely false—tale that Strutton Ground gained its name from the strutting of Peers of the Realm, who sauntered along this little

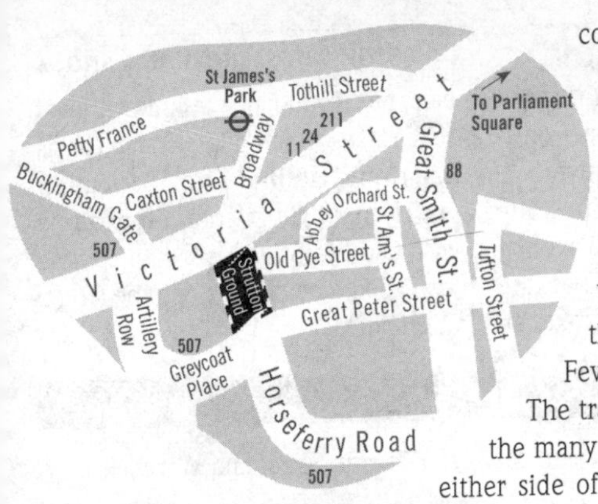

connecting street on their way to Parliament. Today the sauntering has given way to jostling, and the peers to plebeians, as every weekday hundreds of office workers emerge from the edifices of Victoria Street and pop round the corner in search of lunch. Few of the market stalls provide it. The traders don't try to compete with the many sandwich bars and snack joints either side of the street. All you'll find is a couple of fruit stalls, with costers used to selling single apples or bananas to office juniors lunching on the hoof.

Most of the 20 or so barrows contain the type of goods snapped up as lunchtime impulse buys. Thus there's an umbrella stall—never long without a purchase during the winter months—and a good line in low-priced women's clothes. These range from simple tops ('£14.99 in Top Shop, a fiver only here'), to overcoats, via smart office suits, tights, shoes, underwear and gloves. Menswear is limited to sweatshirts, silk ties, socks and underwear, plus a few shirts.

Two traders stock cheap watches, batteries, plugs and blank cassettes and videos, and there's also a stall providing household essentials such as washing-up liquid for workers who won't get home until after their local shops have closed.

A couple of stalls carry goods for use in the office. Buy a bunch of flowers for Mrs Prendergast in Accounts at one barrow, and accompany it with a 'Sorry you're leaving' card from another. You can even buy the pen to write 'Best of luck finding a new job'. Some market traders are recession-proof.

This narrow bustling street, with its three-storeyed buildings, provides a relief from the monotony of the office blocks on Victoria Street. Though most of its present buildings are Victorian, Strutton Ground was first laid out during the 1670s, when the area was surrounded by market gardens. The market most likely started in the 18th century, with the produce of these gardens being sold to the citizens of Westminster. A hay market was once held in Broadway, to the north of Strutton Ground, but this was closed in the 1720s. A relic of that era survives around the corner in Caxton Street: the tiny brick Blewcoat School was built in 1709.

Nearby cafés, pubs and shops

Strutton Ground is crammed with sandwich bars, but if you fancy a sit-down meal try **Café Bianco**, round the corner on Greycoat Place, which offers cheap pastas and pizzas. An English alternative is the **Laughing Halibut** (No.38 Strutton Ground), a fish and chips café with seating in its clean, bright interior. **Finnegan's Wake** (opposite Strutton Ground's junction with Old Pye Street) is a themed Irish boozer with draught Guinness. There are several good food shops along the street. **Stiles Bakery** (No.6) has Eccles cakes and nougat sticks.

Tachbrook Street

Address: Tachbrook Street, between Churton Street and Warwick Way, SW1.

Public transport: ⊖ Pimlico;
⊖/⇌ Victoria;
buses 2, 24, 36, 185, C10.

Opening hours: Mon–Sat 9.30am–4.30pm.

Car parking: difficult; try the multi-storey car park on Semley Place.

Main wares: fruit and vegetables, fish, flowers, greetings cards, children's clothes.

Funny thing about Tachbrook Street: it has everything in place to be the centre of a thriving community, yet even on a Friday lunchtime, customers only arrive in dribs and drabs. The dozen or so stalls are well stocked, but there's little passing trade. While nearby Strutton Ground (*see* p.52) attracts battalions of office workers, Tachbrook Street is very much Pimlico's local market. It is surrounded by a wide mix of housing: well-kept Victorian terraces, home to affluent professionals, and low-rise council flats on the Longmore Gardens Estate. On weekdays, it is mostly old people from the flats who come to examine the stalls.

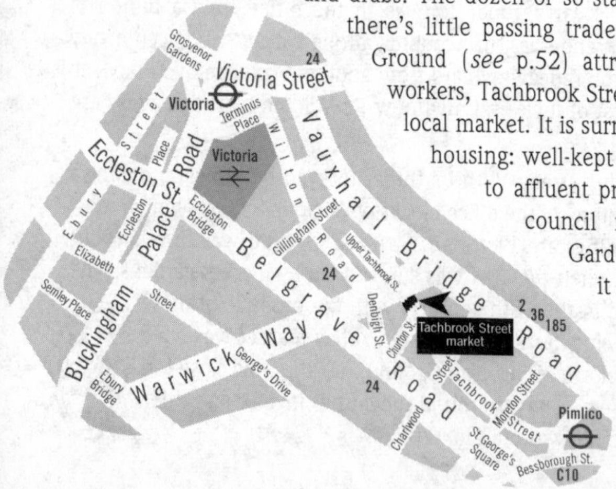

A couple of businesses have been trading on the market virtually since it started in the mid-19th century. **Wright's** fish stall was established in 1876; the family now runs two barrows. One is weighed down with a classy array of expensive fish such as bass, lemon sole, salmon and monkfish, although they also stock whiting and mackerel. The other stall specializes in shellfish, and again there are some auspicious exhibits: fresh scallops in their shells, smoked salmon and dressed crabs get pride of place among the cockles and jellied eels.

John Foster runs one of the market's five fruit and veg stalls, and his family too has been working on Tachbrook Street for over a century. He lists several reasons for the market's decline. For a start, it gets no help from Westminster Council, which has been known to impound traders' barrows left in the street overnight, charging owners £200 for their return. In addition, the price of a pitch is a hefty £3000 a year. Mr Foster also laments the reduction in the area's Spanish population, many of whom returned to their homeland during the last recession. 'They treat fruit as a staple, where the British treat it as a luxury.' The local Tesco's—nearby, but not close enough to attract custom to the market—hasn't helped either.

Most of the greengrocery stalls divide their produce into salad goods (cucumbers, iceberg lettuces and tomatoes), fruit (plums, Spanish navel oranges, grapes) and vegetables (cabbages, potatoes, onions). The best of them, outside **Ivano's** fruit and veg shop (great for dried paprika peppers), has red onions, celeriac and bunches of fresh sage and coriander, as well as the staples. Ivano's also runs a delicatessen on this stretch of Tachbrook Street. Gaze at the display of pizzas, pies and tortillas and drool. The **Bonne Bouche** bakery nearby will also provide lunchtime snacks.

The remaining stallholders supply cut flowers, children's clothes and greetings cards. The traders seem to have little hope that their market will continue for long. Its closure would be a great pity, as central London has too few of these neighbourhood street markets, and the stalls complement the great collection of local independent shops. As I leave, a costermonger with time to kill blows on her cold hands and inspects her box of change. It's nearly empty.

Nearby cafés, pubs and shops

Both the small pedestrianized section of the street that holds the market, and its northern neighbour, Upper Tachbrook Street, are peppered with fascinating small shops. Swoop in from the Vauxhall Bridge Road and you'll come upon **Rippon Cheese Stores** (26 Upper Tachbrook Street), a tiny cheesemonger's packed with British and foreign specimens; **Cornucopia** (12 Upper Tachbrook Street) with its antique clothing for women; and a fine Italian delicatessen, **Gastronomia Italia** (8 Upper Tachbrook Street).

Back towards Victoria Station from the market, at 80–81 Wilton Road, is the **Seafresh Fish Restaurant**, the best fish and chip shop in the area. Slightly further, but worth the walk, is the **Well Coffee House** (2 Eccleston Place), an inexpensive but elegant café run in association with a local church. The branch of the **Slug and Lettuce** chain on Upper Tachbrook Street is a decent, bare-boards pub, with food a notch above the norm: tagliatelle with mushrooms and tomatoes; pan-fried pork with sage, onions and home-fries. There are two notable wine bars along Upper Tachbrook Street. The **Pimlico Wine Vaults** (No.19–22) occupy underground cellars and have a daily changing menu plus a large range of wines by the glass; the **Reynier Wine Library** (No.16) offers a lunch buffet of nibbles to accompany the fruit of its cellars. Both establishments are also wine merchants.

Whitecross Street

Address: Whitecross Street, between Old Street and Sutton's Way, EC1.

Public transport: ⊖/⇌ Moorgate, Barbican, Old Street; buses 4, 43, 55, 56, 76, 141, 172, 214, 243, 271, 505, X43.

Opening hours: Mon–Fri 10.30am–2.30pm.

Best time to go: Thursdays and Fridays.

Car parking: difficult; there's an (expensive) underground car park at the Barbican (entrance on Silk Street or Beech Street).

Main wares: new clothing, shoes, tapes and CDs, watches, fruit, crockery, tools, magazines.

Specifics: look for bargains among the tapes and CDs, the crockery seconds and tools.

Whitecross Street is a narrow medieval thoroughfare which has long been home to a market. It used to run all the way to Fore Street at the edge of the City, but its southern half was destroyed by bombing in the Second World War, and the Barbican Centre was built on the site. The street was named in the 13th century after a white cross that stood near a house owned by the Holy Trinity Priory in Aldgate. Stow, writing in the 1590s, remarks that 'In White Crosse Street King Henry V built one fair house, and founded there a brotherhood of St Giles...the lands were given to the brotherhood for the relief of the poor.' But the street—sited just outside the jurisdiction of the City—became known for less charitable activities: a 17th-century ballad mentions it as the home of a famous brothel, and unlicensed street trading flourished. In the 1850s, Henry Mayhew counted 150 stalls here.

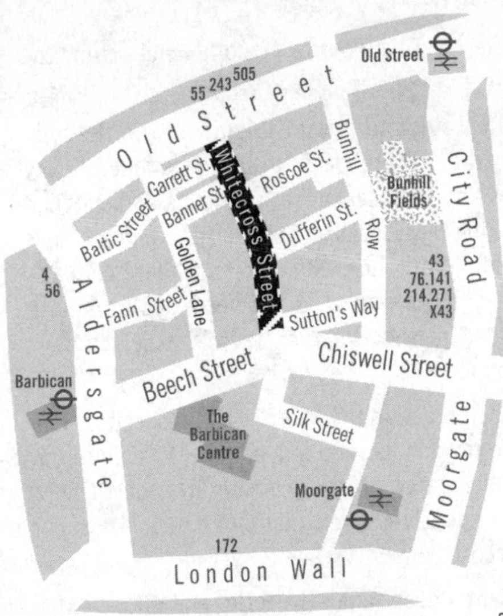

Over the years, Whitecross Street market has geared itself to the needs of local office workers. As soon as the main lunch break is over at 2pm, traders start packing up. Unfortunately, the recession and office relocations have slashed the number of workers in the vicinity over the past five years, while those who remain tend to be chained to their desks by the 'lunch is for wimps' doctrine.

The market has shrunk noticeably as a result. At the start of the 1990s, all manner of traders were attracted here. I remember spotting a dilapidated barrow containing chunks of rock. A sign above read 'pieces of the Berlin Wall, £1'. The stall was suspiciously close to a building site littered with masonry.

But though the market has lost some of its bustle, a good number of stalls still take up pitches between Old Street and Dufferin Street. And there are still enough punters to encourage fly-traders to operate on a Thursday and Friday opposite Roscoe Street. Bootleg videos of new Disney films, balanced on old cardboard boxes, make up their display.

One of the first stalls at the Old Street end carries an abundance of crockery—capacious oven-proof casseroles (£5), mugs, and teapot seconds. It also sells Tupperware containers, china dolls and tinkling wind chimes. Nearby dealers sell greetings cards, pot plants, handbags and padded shirts. **Alexander's Bakery** (No.203) can also be found on this stretch of the street; try its moreish soda bread. For meat, head for **A.L. Hall's** (No.139), Whitecross Street's solitary butcher.

Several stalls sell clothing. Though the stock changes with the season, it is mostly geared to women office workers, and might include smart jackets (from £15), knitwear, suits in black, white and bright red, gloves and skirts—the usual mass-produced stuff. There's also a cosmetics stand, a hair accessories stall and a few jewellery traders: one has silver earrings, the others specialize in cheap trinkets. One stall is filled with men's boxer shorts and socks.

A trader in old boots has been a regular on the market for a few years now. His well-polished stock includes shop seconds and returned goods among the more weathered footwear. Prices start at £10. Four or five other stalls stock the type of footwear worn by women in offices.

A few of the traders gear their stock to the inhabitants of the Peabody Estate, to the east of the market. There's a fruit and vegetable barrow which also sells eggs, pickles and bunches of fresh herbs, a well-stocked tool stall with hammers, masking tape, locks and saw blades, and a couple of stalls selling children's wear, including tiny sheepskin jackets. Children are also catered for at the sizable magazine stand. As well as such diverse publications as *Yachting World*, *Guitar Player* and *Creative Needles* there's a selection of colouring pads and learning-to-read books.

The two stalls specializing in low-priced tapes and CDs are worth inspecting. One is run by the **Cut-Price Music Store** outside its shop at No.145. Most albums go for £2, but choice is limited. The other, more or less opposite, has chart CDs at £10, plus secondhand CDs at £7—expensive, given that stock includes Supertramp's *Crime of the Century*. Tapes cost from £1.

Apart from an electrical goods stall with cheap radios, batteries and phone extensions, that's about it. The stalls peter out near the junction with Dufferin Street. Fifty yards further south, however, the market makes a comeback under a block of flats outside a supermarket. On daft purpose-built stalls with cute little roofs, you'll find greetings cards, children's books, football posters, silk ties, handbags, suitcases, towels and bed covers, more women's clothes, and men's shirts and trousers.

A short walk to the west of the market is Bunhill Fields, one of London's oldest burial grounds, much favoured by dead nonconformists. The last burial took place here in 1854. Within are the graves of William Blake, John Bunyan and Daniel Defoe. It's a beautiful old place, with huge plane trees and well-worn flagstones, quite at odds with the busy roads and modern office buildings around it.

Nearby cafés and pubs

The **Cosy Supper Bar** (No.169), a fish and chips restaurant, is one of the most popular of the several cafés along Whitecross Street. The takeaway queue stretches out of the door on Fridays. The **Barbican Grill** (No.117) is a caff of the old school, serving sandwiches and fried breakfasts, including bubble and squeak. High class vegetarian food can be had at **Carnevale** (No.135), which serves takeaway snacks and salads all day, though you might need to book (✆ 0171 250 3452) for its excellent Mediterranean-style lunches. A relaxed mix of drinkers and diners patronizes the **Molly Bloom**, opposite Whitecross Street's junction with Garrett Street. If you just want a coffee, a good bet is the **Coffee Break** (No.149), a tiny new Italian café.

West London

Portobello Road

Bayswater Road

Address: south side of Bayswater Road, from Clarendon Place to Queensway, W2.

Public transport: ⊖ Lancaster Gate, Queensway, Bayswater; buses 12, 70, 94.

Opening hours: Sun 9.30am–4pm.

Best time to go: morning (early if looking for a car park).

Car parking: plenty of places near Bayswater Road on a Sunday, but spaces are taken up quickly during the summer; try Lancaster Gate.

Main wares: new paintings, drawings, etchings and crafts.

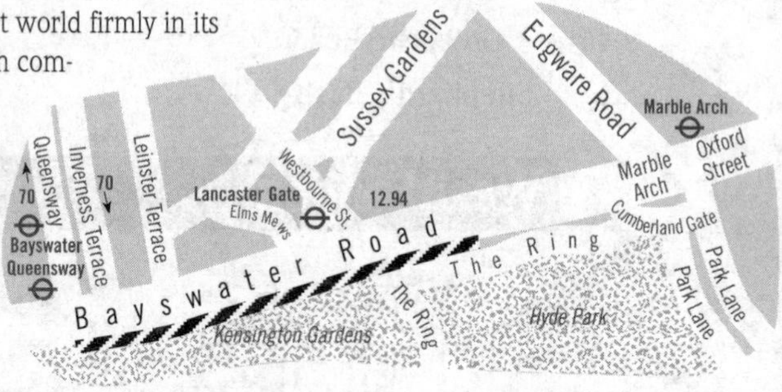

Money has the art world firmly in its grip, but the brash commercialism of Bayswater Road's Sunday art market is almost refreshing compared to the haughty but equally venal commercial galleries of Mayfair's Cork Street. For almost a mile, the railings of Hyde Park are decked with oil paintings, watercolours, sketches and collages by undiscovered artists, would-be artists and con-artists from all over southern England. The quality of work varies enormously: a few are laughingly inept, most are sentimental and dull, but very occasionally you might encounter something eye-catching.

The majority of traders are out for a quick buck (or yen, or Deutschmark), taking all major credit cards. They paint archetypal London scenes, with a reliably high beefeater count each week: mawkish horrors such as cuddly dogs, teddy bears and pussycats; or typically English landscapes (thatched houses, fields of wheat—you know the sort of thing). Spot the influence behind each picture—Monet, Constable and Renoir are the most slavishly copied, but van Gogh, Lichtenstein and even Picasso and L.S. Lowry have their imitators. Many traders display cards from Westminster Council stating: 'All work displayed or offered for sale is entirely the original work of the licence-holder.' Take this with a large pinch of salt and gargle.

Nudes get a look in, and so do reproductions of Impressionist works, but there is also space for a few amateur enthusiasts who dream of selling their first painting.

Some exhibit newspaper clippings, flaunting rave reviews from such organs as the *Bromley & Beckenham Times.* A few artists will draw your portrait while you wait. A brief head and shoulders sketch costs £4, a full-length sketch £15. I spotted one shameless individual charging £75 for a portrait of your favourite pet. Probably the cheapest original works you'll find are the tiny cartoons depicting aspects of London life: five for £5.

It's worth finding the work of painters who steer clear of immediately saleable themes. One specializes in portraits of boxers, another in military paintings. My favourite is Dennis Barrington. His astonishing *End of the Dry Season* is a wild collage involving kippers leaping from the painting.

An increasing number of crafts traders now come to the market. Their stock varies from the amusingly novel (look for the colourful face masks depicting animal heads: there's a great one of a parrot with a huge red beak) to out-and-out tourist tosh. Several sell handmade jewellery and come to Bayswater after spending Friday and Saturday at St James's market in Piccadilly. On Sundays paintings are also hung along the railings of Green Park on Piccadilly (*see* p.52). Embroidered bags, painted table-mats, fridge magnets and hand-painted coins can also be found. Be careful before taking photos at the market, as many traders object to you sampling their works of art on the cheap.

Bayswater Road should be saved for a fine morning, but you shouldn't come here expecting a traditional London street market (head east to Brick Lane, *see* p.115, for the best Sunday morning shindig). Rather, view it as part of an exploration of Hyde Park. Dappled sunlight streams through the plane trees onto the traders as you walk along one of London's oldest roads (Bayswater Road is part of the Roman Via Trinobantia). Only the unceasing traffic mars the peace. Glance across at 100 Bayswater Road, on the corner of Leinster Terrace. Sir James Barrie, the playwright, lived here from 1902 to 1909, during which time he wrote *Peter Pan.*

After a stroll along the market, leave the traffic behind and enter the park. Head towards Marble Arch (perhaps stopping to watch the horse-riding lessons in the paddock on the way) and you'll eventually come to Speakers' Corner. Londoners have exercised their right to free speech here since 1872. Speakers range from the Messianic to the downright dotty: legalization of cannabis, Christianity, world federalism and Islam are perennial topics under discussion. Some heroic characters even continue when no one is listening.

Nearby cafés and pubs

Across the Bayswater Road from the market, near the junction with Elms Mews, is the **Swan** pub, which dates from the 18th century. Despite the traffic, this is a good place to sit outside for a drink under the trees on a sunny day, and the pub also sells food. But my choice for Sunday lunch would be to walk down to Queensway where some of London's best Chinese restaurants are situated. You can eat *dim sum* (inexpensive lunchtime snacks and filled dumplings) at **Royal China**, 13 Queensway, ✆ (0171) 221 2535.

Hammersmith

Address: Hammersmith Grove, between King Street and Beadon Road, W6.

Public transport: ⊖ Hammersmith;
buses 9, 9A, 10, 27, 33, 72, 190, 211, 220, 266, 267, 283, 295, 391, H91, R69.

Opening hours: Mon–Wed, Fri, Sat 9am–5pm; Thur 9am–1pm.

Best time to go: Fridays and Saturdays.

Car parking: there's a car park (paying) just north of the market on Hammersmith Grove.

Main wares: fruit and vegetables, flowers, meat, fish, shellfish, bicycles.

Specifics: Irish foodstuffs.

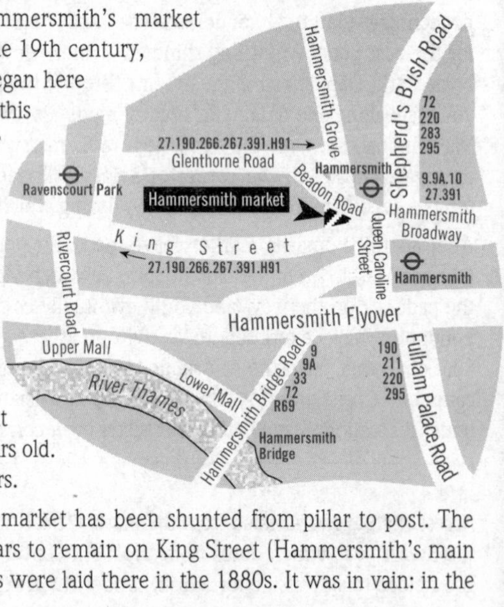

It's uncertain whether Hammersmith's market existed before the middle of the 19th century, but I suspect street trading began here earlier. All the signs point to it: this west London borough is far enough (about 7 miles) from the City not to compete with its markets, and the district has long been well served by transport—it is close to the Thames and is crossed by two great roads from London. An old costermonger interviewed in 1884 thought the market to be a hundred years old. He had traded there for 40 years.

During the past century, the market has been shunted from pillar to post. The traders battled for over 20 years to remain on King Street (Hammersmith's main shopping street) after tramlines were laid there in the 1880s. It was in vain: in the

1900s the market was moved to a side street, Bradmore Lane. But in 1972 that road was swallowed whole when the area was redeveloped and a multi-storey car park, offices, a shopping mall and the Lyric Theatre were built on the site. Beadon Road then became a temporary home for the market. It wasn't until 1978 that the traders were moved to their present site on the southern stub of Hammersmith Grove, just off King Street.

About a dozen stalls are now grouped together on the east side of Hammersmith Grove, with a further half-dozen or so traders operating on and around a tarmac courtyard just off the street. The first stall at the King Street end is well stocked with mostly traditional British vegetables. Two Moët et Chandon umbrellas keep rain off the 'Bobby beans' (French beans) and Brussels sprouts. Next to it is a fruit trader, with the usual apples, oranges and lemons. Another stall has all you need for an old-fashioned English salad: watercress, iceberg lettuce, radishes and eggs. There's a couple of good stalls selling marine life. The shellfish stand has whelks from Norfolk and winkles from Scotland as well as prawns. Vinegar, salt and pepper are kept on white tables nearby. The fish stall (John Tydeman, established 1897) has a fair selection of fish and seafood, including squid and 'uncooked scampi'. At the Beadon Road end of the market, a woman sells cut flowers and pot plants.

Two of the most interesting stalls are set off Hammersmith Grove in a yard. One trader here has about 20 new and secondhand bicycles for sale, with prices for a secondhand model starting at £35. He also sells spare parts and undertakes repairs. And at **Sheahan's Meat Market** you'll find Irish bacon, black and white pudding and Dublin lamb chops. It also stocks a range of other Irish foodstuffs, including soda bread and balm brack (a round currant loaf), plus imported brands—Cidona apple drink, Nash's red lemonade, and Yr sauce—rarely seen this side of the Irish Sea. A cheery crew of Irish butchers greets customers.

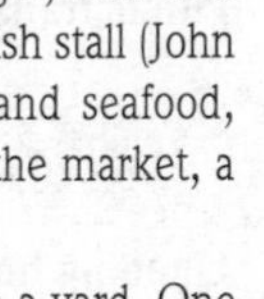

By the entranceway to the yard is another straightforward fruit and veg stall. Near the bike stall is a pet-food business (Wed–Sat) called Crispy's. A children's clothes pitch and a Thai noodle stall (closed on my last visit) complete the picture. At the end of the yard is Hilda's Wool & Haberdashery shop.

King Street and its indoor shopping mall have a disappointingly bland collection of high street shops, and much of the rest of Hammersmith is dominated by the roar of traffic. Two attractions remain: the beautiful river frontage (look out for the poet and designer William Morris's home, Kelmscott House, on Upper Mall) and the small knot of traders that keep the market alive.

Nearby cafés and pubs

Traders and seasoned marketgoers call in for breakfast at the **Broadway Snack Bar**, a basic but friendly old place with a few stools inside, right by the market. There's also a branch of the **Pret à Manger** sandwich bar chain at the junction of Hammersmith Grove and King Street. But if you want to escape the noise and bustle, take a ten-minute walk along Hammersmith Bridge Road to the Thames. Both the **Blue Anchor** and the **Dove** pubs (turn right and walk along the tow-path) serve decent food by the river. Superb vegetarian food can be had at the **Gate** (first floor, 51 Queen Caroline Street, towards the river), which is open for lunch from Tuesday to Friday.

Portobello

Address: Portobello Road, Westbourne Grove, Acklam Road, Golborne Road, W10, W11, ✆ (0171) 727 7684, (0171) 341 5277 or (0171) 373 6099; *see individual markets for details.*

Public transport: ⊖ Notting Hill Gate, Ladbroke Grove, Westbourne Park; buses 12, 27, 28, 31, 52, 70, 94, 302 (Notting Hill Gate); buses 23, 28, 31 (Westbourne Park); buses 7, 23, 52, 70, 295, 302 (Ladbroke Grove).

Opening hours: *see individual markets for details.*

Best time to go: Saturday morning.

Car parking: impossible at the antiques end of the market; there are sometimes spaces along Golborne Road, southwest of its market.

Main wares: antiques, food, new and secondhand clothes, bric-a-brac, crafts, household goods.

Specifics: secondhand clothes under the Westway; junk bargains at the Golborne Road end of the market and on Acklam Road.

Bermondsey might have the edge for antiques, Berwick Street for food, Brick Lane for bric-a-brac and Camden for clothing—but nowhere can compare to the Portobello for an all-in-one experience. Yet it's no homogeneous mass: this Saturday celebration consists of five separate markets roughly stapled together, and it's easy to see the joins.

Portobello Road cuts through the neighbourhood like a cheese iron, taking a sample of all its constituents. The southern stretches, nearest to Notting Hill Gate tube, are opulent and genteel, while the northern tip is scruffy and verging on the lawless. The cutting edge of gentrification, currently just north of the Westway, is

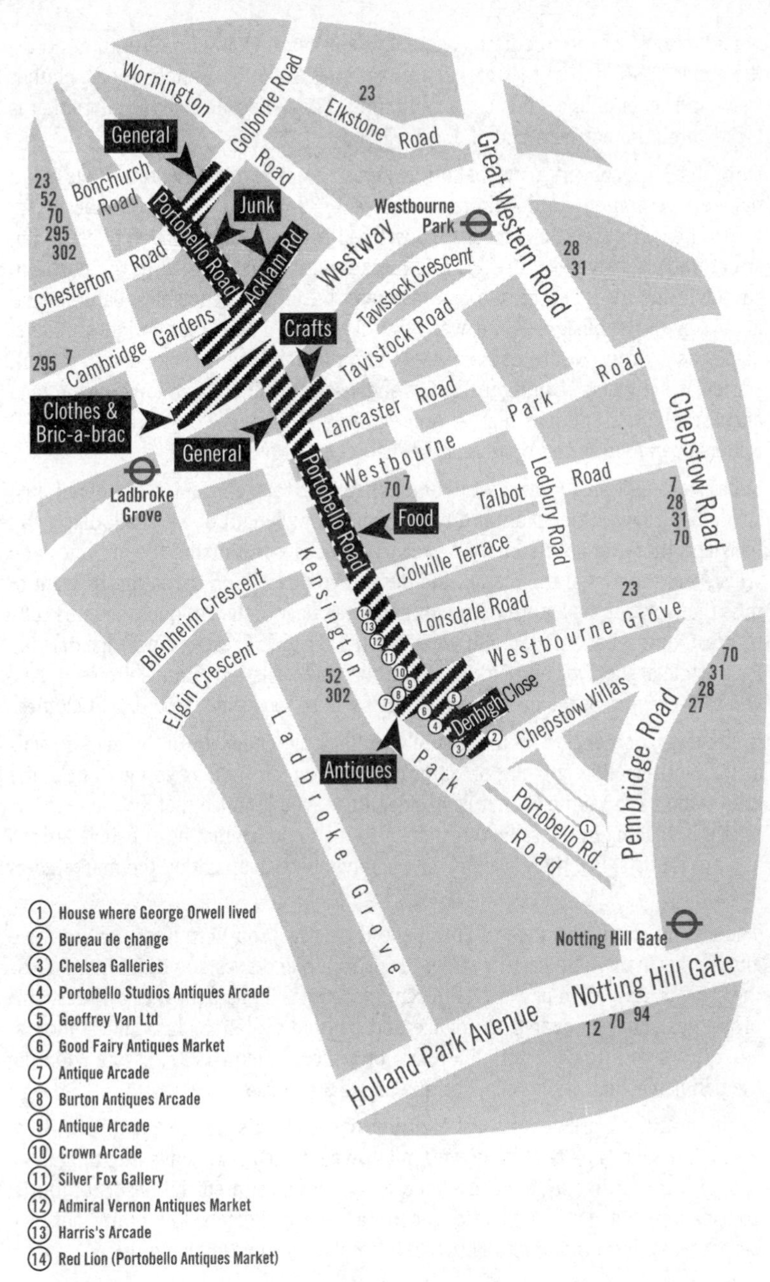
Wornington
Golborne Road
Road
Elkstone Road
23
General
Bonchurch Road
23
52
70
295
302
Portobello Road
Junk
Acklam Rd.
Chesterton Road
Westway
Westbourne Park
Great Western Road
28
31
Tavistock Crescent
Tavistock Road
Cambridge Gardens
Crafts
295
7
Clothes & Bric-a-brac
General
Lancaster Road
Park Road
Chepstow Road
Westbourne
Ladbroke Grove
70
7
Talbot Road
Ledbury Road
Food
7
28
31
70
Colville Terrace
Kensington
Blenheim Crescent
Lonsdale Road
23
Westbourne Grove
Elgin Crescent
52
302
Denbigh Close
Chepstow Villas
70
31
28
27
Pembridge Road
Antiques
Park
Portobello Rd.
Road
Ladbroke Grove
Notting Hill Gate
Notting Hill Gate
Holland Park Avenue
12
70
94
1 House where George Orwell lived
2 Bureau de change
3 Chelsea Galleries
4 Portobello Studios Antiques Arcade
5 Geoffrey Van Ltd
6 Good Fairy Antiques Market
7 Antique Arcade
8 Burton Antiques Arcade
9 Antique Arcade
10 Crown Arcade
11 Silver Fox Gallery
12 Admiral Vernon Antiques Market
13 Harris's Arcade
14 Red Lion (Portobello Antiques Market)

where to look for the trendiest stalls, shops and cafés. Going from south to north, the goods you'll find at the market are: antiques, food, household goods, clothes (new and secondhand), bric-a-brac and junk. The Golborne Road local market is tacked onto the northern end of Portobello Road.

Until the 19th century, Portobello Road was a track leading to Porto Bello farm, named to commemorate Admiral Vernon's 1737 capture of the Caribbean city Puerto Bello. By the 1860s modest houses had been built along much of its length; street trading arrived soon after. The market was at first limited to the northern stretch of the road, and most of its trade was in fruit and vegetables. Saturday has always been the busiest day. It wasn't until the late 1940s that antiques traders, displaced by the closure of the Caledonian market (*see* 'Bermondsey', p.146), started arriving here. During the 1950s and 1960s the antiques trade mushroomed and Portobello's antiques market grew correspondingly. Today, well over 2000 traders operate from this section of the market each week.

Such is the market's size, it would be exhausting to examine it all in detail on a single Saturday. Either saunter down the mile-long length of the road, dipping in here and there, or split your visit over two weeks, scrutinizing the antiques one week, and the rest of the market the next. If you decide on the latter, or want to miss the worst of the Saturday crowds and steer clear of the antiques, take the tube to Westbourne Park station and walk down Tavistock Crescent (perhaps dallying for a while at the Frog and Firkin pub on the way). The ten-minute stroll will take you to the centre of the market: to your left will be food stalls, to the right clothes.

If, however, you decide on the leisurely stroll along the length of the market, start at the Notting Hill Gate end on Saturday morning. As soon as you get out of the tube station and saunter down Pembridge Road, you'll notice that everyone in the crowd is walking in the same direction. You'll also notice that most people around you are tourists. But there's a greater age-range here than among the marketgoers in Camden.

There is no grand entrance to Portobello Road at its southern end; nor are there any market stalls. The narrow street bends round and goes down the hill. Follow the crowds. As you go past the 19th-century artisans' houses (now highly desirable properties), many covered in foliage and painted pastel shades, take a look at No.22, where Eric Blair rented a room for a short time in 1927, before adopting the pen name George Orwell. A plaque marks the house.

At present, the market starts just after Portobello Road's junction with Chepstow Villas, but such is its popularity, you might well come across stalls muscling in on the territory further south. These tend to sell the most predictable sort of tourist codswallop, but you might also encounter one of Portobello's many buskers, perhaps a steel drummer or a Peruvian band playing Andean pipe music.

Antiques market

Portobello Road, from Chepstow Villas to Elgin Crescent (including the west side of Westbourne Grove), W11. Open Sat 7am–6pm.

Tens of thousands of visitors are attracted to Portobello Road's antiques market each week. But even if you balk at tourist tosh and a multinational scrum of punters, it's worth paying a visit. The trick is to avoid the main thoroughfares and the most obvious sites. Rather, explore the edges, the basements and first floors of the many premises that have been partitioned into tiny trading booths where scores of traders set out their wares. Here the stall rents are cheaper and you'll find genuine enthusiasts keen to chat about their collecting obsessions. True, you'll rarely find a bargain, but if you're a fanatic and need just one more perfume bottle, military medal, cigarette card or Dinky toy to complete a collection, then you'll find friendly, like-minded folk who might be able to help you. Outside these premises, stalls are crammed either side of the street. An empty space on this stretch of the road is unheard of—pitches are highly prized at the Portobello; in summer casuals turn up as early as 5.30am to try and bag a pitch.

One of the first sights that comes into view after the junction with Chepstow Villas is a bureau de change (there are several along the upper portion of the Portobello). This gives more than an inkling of what to expect; most traders are thoroughly geared up for foreign visitors and raise their prices accordingly. Many accept credit cards, and some operate the export scheme whereby visitors from outside the EU can have VAT returned on the goods they purchase (ask for a form).

Silver cutlery, pot dogs and magnifying glasses fight for space on one of the first stalls. Next to it, a trader is selling a collection of printer's woodcuts. Denbigh

Close, a quaint cobbled mews cluttered with BMW cars, provides an overflow for a clutch of stalls filled with old clocks, a varied collection of antique cameras, Victorian glass bottles, and elderly typewriters. One trader has marked her wares with price tags that give an address on Bermondsey Street, SE1. Several Bermondsey Street traders make the journey northwest every weekend; hundreds of goods that changed hands at Bermondsey (*see* p.146) on a Friday morning go up for sale at Portobello on the Saturday—often with a hefty mark-up.

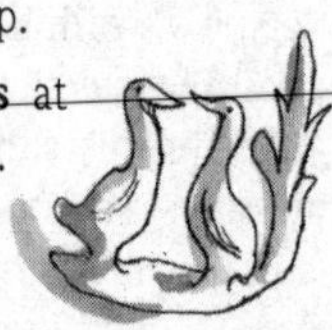

Directly opposite Denbigh Close are the **Chelsea Galleries** at 73 Portobello Road, the first of the indoor concourses of traders. Antique jewellery forms the bulk of their stock: necklaces, old gold rings and elaborate brooches. Upstairs is a café.

Back on the street, there's what looks like a boxful of rubble. On closer examination it turns out to be a collection of fossils, going for £2 each. Fly-traders fill in every inch between the legitimate stalls, selling their usual collection of cigarette lighters and novelty goods.

Portobello Studios Antiques Arcade (at No.101–103) is another gallery filled with traders and bursting with punters. Again, jewellery is the most common commodity, but you'll also find carved ivory, small ornaments, candlesticks, beautiful old pocket watches, silverware, and Graham Symonds, who sells antique wrist watches. His oldest Rolex is a 1913 model costing £700. Upstairs is another cluster of traders dealing in small furniture, decorative objects, antique dolls and old glass display jars. The highlight for me is a business named **Old Father Time**. Its varied collection of timepieces includes a 1941 clock from an RAF operations room, grandfather clocks, and old chronographs with their intricate and marvellous workings open to view. There's also a café here, with filled bagels, pastries and own-made soup. Most of the crowds that jam downstairs seem unaware of the first-floor stalls, so it's possible to have a jostle-free browse.

At 105 Portobello Road is **Geoffrey Van Ltd**, which has yet more traders inside. One small stall, going under the name of the **Dusmet Gallery**, has a couple of ancient sporrans for sale, among a mixture of old books and polished wooden boxes.

The **Good Fairy Antiques Market**, opposite Geoffrey Van, is one of the largest groupings of stalls on the Portobello. About 50 traders are packed into the semi-permanent, covered structure set just off the street. Hundreds of customers block the tiny corridors. Most traders specialize in antique jewellery, but others concentrate on old watches, woodwork tools (well-weathered chisels, lead plumbs), silverware, cutlery (some with ivory handles), and 19th-century prints. One young chap has a collection of old fountain pens going back to 1910, the oldest selling for £120; a nearby stall contains a strange mix of antiquarian books and old opera glasses; yet another trader is trying to sell old golf clubs, a venerable toy steam-engine and a teddy bear.

There are more stalls in the arcades at No.109 (including the **Portobello Print Rooms**, with prints, maps and engravings), and No.113. The latter premises go back quite a way, and lead to a large room at the rear where there is more space to wander among the stalls. Many of the traders here sell antiquarian books, though their collections are small and somewhat disparate. One woman has a selection of embroidered cloths bearing religious homilies. Old glass or pottery bottles, candelabras and light shades can also be found.

The market spills into Westbourne Grove, which bisects Portobello Road. On the east side there are four or five stalls selling new clothes; on the west section there are more antiques stalls out in the street (right up to the junction with Kensington Park Road), plus additional traders housed in indoor arcades. At 296 Westbourne Grove is the **Burton Antiques Arcade**, containing clocks, crockery and glassware; but the best bet is to head for No.290. In the basement, you'll usually be able to escape the crowds and have plenty of time to peruse the traders' goods. Many of these folk are inveterate enthusiasts. Take a look at the magnificent collection of cigarette cards, depicting anything from military uniforms to railway engines. Should you want to buy a set (costing £30–£50 framed), you'll usually have to interrupt the stallholder's conversation with another avid (and often wheezing) collector. He also has a display of old cigarette packets, including brands such as Rich Uncle and Harris's All Gay. Also in this basement is a stall full of rare records (blues, jazz, 1960s). The top of the stall is decorated with a fringe of 45s stuck to a board. A woman asks the stallholder for music to accompany her ballroom dancing team; he duly roots about in his Latin collection.

This basement leads into the next-door premises. Here you'll find more collectors' stalls. One majors in military clothes and medals, another in old radios, a third has sheaves of magazine adverts. There's also a jewellery repairer who offers a bead re-stringing service.

Back onto the Portobello Road, north of Westbourne Grove, the antiques stalls continue to dominate the market on each side of the street. Pewter tankards, old mah-jong sets, brass candelabras, farmyard animal models, kitchenware, magnifying glasses, old pistols and cigarette lighters might all be on view. Coins, stamps and old postcards attract a fair few customers to one stall. The **Crown Arcade**, occupying 119 Portobello Road, has a back entrance down Vernon Yard. Just inside, one trader displays his cherished collection of corkscrews. Next door at No.121, the **Silver Fox Gallery** is mostly full of jewellery traders.

Opposite the junction with Lonsdale Road is the **Admiral Vernon Antiques**

Market ('120 traders plus a bureau de change' reads the sign) which takes up indoor space between Nos.139 and 151 Portobello Road. Jewellery and polished wooden jewellery boxes account for many of the goods, but one dealer specializes in gramophones, stocking models dating back to the days of wax cylinders. Pottery, lace doylies, cameras, pens, oriental porcelain and art deco ornaments are also displayed. A café sells own-made smoky bacon and lentil soup for £1.

Further north, outdoors on Portobello Road, is a stall chock-a-block with telescopes and binoculars; another trader's stock is based around military headgear, including wartime tin helmets. At No.161 is **Harris's Arcade**. Inside, there's a dealer with a fascination for drink. His collection includes a cocktail shaker from Asprey's (the Bond Street store for the dangerously wealthy), and silver wine-bottle holders.

At 165–169 Portobello Road is the oldest of the street's indoor antiques markets, the **Red Lion**. Here Susan Garth 'launched London's first antiques market making the Portobello Road an international institution', according to the blue plaque on the outside of the building. In fact, this indoor market is not now among the more popular sites, and some of the pitches remain unlet. Silverware, crockery and jewellery are among the antiques traded; more out of the ordinary are the lace and cotton nightdresses, plus the collection of old tiles. Yet another indoor market—**'The World Famous Portobello Market'**—can be found at No.177, including a stall full of old teddy bears, and several traders selling paintings. By now you're probably suffering antique-fatigue, and my list of synonyms for 'old' has been exhausted. Fear not: the antiques market finally comes to an end at Portobello Road's junction with Elgin Crescent and Colville Terrace.

Food market

Portobello Road, from Colville Terrace to Lancaster Road, W11. Open Mon–Wed 9am–5pm; Thurs 9am–1pm; Fri, Sat 7am–6pm; organic market (under the Westway) Thurs 11am–6pm.

Yes, food is what's wanted now, and food is what we get. But before continuing along Portobello Road, it's worth taking a short detour up Elgin Crescent where **Mr Christian's Delicatessen and Bakers** at No.11 has a stall outside selling its high-class bread and pastries.

The food market takes up most of the space on the right hand side of the street (as you walk northwards) between here and just before the Westway flyover. The Cain family have the first pitch. All the standard fruits (apples, pears, bananas, oranges) are well presented. The vegetable stall which comes next is also well stocked and pleasing to behold. It does a good line in fresh herbs (rare on London's markets). Sweets and nuts, and flowers fill the next couple of pitches.

This is the longest established section of the market, and some stallholders have been here for years. I heard tell of a man who invited one of the costermongers to his wedding; when he returned to the area 40 years later, the trader still had a stall at the market. Despite the large number of tourists who visit the antiques market, the food traders have kept their prices down; locals make good use of the food market, both during the week and on Saturdays. What has changed is the number of fast food sellers catering for the Saturday crowds. Bratwürst and various other German sausages are dispensed from two vans. The smell of them sizzling mixes with the oriental aromas wafting from a nearby stall selling Thai fried noodles and curries. A kebab van also adds to the atmosphere. **Mr Tasty**, selling West Indian takeaway food (goat curry is a Saturday special), is a reminder that Notting Hill was a centre of London's Afro-Caribbean population. Unfortunately, this community's presence has become less noticeable since the area's gentrification in the late 1980s, but Afro-Caribbeans are still the heart and soul of that huge annual knees-up, Notting Hill Carnival, held on the last Sunday and Monday of August.

Up to three types of mushroom are sold at one of the large fruit and vegetable stalls in the autumn, but there's little in the way of tropical produce—nothing more exotic than a box of mangoes. One man is selling a huge mound of pears (3lb a pound), but not getting much custom. The occasional new-clothes stall has managed to get a pitch on this stretch of the market, but most traders sell inexpensive comestibles such as sweets, eggs and traditional salad ingredients. Two stalls are full of cheap biscuits, sweets and tins of food. Ten years ago there was also a cheese stall where I bought a particularly ripe Gruyère as my contribution to a family meal. It wasn't until we saw a battalion of maggots shuffling towards the candlelight that we realized something was amiss. By that time, half the cheese had been eaten. Sadly that stall has gone.

Near the junction with Westbourne Park Road there's a fishmonger's barrow with a fair choice of seafood and fish (squid, smoked salmon, mackerel, crabs, smoked haddock and mussels). But farther on **G. Piper & Son** has a more exotic collection, including fresh king prawns. Afro-Caribbean women (who tend to be discerning fish-buyers) are among the people queuing. They also frequent the nearby butcher's stall that sells fresh chickens, spare ribs and oxtails.

At this point we must interrupt this Saturday excursion for a word about Thursdays under the Westway (just 100 yards further north from the daily food stalls). From 11am to 6pm each week, a small market devoted to organic food takes place. Here you'll usually find a couple of well-stocked fruit and vegetable stalls (with squash, yams, cabbages, apples, oranges and organic free-range eggs among the produce); an enticing bread stall displaying a variety of loaves (soda bread, barley bread, rye bread and sun-dried tomato focaccia); a meat caravan run by Longwood Farm (an organic farm in Suffolk), which displays a few organic cheeses, butter and unpasteurised milk, as well as all the usual cuts of beef, pork and lamb; and finally a stall reminiscent of a Women's Institute market, with jars of jams and chutneys (including apple butter and grapefruit marmalade), honey, olive oils and home-made chocolate and almond torte (£1 or £1.50 a slice)—all organic.

Back to Saturdays, when the market undergoes another transformation after the junction with Lancaster Road.

Clothes and bric-a-brac market

Under the Westway, from Portobello Road to Ladbroke Grove, W11; Acklam Road, W10; Portobello Road, from the Westway to Bonchurch Road, W10, © (0171) 229 6898. Open Fri 7am–4pm; Sat 8am–5pm; Sun 9am–4pm.

From Lancaster Road to the Westway, stalls contain everyday goods such as haberdashery, new bags, electrical goods, fabrics, crockery, kitchen-ware (enamel breadbins, cheese graters), leather belts, shirts, hair-care stuff, children's wear, leggings and tops; there are also plans to hold a Saturday crafts market on the pedestrianized section of Tavistock Road, just off Portobello Road. But in the gloom beneath the huge concrete slab of the motorway flyover, the atmosphere changes palpably, becoming more like that of Camden. Here you will find soul and funk music stalls selling records and CDs, hippyish jewellery, brassware, candlesticks, or silk ties and shirts. Songs from Bob Marley's *Natty Dread* album mix with the hum of overhead traffic and the echoing hubbub of the market crowds. Spicy aromas emanate from the Makan Malaysian takeaway under the bridge.

On Fridays, retro fashions (1960s clothes, old Levi's and the like) are sold in this area, with a high percentage of dealers among the customers. At present, bric-a-brac holds sway on Sundays, but there are plans to include designer clothes traders from April 1996. On both these days, there's a more relaxed feel to the place; on Saturdays, business is brisk and the crowds are much bigger.

Hip flasks, candelabras, jewellery, art deco ornaments, coffee percolators, glass-ware and clocks are gathered together in the area outside the Portobello Green Arcade every Saturday. As at Camden and Greenwich, several stalls specialize in secondhand jeans (old Levi's go for as much as £35) and leather jackets. The best place for these is under the curvaceous tarpaulins that cover the couple of dozen stalls near Portobello Green. Army surplus clothes, including balaclavas and huge army boots still smelling of the barrack room, and a few designer stalls (look out for one selling bright orange furry rucksacks) can also be found here, as can a stall packed with old vinyl records from the 1950s onwards.

Follow the Westway westwards and the Camdenesque nature of the market becomes even more apparent. Sheltering under the roadway are a mixture of crafts, cassette-tape and bric-a-brac stalls, together with more new and secondhand clothes. Further along, the stalls sell aromatherapy oils, coins made into pendants, collections of old glass bottles, secondhand books and dance mixes on tape. One dealer jams along with a tambourine to his mix of jazz-funk. Nearby is a fabulous collection of buttons, from toggles to great black discs two inches in diameter. Clothes designers also inhabit this stretch of the market: **Red Hat No Knickers** has a stock of own-made headgear, and at **Groovy Baby** you can kit out an infant with Sex Pistols T-shirts or Groovy Baby bibs. Here kitsch is chic: why not buy a telephone coated in Astroturf or a 3D portrait of the Virgin Mary? Designer mirrors also make an appearance; one has a furry fringe with the words 'Miaow, sex kitten' written on it.

Stalls continue under the Westway as far as Ladbroke Grove. You might also encounter bootleg tapes and rock videos, a dealer specializing in Brazilian music and football shirts, ethnic jewellery, secondhand records (Pink Floyd albums 50p), and a stall full of pastries (croissants 40p). There are two takeaway stalls, one selling Indian food—*sag aloo* (spinach and potato curry), and *keema* (minced lamb curry), for instance—the other with West Indian dishes (jerk chicken, fried plantain, and peanut cake for afters). Burning joss sticks further flavour the air.

To discover the rest of the market you now need to retrace your steps back to Portobello Road. Cross the street—perhaps perusing the CND stand on the way—and you arrive at Acklam Road, where a small tarmacked area is home to about 30 more stalls. Here the market's character changes into something more like the poorer areas of Brick Lane: one trader sells old televisions and hi-fi, another has dog-eared secondhand books (both hardback and paperback), while a third sells leatherwear. A suitcase without an obvious owner lies open to view. Within is a display that no pop-artist could have imagined: a frying pan, the hand-set of a telephone, and an empty tin of Cadbury's Smash. One stall has boxes of old records going for £1 each, or four for £3; a couple of avid collectors expertly flick through them. Next to it, a trader is selling both new and secondhand work overalls. Around the edges of the tarmac, forlorn piles of clothing are laid on the ground next to a sign reading '30p each'. Their owner waits for anyone to take interest.

Back on Portobello Road (heading northwards), the standard of goods and the prices are noticeably higher than on Acklam Road. There's a good secondhand record pitch with well-ordered stock, and a book stall with old copies of Iris Murdoch novels. You can almost see the gentrification process spreading north along this portion of Portobello. Le Bistroquet at No.299 and the Portobello Café at No.305 are two new examples of trendy spots that have sprouted in the mid-1990s.

There are a couple more designer clothes pitches on the stretch up to Oxford Gardens (one selling hats), but from here northwards the market becomes more raggedy, the piles of goods less ordered, and the prices lower. Along with Acklam Road, this is the one section of the market where you might still find a bargain. Secondhand clothes, hung on rails further down the road, are now piled on tables willy-nilly. North of here, they might be dumped on the pavement. Stallholders and their stock change every week, but there's plenty of wheat among the chaff. Perhaps you'll find some traditional West African jewellery. Or a collection of fire-grates. Or a haberdashery stall. I encountered a trader trying to rid herself of a box-load of stick-on finger-nails, and a chap attempting to flog a Harrods mink coat for £150—'It would cost £3000 new.'

Two regulars at this flea market section are a trader who sells decent new hardback books at a discount, and a secondhand bike seller who ingeniously arranges his machines to lean against each other. The convoluted mass contains about 20 bikes yet only takes up the area of one pitch. About 20 yards up the road, a punter has found a bargain. She gleefully clutches her purchase, a 50-year-old pressure cooker that looks more like a First World War mine. 'I'm going to try and sell this to the Design Museum.'

If you're an inveterate rummager, it's almost impossible to escape this section of the market empty-handed. At the discount tape and CD stall, I found a new double tape of blues classics for £2.99.

Just before the junction with Golborne Road, there's an argument going on at one stall. Does the secondhand radio-cassette player work? A nearby trader with a few old batteries steps in to solve the dispute. Like the curate's egg, the machine is good in parts: the radio works, the cassette player doesn't.

A few traders take pitches to the north of Golborne Road at the northernmost end of Portobello Road. One stallholder has secondhand books and a top hat; another hopes to get rid of a radiogram and a typewriter. The next stall has a stock of old postcards, sold by a trader who either couldn't get, or couldn't afford, a pitch at the antiques end of the market. Crowds are thin here and stalls begin to straggle. The final pitch is just before the Brasserie du Marché aux Puces, a smart and classy brasserie at 349 Portobello Road.

Golborne Road

Golborne Road, between Portobello Road and Wornington Road, W10. Open Mon–Sat 9am–5pm.

Golborne Road market is, in effect, a separate, local market with a self-contained set of about 30 stalls that complement the small shops and cafés along the street. It is open during the week, though best on Saturdays, and serves the community that lives in the nearby tower blocks and terraces. The area is markedly less moneyed than the southern stretches of Portobello Road. Here most of the weekly essentials are sold: vegetables from **E. Price's** stall, a traditional barrow 'noted for potatoes'; new clothes and training shoes; bedlinen; toiletries; a variety of household goods from disinfectants to cheese graters and crockery; cakes and sweets; fruit and salad food. A baker's stall has stocks of bread pudding and onion bhajis, as well as a choice of loaves. At the Afro-Caribbean food stall there's a fair selection of tropical fruit and vegetables, including coconuts, plus yam flour and salted fish.

The small secondhand section of the market carries on the theme already established on the northern reaches of the Portobello. Rickety chairs are placed out on the south side of the street, and there's a pitch full of well-worn tools and a hodge-podge of electrical components such as old radio valves. Secondhand CDs, a fishing reel and a pair of gum boots could also be snapped up. Prices seem to fluctuate depending on how wealthy the customer looks. There's none of the cream-tea pretensions of the antiques market here.

Golborne Road is a focal point for Moroccans living in London. The burger van at the market serves halal meat and has fiery *harissa* sauce to sprinkle on the buns. A group of Moroccan men are usually gathered round the van for a chat. The road is also a meeting place for local Portuguese, who congregate in the Oporto café (at No.62a) or the Lisboa Patisserie (*see* below). If you can find space at either, rest your legs and order a *galao* (milky coffee) before walking back to the tube at Ladbroke Grove.

Nearby cafés, pubs and shops

Anyone interested in food should make a pilgrimage to **Books for Cooks** at 4 Blenheim Crescent, just off Portobello Road's food market. It has London's best collection of new and secondhand books about food; cookery demonstrations often take place at the back of the shop on Saturdays, with the food served in a tiny café. The **Portobello Star**, at 171 Portobello Road, is a cosy old pub popular with traders. It serves pub food such as chilli con carne (£3.50). **Applewood Farm Shop** at 206 Portobello Road has a range of fresh produce, and on Saturdays runs a crêpe stall outside. The

Original Soul Bar at 265 Portobello Road is one of the funkiest Portobello venues. On Tavistock Road, just off the Portobello near the Westway, is the **Coffee Shop**, a vegetarian snack bar with dishes such as vegetarian moussaka and pastas. You'll often find some of Portobello's liveliest buskers performing nearby. One of the best spots for a budget meal is **Le Bistroquet**, a trendy eating and drinking spot at 299 Portobello Road. Breakfast (including a vegetarian option) is served until 5pm, and full meals (Italian and French influenced) are low-priced: a three course meal costs only £8.

Golborne Road's Moroccan community meets and eats at the **Marrakesh Café** (91 Golborne Road), which serves meals such as dried bean soup and vegetable couscous. The Portuguese have the **Lisboa Delicatessen** (54 Golborne Road), with its stocks of salt cod, *choriço* and Portuguese wines, and the **Lisboa Patisserie** (57 Golborne Road), which has seats outside and is great for a coffee and a *bolo de nata* (custard cream).

Shepherd's Bush

Address: east side of railway viaduct between Uxbridge Road and Goldhawk Road, W12, © (0181) 743 5089.

Public transport: ⊖ Shepherd's Bush, Goldhawk Road; buses 49, 72, 94, 95, 207, 220, 237, 260, 283, 295, 607.

Opening hours: **market** Tue, Wed, Fri, Sat, 8.30–6; Thur, 8.30–1.30. **Steptoe's Yard West Antiques & Bric-a-Brac** Wed, Fri, Sun 7am–3pm; Sat 6am–3pm.

Best time to go: Friday or Saturday morning.

Car parking: try the side streets to the west of the market, between the Uxbridge and Goldhawk roads.

Main wares: fruit and veg, household goods, clothing, electrical goods.

Specifics: Afro-Caribbean foods, pots and pans, men's suits, fabrics.

I once asked a Brazilian restaurateur where in London he could find the ingredients to make his wonderful Bahian stews. His reply, of course, was Shepherd's Bush market. Along with Brixton in the south and Ridley Road in the east, Shepherd's Bush is the epitome of cosmopolitan London. Here you'll find Afro-Caribbeans selling to Arabs, Bangladeshis selling to the Irish and Africans selling to Brazilians.

Like much of Brixton, the market clings to a Victorian railway viaduct. It runs the distance between Uxbridge Road and Goldhawk Road, about quarter of a mile, occupying land originally intended to be an access road to the underground station.

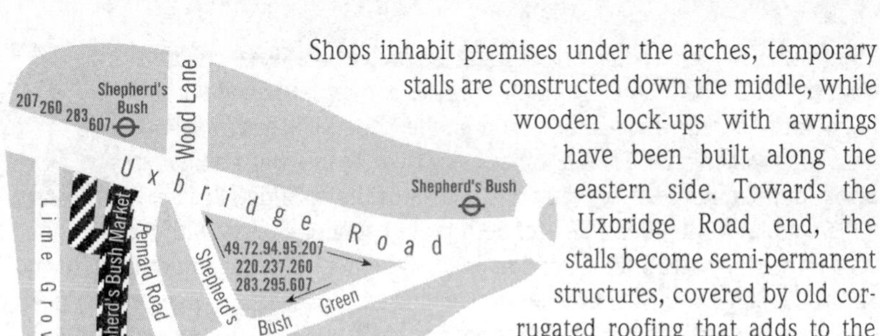

Shops inhabit premises under the arches, temporary stalls are constructed down the middle, while wooden lock-ups with awnings have been built along the eastern side. Towards the Uxbridge Road end, the stalls become semi-permanent structures, covered by old corrugated roofing that adds to the shanty-town appeal of the place.

Trading started here in the summer of 1914, but did not go on for long. During the First World War the market had to make way for the army, which billeted troops and stabled horses under the arches. After the war the market resumed, gaining in popularity and spreading to the west of the railway (this site was closed and redeveloped in 1969). When the area was badly bombed in the Second World War the market was threatened with closure, but the costermongers helped to clear the rubble and trading resumed within days.

Today, the first stall you encounter from the Goldhawk Road end sells a large but atypically staid choice of fruit and veg: potatoes, onions and broccoli; oranges, grapefruit and apples. The record shack next to it is more in tune with the market. Its range includes ex-chart bands, Irish music and reggae records, plus videos of African and reggae bands. All manner of household goods can be found at the market: fly spray, bin bags, umbrellas, leather purses, briefcases, bags, and plenty of toiletries, bedlinen and cosmetics. New householders should head for the lock-up with a vast collection of crockery and china, and a nearby business with scores of stainless steel pots and pans from little milk pans to huge cauldrons, plus gargantuan Thermos flasks. They might think twice, though, before buying some of the new wooden furniture: a mock-marble-topped table costs £325. Shepherd's Bush is also a magnet for dressmakers, with its haberdashery, lace and colourful textile stalls. **E. Mills & Son's** lock-up is packed with fabrics, rugs and linoleum, while nearby you can buy pillows, foam rubber and cushions. Toys, petfood, jewellery, watches and small electrical bits and bobs are also sold here. One stall is packed with tourist stuff—policemen's helmets and Union flags. Strange, since few tourists visit Shepherd's Bush.

The market is a good source of clothing. As well as the usual children's wear, lingerie, cheap shirts, women's dresses and tops, there are beautifully embroidered African tunics and clothes; silk nightwear for both men and women; and a flamboyant choice of women's hats (including plenty of frilly numbers for weddings). Towards the Uxbridge Road end, there's a fork in the thoroughfare. Both prongs continue (each with lock-ups and stalls) until they reach the Uxbridge Road. Take the left prong under the railway and you'll find a couple of excellent-value men's tailors selling a large stock of new suits from £40 upwards and jackets from under £20.

The spirit of the market is to be found in its ethnic diversity. Take a look at the Asian-run stalls selling incense sticks, decorated tool boxes, plastic flowers, pictures that are also clocks, and hubble-bubble pipes. Or the Afro-Caribbean hair-care lock-ups with their collection of wigs. One trader stocks pictures and prints: a portrait of a black Christ on the cross lies next to one of Malcolm 'By any means necessary' X. Two Arab women in yashmaks peruse the stock. Another stall, **Raf and Ras**, has T-shirts emblazoned with Rastafarian slogans. The prize for cultural diversity goes to the small music lock-up in the middle of the market. One rack of cassettes is devoted to Arabic crooners (judging by the pictures), but there are also tapes of Irish jigs, African music and a small but immaculate Andy Williams collection. The owner of the joint flips another cassette into the system and loud, lazy Chicago blues pulses out of the large speakers.

Nowhere in west London can match Shepherd's Bush market for Afro-Caribbean foodstuffs. One large fruit and veg stall sells three types of mangoes; another has about ten varieties of sweet potato, including Ghana yam, cassava and eddoes. Then there are green plantains, green bananas and strange fruit called garden eggs (yellow aubergines, about the size of a chicken's egg). Asian and cockney traders cater for West Indian customers, so the halal meat lock-up sells fresh goat's meat, while at the fishmonger's, **W.H. Roe's** (great name, great stall) you might find red bream, blue runners, grouper, and live crabs blowing bubbles.

The Caribbean feel of the market is most intense at its northeast corner near the Uxbridge Road exit. Several traders as well as customers hail from the West Indies. Singed cow's feet, Uncle John's sweet bread and lots of dried fish are sold under the corrugated shelters. One woman has bottles containing strange red liquid that could be palm oil; piled at the back of her hut are tins of palm nut cream soup. Next door at the record shack, soca holds sway.

But you don't have to stray far from this stall to find a complete incongruity: a stall full of secondhand goods (crockery, glassware and the like) run by an old woman who wouldn't look out of place in a church fete in Suffolk. Pulp fiction (mostly Mills & Boon romantic novelettes) dominate a nearby bookstall, while a large video stall has a good stock of children's films and sports videos.

The Arabic influence on the market's foodstuffs is most evident at the fast food stall towards the Goldhawk Road end. Falafel, *fu'l medames* (broad beans with olive oil, lemon juice and garlic), *segot* (spicy sausages), fried aubergine and lamb kofta are all served with pitta for about £2 each. In addition, a couple of traditional caffs occupy lock-ups on the market, with tables and chairs outside. Breakfasts and fry-ups account for most of their menus, but one, **The Pantry**, also does squid omelette. For pudding, head for the sweet and biscuit stall which stocks popcorn, candy floss and jammy dodgers.

As is the case with many successful markets, Shepherd's Bush has spawned an off-shoot run by a private operator. **Steptoe's Yard** is a car-boot affair, just to the east of the market off the Goldhawk Road. It is held in a sizeable yard down a short cobbled drive and makes a good secondhand complement to the main market. There are about 50 stalls in all. You might find new-looking televisions and hi-fi, worn shoes, secondhand suits, an old packet of Durex Gold. One stall displays an ancient wooden toilet seat next to secondhand fluffy toys. Another has a few bottles of 'Zardor' men's aftershave, a solitary old pepperpot, and six packets of Cheesy Wotsits. But there are some genuine car-booters here as well, selling old fondue sets (the classic unwanted present), disks for obsolete computers, tatty books and oily tools. A doughnut van provides the nourishment. I didn't stay long: the man in charge, a beefy chap with a forthright manner, accused me of being a KGB agent.

Fact is, I couldn't resist another peek at the Caribbean section of the main market. Just smell the dried fish, black as liquorice, open to the air or in weathered plastic bags; or listen to the easy chatter of the stallholders, grouped round the radio and chuckling as the West Indian cricketer Brian Lara hits yet another four over mid-off. And for a moment you're out of London, out of Europe even. A blast of celebratory soca sends you on your way. Can shopping really be this much fun?

Nearby cafés and shops

The permanent shops by the stalls don't quite qualify as part of the market, but several are worth exploring. Take a look in **International Cash & Carry** (160 Shepherd's Bush Market), with its alluring collection of exotic food and drink: a wide choice of rum (with names like Wray & Nephew and Conquering Lion Overproof Rum), Jamaican syrup, dragon stout, sorrel (not the green-leafed plant, but a drink made from the pink flower heads of a type of hibiscus), sarsaparilla, and stranger still, bamee, mauby bark, Irish moss, strong bark, chene root and casareep. **Moon Foods Cash & Carry** (183 Shepherd's Bush Market) has huge bags of rice, passion fruit cordial, enormous tins of vegetable oil, bags of spices and nuts, salt fish and best Jamaican ackee. If you're not tempted by the market cafés, try **A.H. Cooke's**, round the corner from the market (48 Goldhawk Road), a west London outpost for traditional pie and mash. **Blah Blah Blah** (78 Goldhawk Road) is a hippyish restaurant serving vegetarian food from around the world.

North London

Camden Passage

Camden

Address: Camden Lock, Buck Street, Electric Ballroom, Chalk Farm Road, Camden High Street, NW1; *see individual markets for details.*

Public transport: ⊖ Camden Town, Chalk Farm;
⇌ Camden Road;
buses 24, 27, 29, 31, 134, 135, 168, 214, 253, 274, C2.

Opening hours: *see individual markets for details.*

Best time to go: about 10am on Sunday.

Car parking: try the side streets north of the Chalk Farm Road, but expect to walk a long way.

Main wares: secondhand clothes, designer clothes and jewellery, antiques, books, crafts, furniture.

Specifics: street fashion and accessories.

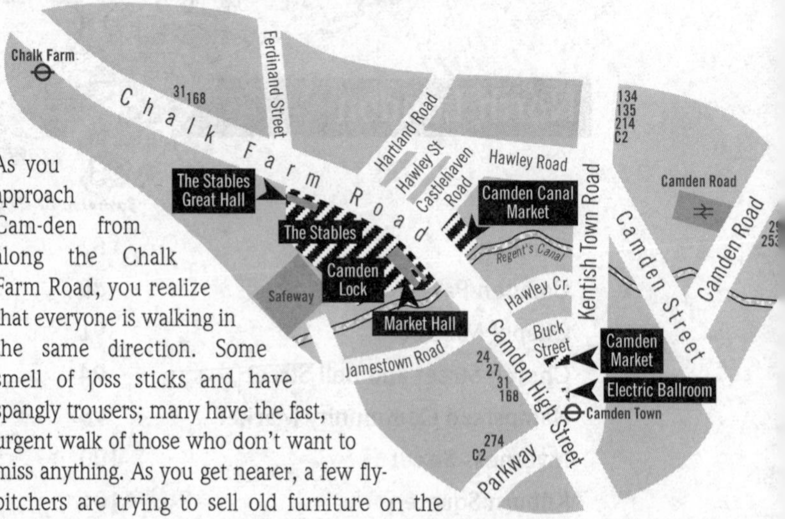

As you approach Cam-den from along the Chalk Farm Road, you realize that everyone is walking in the same direction. Some smell of joss sticks and have spangly trousers; many have the fast, urgent walk of those who don't want to miss anything. As you get nearer, a few fly-pitchers are trying to sell old furniture on the pavement. Their presence is a sure sign of a successful market.

You are heading for London's biggest weekly street festival. Along Camden High Street, north of the tube station, there's a carnival atmosphere. The road is jammed with traffic as crowds overflow from the pavements. Shops and cafés join in the street life by placing their wares outside, and hawkers use any available space to milk the passing throng.

Camden market first opened in 1974 at a disused timber wharf beside the Regent's Canal. At first it consisted of craftsworkers who had colonized the Victorian waterside warehouses, selling their goods in the old cobbled yard. Since then it has grown alarmingly, sprouting new shoots at half a dozen sites around Camden. It now vies with Petticoat Lane and Portobello Road for the title of London's most famous market. And for popularity, Camden wins hands down, attracting hundreds of thousands of tourists and Londoners each week.

The market came into being after the British institutions of church-going and Sunday lunch had crumbled so, unlike the older East End Sunday markets, it continues into the afternoons and reaches a zenith at 2pm when its clubbing regulars have woken up and are ready for the day.

The traditional fruit and veg market of Inverness Street is also in the centre of Camden. It is quite different in character from the weekend clothes and crafts market, so is listed separately (*see* p.100).

The Stables

Off Chalk Farm Road, opposite junction with Hartland Road, NW1, ✆ (0171) 485 5511. Open Sat, Sun 8am–6pm.

The Stables is without doubt the most vital of Camden's markets. Prosperity hasn't yet had time to prettify and package it, so you'll still find some of the rough and ready spirit of 1970s Camden. Rave music, mixed with indie tunes and reggae, is never out of earshot. Within the gates of the former goods yard, trading takes place both outdoors on cobbled thoroughfares and any available piece of wasteland, and under cover of the ramshackle Victorian sheds and a succession of railway arches.

Camden is very different from the established antiques markets such as Portobello Road or Camden Passage in Islington. Many of the traders are young and hip, which means they may let an unfashionable hunk of Victoriana through their grasp without realizing its worth. But when it comes to 20th-century fashions, which account for most of their stock, these traders are totally clued-up. Where else would a pair of tarnished 1950s cats'-eyes sunglasses cost £12.50; or old BOAC bags be sold as fashion accessories?

Though most stalls are run by Londoners with an eye for street fashion, bigger business is already making hay at the Stables, as evidenced by a huge stall of 'vintage' Levi's where secondhand denims are sold for upwards of £20 each. And one section, **The Gin House**, sells stuff that would have enraged the post-hippy generation that first populated the market: a stag's head for £42; a shooting stick for £10. But it's impossible not to admire the collection of old cricket bats, redolent of linseed oil and high summer, or the huge battered leather suitcases plastered with freight stickers from around the world.

There are still grungy bargains to be had at the Stables, if you don't mind a bit of wear and tear. Most of the best clothes stalls are outside, just to the left of the entrance, up a cobbled walkway that leads to the Stables Great Hall. Well-worn leather jackets in a variety of styles cost from about £10; secondhand printed T shirts sell at the not-so-giveaway price of £5.

Camden fashion doesn't stop at clothing. Many of the market's teenage customers of the 1970s and 1980s now have their own flats to furnish, so there's plenty of stripped pine furniture about, some of it roughly painted in Mediterranean turquoise. Most of the renovated furniture is kept within the murky confines of the railway arches, though antique pieces can be found in the Stables **Great Hall**. This large Victorian structure, once a hospital for horses, also contains old kitchenware, cigarette tins, books and various household goods from the 1920s to the 1970s.

Outside the Great Hall, secondhand street fashions are interspersed with traders selling bootleg tapes of live gigs, concert videos and army-surplus gear. You might also encounter club DJs selling cassettes of their rare groove, samba or techno mixes: it's near impossible to avoid moving to the beat.

Outside **Old Times Square** and **Antique Alley** (both converted railway arches) are stalls displaying African crafts, candlesticks and holders, glassware, South American gourds, designer fabrics and jewellery. There's also a trader selling old guitars and a collection of 1960s records. In an old building opposite the arches is a room full of American gear: US licence plates, work-wear from the 1930s to the 1950s, and reproduction posters from Jimi Hendrix concerts.

Walk into **Objets d'Arch**, under one of the railway arches, and you wonder why you ever bothered to bring back souvenirs from your travels—they are all here, including African masks, shields and spears, and multifarious crafts and glassware. Next to it, **Collectors' Arch** has loads of old cutlery, silverware and crockery. The next arch has been taken over by a futon store; others contain stalls selling old Dinky toys, 1950s children's annuals, 'carefully used' American clothing, wood-carving tools, new football scarves, and 'reclaimed' stripped pine furniture.

Camden is not without its shysters: one notice reads 'Did you know that your quartz watch emits harmful electromagnetic radiation? Have it neutralized here, £1 only.' Another trader is trying to sell a rock, describing it as masonry dislodged from St Paul's Cathedral during the Blitz—yours for £40.

Outside, a crêperie stand attracts mid-morning brunchers. If the weather's bad, eat instead inside the converted tube train in the central space of the Stables.

There are more railway arches behind the Stables Great Hall and one of these contains **Camden Green Market**, fronted by an organic café. On the menu is 'hot organic soup', whatever that is. Inside the arch, traders sell organic cheeses (including some ferociously flavoured goat's cheese), organic fruit and veg, a variety of organic breads, and organic herbs.

Further into this Victorian labyrinth of dank, dark arches, named the **Catacombs**, are some of Camden's most colourful traders. Clothes from the 1950s are sold by a chap with bright orange and yellow hair who demands a tip if you photograph him; another trader seems in a trance in his dimly lit dungeon which is decked out in shawls and strewn with strange ornaments. In other arches you might find restored carriage clocks, old musical instruments, old wooden carvings, and Indonesian or Indian woodwork and artefacts. A nearby café specializes in East African curries.

All the above can be found to the left of the main entrance to the Stables. If, however, you turn right, you come across more old buildings filled with antiques stalls, where you might find anything from a 1920s accordion to a silver cutlery set. Further along, the **Long Stable** is full of retro clothes, many from the 1960s. Appropriately, Velvet Underground tracks are played at the record stall.

On a fine day, the benches outside the Long Stable make a good stopping point to rest and watch the crowds pass by (if you can get a seat). Fast food huts supply the nourishment, from the traditional pie and mash to ultra-exotic Burmese cuisine, and cater for vegetarian tastes with falafels and vegetarian pizzas.

Soon after this point, the Stables merges with Camden Lock market.

Camden Lock

Camden Lock Place, off Chalk Farm Road, NW1, © (0171) 284 2084. Open Sat, Sun 10am–6pm; a few stalls open throughout the week.

This is where Camden Market started in 1974. If you arrive early on a fine day, it's still a place of great charm. Longboats chug down the canal watched by couples relaxing on the banks; traders lay out their wares on stalls in the cobbled yard; and buskers play a few chords before the crowds arrive.

The Lock market was started by craftsworkers selling their handmade goods, but nowadays artisans are a minority among the 400 or so traders. Businesses here have become prosperous, more conformist and consequently less exciting. New clothes as well as old are sold, and many traders in Andean, Asian, or African artefacts and clothes seem to be professional importers. Yet there are stalls still worth finding: don't miss the pitch full of percussive instruments, from African talking

drums to Irish bodhráns; or the hand-crafted ocarinas (pot flutes); and there's always some new handmade jewellery to be examined.

The **Middle Yard** of Camden Lock has rows of stalls displaying new clothes from young designers (bright mini-skirts, tops in unbleached fabrics), designer jewellery, knit-wear, kinky leatherwear and multicultural fast food. There is still space for the part-timers who make food and drink to sell here. One week you might find organic carrot cake, the next spiced cider and homemade lemonade.

The **Market Hall** of Camden Lock is an impressive building with elaborate wrought-ironwork. Stalls fill the ground floor and a first-floor gallery. Many display crafts from around the world, bought cheap and sold dear: Indonesian batiks, stone sculptures from Africa, cassette tapes from Latin America. Local craftsworkers get a look-in here as well, with hand-painted plant pots, jewellery and glassware.

On the first floor is a fairly good bookstall selling new fiction. Another stall sells new suits cut in the collarless tunic style favoured by the Beatles in 1964. Part of this hall leads to **Dingwalls Gallery**, which contains more clothes (including tutus and colourful designs on sweatshirts and T-shirts). Shops line the outside of the market hall; most of these, and several of the indoor businesses, trade through the week.

Camden Canal Market

Off Chalk Farm Road, south of junction with Castle Haven Road, NW1. Open Sat, Sun 10am–6pm.

This outcrop of the market is reached down a sloping covered walkway opposite Camden Lock. The dawdling crowd peruses the clothes, electrical goods, jewellery and reggae stalls on either side of the walkway. One trader has a serene expression and a stock of pot-pipes and king-sized Rizla papers. At the end of this corridor is a small outside courtyard filled with stalls. There are some secondhand clothes, but most garments—including colourful shirts and Latin American knitwear—are new. One trader even sells wax jackets and green wellies—symbols of the landed elite, here in Alternative Camden.

Off the courtyard, an indoor section contains dozens of stalls full of all manner of secondhand goods, plus a few tacky new things. In unsung parts of Camden like this, you can still happen upon a goldmine. Lovers of old western books will find a stall dedicated to their passion (look out for the Hopalong Cassidy series). And if you agree that Britain's prime contribution to world culture is the public house, head for **Pub Paraphernalia**, a stall packed with genuine artefacts from British boozers—such as tankards and Guinness water jugs—as opposed to the bogus pub signs found at some tourist markets. There's even a stall selling a few secondhand Levi's for £5: the lowest price in Camden. One trader specializes in Chinese opium pipes, while another has a large stock of New Age books, and a third is selling his collection of pipes and cigarette lighters. Several stock household artefacts from the 1920s to the 1970s of the type that can also be found at the Stables. Look out for the collection of old sewing machines. If you're desperate for currency, visit the bureau de change at this market.

Camden market used to have many secondhand record stalls, but in these post-vinyl days they are dying out. One of the best is here, with LPs and singles well ordered by genre. Punk, indie and 1960s bands are especially well represented.

Camden Market

Camden High Street, at junction with Buck Street, NW1, ✆ (0171) 938 4343. Open Thur–Sun 9am–5.30pm.

This is one of the most crowded parts of the market, and it can get quite claustrophobic in the narrow alleyways between stalls. It is still worth heading into the den, though, if you're after clothing or jewellery. But be warned: the Carnaby Street process is well underway here, turning street cred into straight crud.

Some of the prices are plain daft: secondhand flared jeans cost as much as £25. There are also the wax coats, cheap jewellery and digital watches, and the leather belts popular with heavy metal fans, that can be found at many London markets for a good deal less. If you're prepared to squeeze yourself through the crush, though, you might discover a few gems: jolly handbags and hats made from recycled clothes; secondhand boots and shoes, all at £5; secondhand suede jackets for only £15; old leather and velvet jackets at £10 each. As well as fashionwear, there are a couple of stalls displaying hippyish artefacts, and a trader specializing in music videos.

Electric Ballroom

Camden High Street, south of junction with Dewsbury Terrace, NW1, © (0171) 485 9006. Open Sun 9am–5.30pm.

The Electric Ballroom is a deeply dark nightclub that opens its doors on Sundays for clothes trading, and occasionally on Saturdays for record fairs. To help the show along, DJs play dance tracks throughout the day. Yep, it's mighty hip in here, but the fashion industry is ready to pounce. You can almost see the marketing managers waiting in the wings, as street fashion is accommodated into the business system and a quick buck is made from old clothes.

But young designers still use the Electric as their showroom. Most of their wares are new clothes made from old, in new styles subverted from old. Clubwear, bright, shiny and lurid, is also on display: one stall is devoted to Lycra, while at another, PVC skirts go for as little as £5. Skimpy tops from **Sonia Au-Yeung** (SAY!) attract plenty of interest, and **Cheap Trash** has a stock of cheerful feminist T-shirts in support of SCUM (the Society for Cutting Up Men).

The designers are joined by those entrepreneurs who trawl the jumble sales and charity shops of England for 1950s stilettoes, 1960s zoot suits and 1970s skinny-ribbed sweaters—anything retro, in fact. One stall has been here for years, selling entire men's outfits: suits, shirts and ties, ranging from early 1960s FBI-style black suits to late 1960s lounge-lizard velvet jackets. A run-of-the-mill suit that was bought for 50p at a jumble sale now costs £50. That's fashion for you.

On the Electric Ballroom's stage every Sunday, a hairdresser (completely and worryingly bald) lops off the locks of exhibitionists, while the crowd passes by. Further diversions from clothes shopping are provided by DJs selling club-mix tapes. And you might even encounter the local palmist, who will divulge your future as you sit halfway up a staircase at the back of the hall.

Nearby cafés and shops

Many of the varied fast food joints in the market itself are mentioned above, but if you want to escape the crowds, try **John's Café** (39 Chalk Farm Road). The trendy goings-on down the road seem to have passed by this basic caff. If, on the other hand, you want to tune in to upbeat Camden, order a cocktail at **WKD** (18 Kentish Town Road), one of the funkiest venues for a drink and a snack.

Several interesting shops are sited around Camden Lock, including **Compendium** (234 Camden High Street), one of London's best local bookshops; it has particularly good feminism, politics and Third World sections.

Camden Passage

Address: Camden Passage, off Islington High Street, N1, ✆ (0171) 359 0190.

Public transport: ⊖ Angel;
buses 4, 19, 30, 38, 43, X43, 56, 73, 171A, 214.

Opening hours: **antiques and bric-a-brac** Wed 7am–2pm; Sat 8am–4pm; **books** Thur 7am–4pm.

Best time to go: Wednesday.

Car parking: parking meters on the side streets east of Camden Passage.

Main wares: antiques.

Specifics: old cutlery, military clothing and artefacts (Sat only), crockery.

Don't confuse this with the weekend kerfuffle at Camden Town (*see* p.82). Camden Passage is in the heart of Islington, where old goods are sold to the nouveaux riches; where quaintness is quantified in quids; and where collectors fork out for silver spoons.

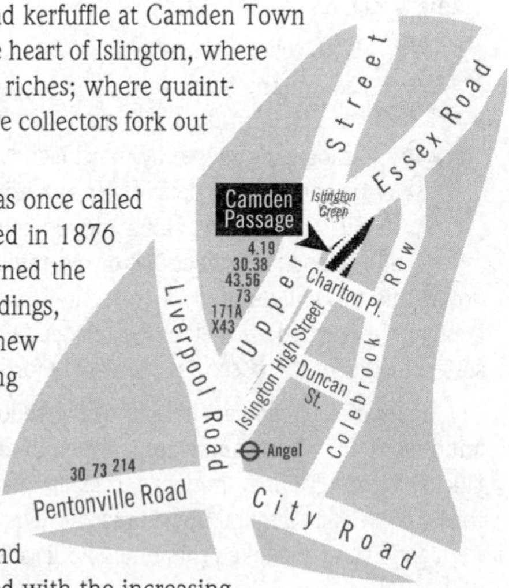

The narrow, flagstoned walkway was once called Cumberland Row, but was renamed in 1876 after the Earl of Camden, who owned the land. Despite the venerable surroundings, the antiques market is a relatively new affair, dating from 1960. The timing was spot-on. In 1960 Islington was just starting to become fashionable again, with middle-class couples moving into the area and renovating its beautiful Georgian and early-Victorian houses. This, coupled with the increasing popularity of antiques, ensured the market's success.

Get yourself in the mood by walking through the **Mall** antiques arcade, which occupies a renovated tramshed to the south of the Passage. Bijou shops packed with *objets d'art* line a central walkway. Exquisite china from Vienna, wooden sailing boats, 19th-century paintings, grandfather clocks—most stuff is in impeccable condition and seriously expensive. Take heart: the market proper is not quite as exclusive.

Apart from a couple of restaurants, virtually every shop on the northern stretch of Islington High Street and Camden Passage now sells antiques. Every inch of space is used. Take the **Angel Arcade** (near the northernmost end of Islington High Street), which occupies only part of one terraced house yet contains 20 antiques shops. China, Victorian ornaments and old brassware are everywhere, but on Saturdays (from 8am to 2pm) the most fascinating events take place in the basement, which hosts the **London Military Market**. Belts, buckles, badges, and bayonets from the Second World War form the bulk of the stock at the Military Market, yet there's plenty of older and newer stuff. A policeman's helmet, circa 1980, costs £36; an NYPD officer's hat goes for £28. Though there's a couple of female traders, women are rare in this subterranean bunker. Smell the odour of khaki encrusted with ancient sweat as you pass the old uniforms; gaze in wonder at the preposterous helmets worn by German cavalry officers in the First World War; note the unnerving look in the eyes of traders obsessed with Nazi memorabilia. Then reflect on the paltry price asked for service medals from the 1914–18 carnage (as low as £3); or sort through the mixture of German and Soviet medals awarded during the mutual slaughter on the Eastern Front (an Iron Cross First Class fetches about £50).

It's a relief to ascend the staircase and reach the open air. Turn right, continuing northwards, and you soon reach Camden Passage. In every available space, trestle tables are set up in clutches between buildings; most are covered by translucent shelters. The first batch of stalls is just off the Passage on **Pierrepont Row**. Silver cutlery and tableware, jewellery, glassware, china and old coins are ten-a-penny, but there are also more esoteric collections of old radio valves and early cameras. Further down this tiny cul-de-sac is a collection of small antiques shops, single-roomed cubby holes packed with elderly artefacts. One specializes in 1920s fashion accessories: frocks for the bosomless, jewellery for flappers.

The fleamarket arcade at the end of Pierrepont Row contains two small floors of antiques stalls. Silver tableware is much in evidence, but you'll also find carriage clocks, Victorian prints, miners' lamps, fascinating old postcards, glass bottles, buttons, baubles and general bric-a-brac. Upstairs is the minute **Art Café**, a good place for a coffee and a smoked salmon and dill sandwich, if there's room.

The next outcrop of the market occurs at the junction with Charlton Place. On Thursdays a small book market takes place here (mostly paperback fiction, though also some hardback reference books), but on Wednesdays and Saturdays half a dozen more antiques traders set up their trestle tables. Among their stock you might find paintings, writing cases, old kitchen equipment, huge old keys, crockery, and antique spectacles.

Farther along Camden Passage, a few of the antiques shops put wares out onto the walkway. Near to the Camden Head pub (worth popping into for refreshment), the Passage widens and several traders exhibit their stock on the pavement. This is the cheapest, but also the dodgiest part of the market, and there's a fair amount of junk: cub-scout caps, cigarette cases, candlesticks, pottery, broken binoculars. One hopeful soul is trying to sell a piece of driftwood that, he claims, was part of HMS *Victory*. Dodges like this tell you that the market is popular with tourists, and indeed many nationalities can be spotted here, especially North Americans.

Opposite the Camden Head is a more official part of the market, also under shelter. About half a dozen traders try to sell a wide variety of goods: old lace, policemen's helmets, domino sets, magnifying glasses. The largest part of the market is but a few steps on from this outcrop. Opposite Islington Green, at the end of Camden Passage, are about 30 stalls under cover. Again there's a good choice of silver cutlery, candlesticks and tableware, but also many Dinky toys and toy soldiers. Prices are high: even the smallest well-used toy car, devoid of paint, might cost £5. A couple of crafts traders sell gaudy jewellery and old silver coins, cunningly cut in two and described as 'lovers' pendants'. As with virtually every other object at Camden Passage, you'll be able to get a substantially lower price by haggling.

Nearby cafés and pubs

Islington is replete with great eating and drinking places. **Alfredo's** (4–6 Essex Road, 50 yards north of the market) is one of the best caffs in London, serving low-priced pies, fried breakfasts and custard-swamped puds in basic art deco premises. A more refined, but still cheap, lunch can be had at the **New Culture Revolution** (42 Duncan Street, just off Islington High Street). It's a Chinese dumplings and noodle bar with an emphasis on healthy, meal-in-one dishes. Upper Street has some of the area's best pubs, including the **Slug and Lettuce** (just north of Islington Green) and the famous pub theatre, the **King's Head** (a ten-minute walk north up Upper Street).

Chapel Market

Address:	Chapel Market, N1.
Public transport:	⊖ Angel; buses 4, 19, 30, 38, 43, 56, 73, 171A, 214, 279, X43.
Opening hours:	Tue, Wed, Fri, Sat 9am–4pm; Thur, Sun 9am–1pm.
Best time to go:	Saturday, Sunday.
Car parking:	try the side streets off Liverpool Road to the north of the market.
Main wares:	fresh food, clothes, household goods.
Specifics:	fresh fish, fruit and veg, clothes.

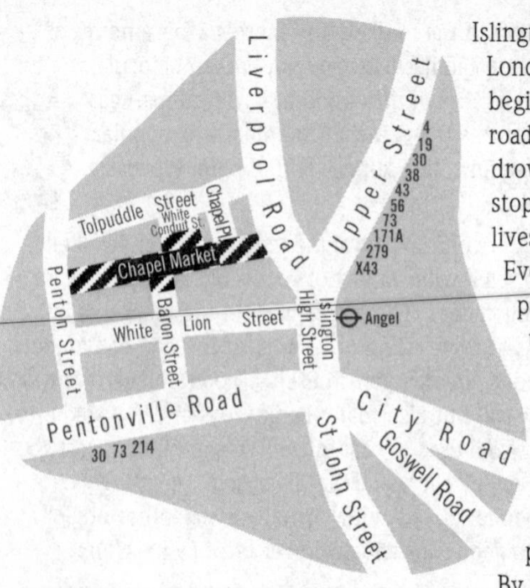

Islington has been linked with London's markets from its medieval beginnings as a village on the main road north of the city. For centuries, drovers used the place as a final stop-off point before guiding their livestock to Smithfield market. Even today you can see the high pavements of Upper Street, built to prevent mud and dung from the road splashing pedestrians.

Chapel Street was built in 1790 (the writer Charles Lamb was one of the first residents), but the market probably dates from the 1860s. By then, Islington contained two distinct strata of society living in close proximity. Gentry from the beautiful squares of Barnsbury (north of the market) would have steered clear of the mayhem of Chapel Street, which catered for the new working-class communities of Pentonville and Angel. The market gained official recognition in 1879, and in 1936 Chapel Street was renamed Chapel Market.

Today, Islington still contains a fascinating social mix. In the 1960s and 1970s, its larger houses were rediscovered by prosperous folk and it became fashionable among socialist-leaning professionals—it's no coincidence that the Labour leader Tony Blair lives here. At Camden Passage (*see* p.89), the residents of exquisite Victorian terraces can be seen browsing for their antiques.

Chapel Market, on the other hand, continues to provide basic foodstuffs, clothing and household goods. True, you might find a Greenpeace stall full of middle-class lefties selling T-shirts, or a group of local teachers with a petition, but that all adds to the fun. Despite the proximity of several supermarkets (Sainsbury's has had a store on Liverpool Street for a century), street trading thrives and Chapel Market remains one of London's best.

During the week, stalls are concentrated at the Liverpool Road end, but at the weekend they stretch more than two hundred yards to Penton Street. A large stall selling greetings cards and party goods (streamers, balloons and, from November, Christmas decorations) seems to be a permanent fixture at the eastern end. Then there are several fruit and veg stalls, well stocked but without anything too exotic (you might find avocadoes, but mangoes are rare).

The clothes stalls dotted along the street supply all age-groups: frilly clothes for toddlers, Naf Naf tops for teenagers (sold at half price), sensible frocks for women (to be replaced by sensible jumpers in winter), T-shirts, tracksuit bottoms, football strips and scarves, jeans, socks, underwear and lingerie. In the markets of east or southeast London, barrows piled high with a jumble of low-priced garments attract crowds of elbow-wielding bargain hunters, but in Chapel Market such a stall is almost deserted—further evidence of Islington's changing social make-up.

There's usually a fair choice of fast food: perhaps some Thai noodles or freshly made apple fritters; definitely winkles or peeled prawns. The two wet-fish stalls brim with fresh conger eel, Dover sole, mullet, sardines, and (the sign of a good fishmonger) fish heads for stock. But as with the fruit and veg, you won't find much geared towards Asian or Afro-Caribbean shoppers. For jackfish and snappers, take a ten-minute ride on the No.30 bus to Ridley Road market (*see* p.134).

The rest of the traders stock everyday goods for locals: towels, cut flowers, cosmetics, haberdashery, electrical equipment (from Walkmans to kettles and answerphones), carry cots, sweets, cheap tapes and CDs, petfoods, toys, leather clothes and bags, pot plants and household goods such as dusters, freezer bags and cling film. There's also a key-cutter and, right at the end of Chapel Market, a tool stall.

At weekends, a few traders take up pitches in neighbouring side streets. On Chapel Place you'll find handbags, curtain material and perhaps a candlestick stall; White Conduit Street has a large cut-flower and plant stall, and a trader with a large stock of secondhand pulp fiction. But Baron Street has the best entertainment. Here, a couple of weathered old traders (who can also be found on Sundays at Brick Lane) sell extremely cheap tinned food, biscuits, chocolates and nuts. This is old-style Islington, where French loaves are 'bagwets' and three tins of ham cost a nicker. No one minds that the sell-by date is fast approaching, if not gone. A huddle of elderly locals surrounds the stall, bantering with the traders. The best show is saved for new, fancy lines:

Trader:	'Ever tried a drop of fruit tea?'
Customer:	'Not likely, have you?'
Trader:	'No, of course I haven't. I don't like the bleedin' stuff.'
Customer:	'What d'you want it for then? Give it away.'
Trader:	'Well it's no good if you don't like it, is it?'

Allow yourself a secret smile: half a mile away, the burghers of Barnsbury will be paying through the nose for fruit tea at their wholefood shops.

Although **M. Manze's** pie and mash shop at 74 Chapel Market is no longer run by the Manze dynasty, it's an unyieldingly traditional place, right down to the marble-topped tables and wooden benches worn smooth by generations of costermongers' buttocks. In 1997 the caff will celebrate its centenary, if the owner can manage to survive the competition from McDonald's. There are plenty of decent restaurants and pubs along Upper Street (*see* 'Camden Passage', p.89), but the best place for a coffee and a croissant is **Pâtisserie Bliss**, just south of Angel tube at 428 St John Street.

Church Street and Bell Street

Address: Church Street, W2 and NW8;
Bell Street, between Edgware Road and Lisson Street, NW1
Alfie's Antique Market, 13–25 Church Street, NW8,
✆ (0171) 723 6066.

Public transport: ⊖ Edgware Road;
buses 6, 16, 16A, 18, 27, 98, 139.

Opening hours: **Church Street** Tue–Sat 9am–5pm;
Alfie's Antiques Market, Tue–Sat 10–6;
Bell Street Sat 9–5.

Best time to go: Saturdays.

Car parking: try the side streets off the Edgware Road to the north of Church Street (it's free at the parking meters on Saturdays).

Main wares: **Church Street** fruit and vegetables (Tue–Fri); antiques, clothes, household goods, plants and flowers, fruit and veg, meat, fish (Fri, Sat).
Bell Street general junk, secondhand clothes.

Specifics: antique jewellery, cheap packaged food, fruit and veg, old clothes.

Barely outside the West End, the neighbouring markets of Church Street and Bell Street offer a wealth of junk, antiques and traditional street-market clobber every Saturday. Though Madame Tussaud's is little over half a mile away, few tourists come here. The markets are mostly left to a cosmopolitan band of local shoppers: lads from the nearby council flats, tweedy antiques collectors and Arab women in yashmaks.

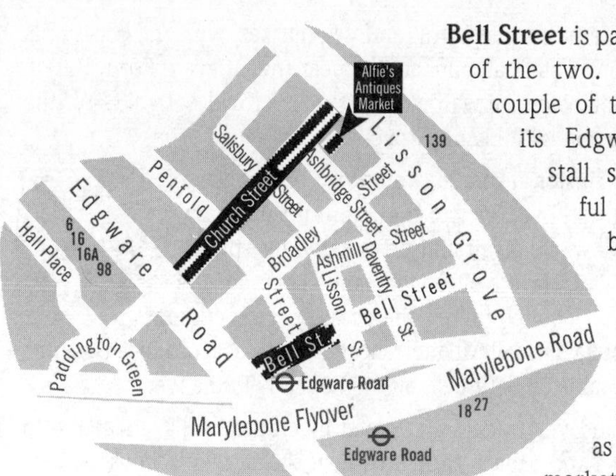

Bell Street is patently the poor relation of the two. On weekdays, only a couple of traders take pitches at its Edgware Road end. One stall sells hundreds of useful bits and bobs: razor blades, haberdashery, padlocks and batteries. On Saturdays, it is joined by a couple of dozen junk stalls that straggle along the road as far as Lisson Street. The market is informal in the extreme. At one pitch a genteel woman might spread a tablecloth over her trestle table and display old jewellery like exhibits at a village tombola. Occasionally, a collection of old suits, jumpers and dresses will be hung on a clothes rail from a defunct store. More often, piles of junk are scattered over a table, or even ditched onto the pavement.

You won't find the retro-fashion prices of Camden here: a double-breasted suit in good nick might fetch £15. But some wares—like the pile of broken tools and door handles, sold by a couple of gents more interested in their cider bottle—have only curiosity value. It's tempting to muse on the lives of some of the traders, as evidenced by the goods they ply. One sad mound has a baking tray once used as a palette, together with catalogues from art exhibitions and a few half-completed sketches. A nearby trestle table is covered with men's secondhand shoes in reasonable repair; don't ask after the first owners—it's likely they're all dead.

You might find a priceless antique being sold for peanuts along Bell Street, but it's doubtful. More typical are the collections of elderly liquidizers, fluffy toys grey with use, and chipped crockery. A threadbare gent warns young boys away from his pile of well-worn, soft porn magazines: 'Don't look in there or your eyes'll go blind.'

Few cars venture down Bell Street, so the market is perfect for a peaceful potter, before taking one of the side streets north and walking the hundred or so yards towards the tumult of **Church Street**.

Church Street market can be traced back to 1830, when the Portman market began trading in meat, fruit and vegetables near Lisson Grove. At the turn of the century, plans to provide indoor premises near Marylebone Station faltered, so the market moved to its present location in 1906. From Tuesday to Thursday Church

Street is little more than a minor local fruit and veg market, with the occasional household goods and clothes stall, all bunched up near the Edgware Road. But on Fridays and especially Saturdays, upwards of 200 stalls crowd both sides of the street right up to the junction with Lisson Grove.

Most fruit and veg stalls cluster at the Edgware Road end. A few of these costermongers are well over 70, but they still turn up every week. One trader always wears a suit and tie to serve his spuds; another puts up notices like 'Have a bit of good and cheap, for the doctor,' over his tomatoes. Though there's the occasional experiment with mangoes or even loquats (small Mediterranean fruits), most produce is run-of-the-mill. Prices are reasonable on Saturday, but higher early in the week.

On Saturdays the fruit and veg traders are joined by clothes stalls stocked with leather jackets, children's and babies' garments, new shoes, men's trousers, low-priced shirts, women's smart jackets, jeans, pyjamas, glittering nightclub outfits, underwear, and even leather trousers.

An old stall by the junction with Penfold Street has been a Church Street regular since 1968. The trader, a ruddy-faced, white-haired woman, looks for all the world as if she has brought in the eggs, cheese and homemade jam straight from her farm—unlikely, given her London accent. A relative newcomer is Dave Mailer, who runs London's first South African takeaway from his small caravan on Church Street. Chicken *peri peri* (hot stuff), *Boereworst*, and *frikadell* (100 per cent beef) are on the menu. Business is brisk.

There are two or sometimes three cheap food stalls on Church Street; they usually have a similar stock of tins, packets, biscuits and chocolates. They all sell in bulk (three bags of peanuts for £1, say); they only trade here on Fridays and Saturdays; and all of them tend to sell out by the early afternoon. Outside one is a sign: 'Mark won't be here today. He got five numbers and the bonus on the lottery and has gone on holiday. Lucky b******.'

The Church Street area of Edgware Road still has a good supply of hi-fi and electrical goods stores, though several have been demolished recently. The market also has a fair selection of Walkmans, radio cassettes, headphones and blank tapes and videos. One stall stocks more expensive stuff: CD players and televisions. Duvets, towels, petfood, saucepans, plant pots, handbags, suitcases and cut flowers can also be found on the middle section of the market.

On Saturdays there's space for specialist stalls: one just selling watches; another with nothing but umbrellas; a large fabrics stall; a hat stall selling felt and lace creations; haberdashery and net curtains. In summer, the plant and herb stall and the gardening pitch draw a crowd; the cosmetics and perfumes stall, and the one selling hair accessories, are popular all year round. The butcher's has chickens, gammon and sucking-pig; the fish stall has plaice, cod and coley. There's also a shellfish stand with crabs, roll-mop herrings and mussels; occasionally, the trader will cook king prawns in a huge pan, and sell five of them hot with a wedge of lemon for £2. Nearby, a wholefood stall has bags of dried herbs, cereals, pulses and dried fruit.

At the junction with Salisbury Street, a few fly-traders sell fake designer goods, perfumes and pirate videos. By this point, the shops on either side of the street have undergone a noticeable change. The butchers', bakers' and caffs occupying postwar buildings have been replaced by antiques shops trading from well-kept 19th-century terraces.

The market takes some time to catch up with this change, and for a while the women's clothes (smart jackets, fashionable bodies, lingerie), cheap jewellery, shoes and electrical goods continue. But from the junction of Ashbridge Street, there are two lines of stalls on the south side. The second line is gathered on the pavement outside **Alfie's Antiques Market**, which takes up all the terraced premises between 13 and 25 Church Street. The outside stalls have a mixture of old crockery, jewellery, cutlery, paperweights—rather like stands at a car-boot sale, save that every article is (or is purported to be) valuable. Not all the traders are as reputable as they might be: one asked £850 for a simple silver bracelet when he saw the potential customer was an Arab woman.

Inside Alfie's, the traders inhabit permanent premises and are mostly middle-class folk who chat quietly to each other in the corridors. Up to 370 dealers occupy the 35,000-square-foot space, which includes a basement and three floors plus a roof-top café. Silverware, old jewellery, furniture, Victorian prints and general bric-a-brac make up the majority of the exhibits, though you are also likely to find picture frames, leather armchairs, carriage clocks, toy cars, toy soldiers, antiquarian books and wooden

Church Street

writing cases. One of my favourite stalls is in the basement and sells antique kitchen equipment; the old pots, pans, milk jugs and enamel storage jars are displayed on shelves as though part of a 19th-century scullery. Inevitably Mrs Beeton makes an appearance. Compared to Portobello Road, the crowds are thin here and browsing is painless. Traders are experts and know the value of their stock, but they are often willing to lower their prices.

Together, Church Street, Bell Street and Alfie's reveal something of the scope of street trading in London. If you've little time in the city, come here on Saturday and spend a morning joining in the bustle.

Nearby cafés and pubs

On a fine day, an outside seat at **Lindsay's Roof-Top Café** in Alfie's Antiques Market is the best bet. Breakfasts, salads and inexpensive lunches are served. Edgware Road has plenty of cheap cafés. The **Metropolitan Café** at No.340 has pies, fried breakfasts and steamed syrup puddings. Traders tend to eat at the **Market Grill** on Church Street near the junction with Salisbury Street, which sells a few Thai dishes along with fried breakfasts and sandwiches. They drink at the **Traders Inn** opposite. A 15-minute walk south on the Edgware Road will bring you to a collection of Lebanese restaurants; try the **Ranoush Juice Bar** for fresh fruit juices and cheap Middle Eastern snacks.

Hampstead Community Market

Address: 78 Hampstead High Street, NW3, ✆ (0171) 794 8313.
Public transport: ⊖ Hampstead; ⇌ Hampstead Heath; buses 46, 268.
Opening hours: Sat 10am–6pm; permanent stalls Tue–Sat.
Best time to go: Saturday.
Car parking: try the side streets south of Hampstead, but expect a long walk.
Main wares: crafts, books, fruit and veg, wholefood, fish.
Specifics: hot snacks, fish, secondhand books.

Ever since Alexander Pope came with his friend John Gay to take the waters at Hampstead Wells, this borough-cum-village has attracted the literati. These days the place has fallen victim to its beauty, and only rich literati can afford to live here; behind the door of every 18th-century cottage lurks a corpulent novelist or a millionaire literary agent. But Hampstead's beauty is undeniable; to wander its streets (especially away from the busy main roads) is to immerse yourself in sophistication and gentility. **Keats's House** (Wentworth Place, Keats' Grove) attracts many visitors to the area, while a stroll on **Hampstead Heath** is *de rigueur* for both visitors and locals on fine weekends.

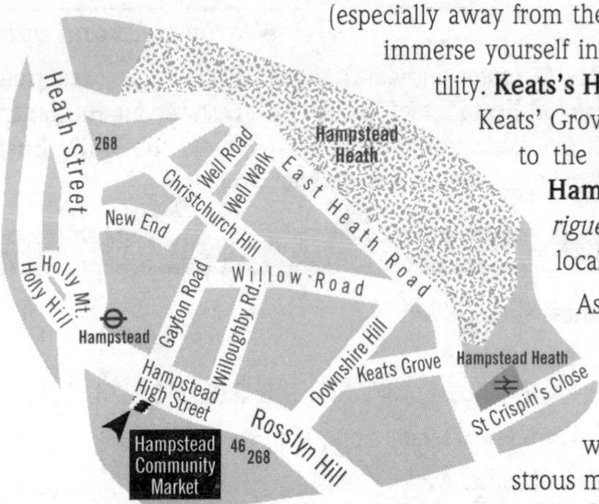

As a rule, affluent areas do not have thriving street markets, and the rule is obeyed here. The folk who fortify their monstrous mansions on the Bishop's Avenue north of the Heath would as likely frequent a fruit and veg mart as campaign for an equal distribution of wealth. Yet Hampstead Community Market, though small, does have a certain Women's Institute-style charm. It is held indoors in a building akin to a village hall. Notices are displayed near the entrance advertising local events, and there's a collection of swirly paintings by under-fives around a serving hatch. Snacks and inexpensive hot lunches (perhaps chicken in Creole sauce, or carrot cake) are served to marketgoers every Saturday. Trestle tables covered with tablecloths are arranged lengthwise, and diners sit on small school chairs to tuck in to the homely, nourishing food.

About 15 stalls are set up around the hall. There are two or three antiques stalls, but the crafts traders are more numerous, selling dried flowers, hats, paintings, jewellery, mother-of-pearl buttons, cushion covers and pottery. As you'd expect in Hampstead, there's at least one book stall, stocked with weighty biographies and highbrow novels. Most are secondhand and in good condition; prices start at £1.50.

Next door to the Community Centre, four permanent wooden stalls sell food. The first is well stocked with fruit and vegetables; the second is a deli/sandwich stall; the third sells wholefood (cereals, nuts, dried fruits and herbal teas); while the fourth has a wealth of seafood and fish geared to local tastes and pockets (wild salmon, sea bass, Dover sole, Tiger Bay prawns). But all in all, prices at the food stalls aren't as high as you'd expect for the area. Hampstead Community Centre, which established the market in the mid-1970s, should be praised for ensuring that some basic commodities are provided here. The food stalls are a godsend in an area that could easily be swamped by antiques shops.

Nearby cafés and pubs

Hampstead is awash with tea rooms and cafés, though tweeness is a recurrent problem. **Louis Pâtisserie** (32 Heath Street) is one of the best, serving Hungarian-style cakes and pastries. Of Hampstead's many old pubs, try the **Holly Bush** (22 Holly Mount), a cosy old place serving standard pub grub.

Inverness Street

Address: Inverness Street, NW1.

Public transport: ⊖ Camden Town;
buses 24, 27, 29, 31, 134, 135, 168, 214, 253, 274, C2.

Opening hours: Mon–Wed, Fri, Sat 9am–5pm; Thur 9am–1pm.

Best time to go: Friday and Saturday.

Car parking: try the streets north of the Chalk Farm Road, but be prepared for a long walk.

Main wares: fresh food, household goods.

Specifics: fruit and veg, cheese.

Camden Town sprang up in the 1840s, in the wake of the railways. Workshops and factories clustered along the lines running north out of London, and workers' housing followed. Until the 1970s, Camden remained a largely working-class district; then, helped by the opening of Camden Lock market (*see* p.85), it became one of London's most fashionable areas.

Inverness Street is a spirited survivor from earlier times, a small street market that supplies local people with extremely cheap fruit, vegetables and household goods. Even on Saturday there are only about 30 stalls. At the junction with the High Street, the worst of them attempt to divert crowds heading for the newer and more famous weekend markets. One sells cheap jeans, another flogs rubbishy tourist postcards, Union flags and dolls. But as you proceed down Inverness Street, the market gets back to basics, with stalls full of food. The cheese seller (Wed–Sat) has about 30 varieties including Wensleydale, Cheshire, Long Clawson Stilton (£4.10 per lb), Roquefort (£8.50 per lb) and *chèvre*. A fishmonger trades at the market from Thursday to Saturday and brings along a fair selection of seafood (whelks, mussels, crabsticks) and white fish. There's also a butcher's stall; along with eggs, bacon joints and saveloys, it sells boiler chickens with their heads still on for £2.

At the westerly end of the market, a chap piles all manner of useful household goods round him, from cheap coloured candles to tablecloths and napkins. Other traders sell toiletries and detergents, petfood, potted plants and flowers. But the market is best for fruit and veg, which is cheap and plentiful with eight or nine large stalls devoted to it. The strongest lines are in traditional produce. In season, you might find 2lb of grapes for £1; 2lb of tomatoes for 50p; and bananas at 20p per lb. But mooli, fennel, beef tomatoes, asparagus, limes, kohl rabi, medlars, plums, mangoes and raspberries also appear. A couple of the costermongers also turn up on Sundays to get their share of the mass action. Unsurprisingly prices are raised.

Despite local competition from both Safeway and Sainsbury's, Inverness Street still holds its own. And while the traders sell produce at a fraction of supermarket prices, it's easy to see why. Would that all localities had such a resilient market.

Nearby cafés and shops

The **Beigel Bar** at 12 Inverness Street is the nearest place for a bite, selling filled bagels, hot salt-beef sandwiches and homemade soup. The street also has a couple of interesting specialist shops: **Megacity Comics** (18 Inverness Street) stocks sci-fi comics, and **Shakedown** (No.24) is an independent record and CD store. *See also* 'Camden', p.88.

Kilburn Square

Address: west side of Kilburn High Road, opposite Quex Road, NW6, ✆ (01494) 871277.

Public transport: ⊖ Kilburn Park;
⇌ Kilburn High Road;
buses 16, 16A, 28, 31, 32, 98, 206.

Opening hours: Thur–Sat 9am–5.30pm.

Best time to go: Saturday.

Car parking: try the side streets to the west of the Kilburn High Road.

Main wares: clothing, petfood, household goods, cassettes and CDs.

Specifics: Afro-Caribbean literature, petfoods, tropical fish, Irish music.

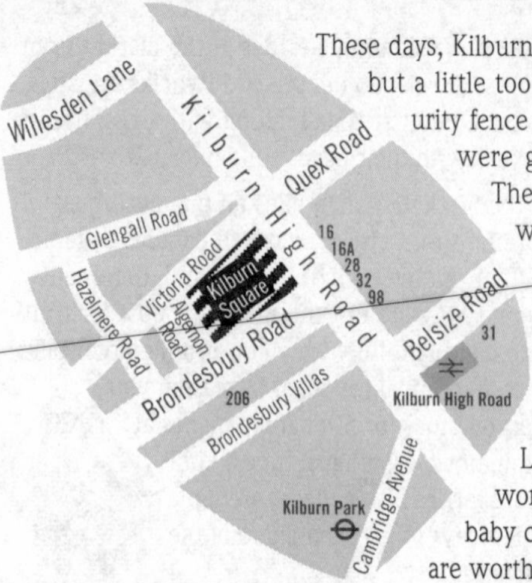

These days, Kilburn Square market looks neat and new, but a little too well-ordered. A blue and grey security fence was put up in 1994 and stallholders were given permanent lock-up premises. The market was nothing special before, when temporary stalls were set up on this dreary concrete square, but now some premises are empty or closed even on a Saturday.

Many of the 40 or so traders sell clothing of the type common at London's street markets: jeans, women's jackets, tawdry nightclubwear, baby clothes, socks, shoes. But a few stalls are worth closer inspection. **Books & Images** stocks Afro-Caribbean literature and artefacts, including many books on black politics and history; a new age stall called **Live and Let Live** will replenish your stock of crystals; **Nefertiti** is an Afro-Caribbean hair and beauty centre; **Paul's Aquatic World** sells tropical fish together with all the accompanying gubbins (and guppies); and the **One-Stop Pet Food** stall deals in dog baskets and bird cages. There's only one (albeit large) fruit and veg stall, but it's also possible to buy seafood and cheap biscuits and cakes. Other basics are sold by the household goods stall.

Though Kilburn is a centre of the London Irish community, there's little to remind you of it at the market. The one exception is the cassette stall which has a large collection of Irish music, from Daniel O'Donnell upwards. It is one of the few temporary stalls, trading in the middle of the market under umbrellas.

At junctions up and down the Kilburn High Road solitary vendors set out their wares. Two of them can be found outside the Cock public house, 50 yards north of the market. One sells socks and underwear, the other haberdashery. Hardly enough to make a market, but these hawkers seem more in keeping with the unfettered traditions of London street trading than the enclosed stallholders down the road.

Nearby cafés, pubs and shops

A snack bar in the market sells fried breakfasts, jacket potatoes and ice-creams. Kilburn High Road is a busy main street with many of the usual chainstores, but it does contain the occasional gem. Watch out for Irish white pudding at the butchers', soda bread at the bakeries, and Irish stew at the caffs (take a trek north on the High Road to find all three). The most famous Irish pub in the area is **Biddy Mulligan's**, at the junction with Willesden Lane.

Nag's Head and Grafton School

Address: Nag's Head, Seven Sisters Road, southwest of junction with Hertslet Road, N7, ✆ (0171) 607 3527;
Grafton School, off Hercules Place, N7.

Public transport: ⊖ Holloway Road;
buses 4, 17, 29, 43, 153, 253, 259, 271, 279, X43.

Opening hours: **general** Mon, Tue, Thur 8am–5pm;
secondhand and antiques Wed 8am–5pm;
new goods Fri 8am–5pm, Sat 8am–5.30pm;
flea market Sun 8am–2pm;
Grafton School market Sat 8am–4.30pm.

Car parking: you can park for an hour (Mon–Fri, unlimited at weekend) on the northbound carriageway of the Holloway Road near the junction with Seven Sisters Road, but spaces are limited; otherwise try the side streets to the north of the Seven Sisters Road.

Main wares: bric-a-brac, new and secondhand clothes, household goods, fruit and veg, fish, secondhand electrical goods and records.

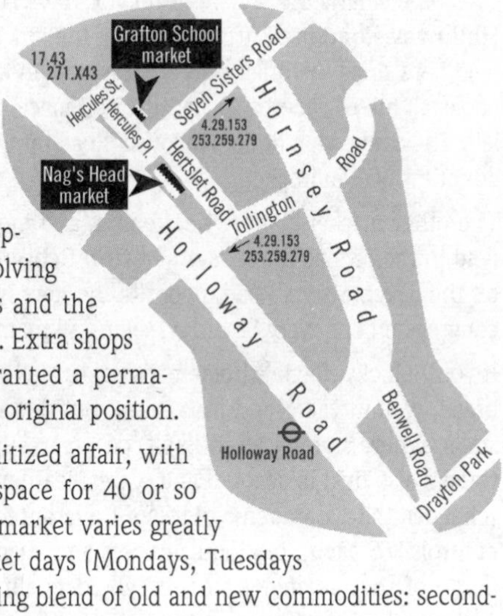

Until a few years ago, the **Nag's Head** market occupied a patch of wasteland near the pub that has given its name to the busy junction of Holloway Road and Seven Sisters Road. However, developers planned to build a shopping centre there. After a battle involving locals, stallholders, the developers and the council, a compromise was reached. Extra shops were built, but the market was granted a permanent though smaller site close to its original position.

It's now a compact, somewhat sanitized affair, with roofing covering the traders and space for 40 or so stalls. As was always the case, the market varies greatly through the week. On mixed market days (Mondays, Tuesdays and Thursdays), you'll find a satisfying blend of old and new commodities: secondhand clothes, bric-a-brac and electrical equipment; new clothes, fresh food and household goods.

On Wednesdays everything is secondhand. Again, there's plenty of bric-a-brac, but also cheap clothing, shoes (including some great leather winkle-pickers for a fiver) and well-worn household goods.

On Fridays and Saturdays, only new goods are sold, and consequently the market is relatively bland. There are a couple of big fruit and veg stalls, but the variety of produce and the prices aren't exceptional. The two fish stalls are better; along with North Sea regulars, they stock milk fish, jackfish and snappers (popular with the Afro-Caribbean locals). Clothing ranges from sensible striped shirts (three for £10), to skimpy tops for teenagers, printed with slogans like 'single and desperate'. A couple of stalls sell cassette tapes and videos—you may not have heard of the artistes, but the prices (three cassettes for £5; videos £1.50 each) are rock bottom. Electrical bits and bobs, tools, cheap jewellery, toiletries, stationery, toys, greetings cards and a butcher's van complete the picture.

Every Sunday the market changes character yet again. Though a few new goods are sold, secondhand clothes and bric-a-brac are to the fore, giving a flea-market feel to the place. As Holloway isn't on the tourist map, and competition from Camden and the East End markets is fierce, you're likely to find bargains among the crockery, ornaments and glassware, if you're prepared to root around.

Two other markets are held in this locality. The first is on the wide pavement of **Holloway Road** itself, to the south of the junction with Drayton Park. It has been held here since Victorian times, but is now in its death throes. A large secondhand bookstall full of paperbacks and the odd piece of secondhand furniture is all that is left. The conversion of the Holloway Road into a non-stop four-lane speed track has doubtless had an impact.

The other market is more heartening, and more like the Nag's Head of old. It is held in the tarmac grounds of **Grafton School**, down Hercules Place (a walkway off the Seven Sisters Road, opposite the new Nag's Head market). About 70 stalls congregate here every Saturday, selling all manner of new and old goods.

If you're lucky, Suzie's homemade cakes stall may be there, with its enticing soda bread, walnut cakes and fruit cakes. But there are always plenty of car-boot-style stalls, where homely junk is placed on trestle tables. Many of the professional traders also deal in secondhand wares: leather jackets from £5, jeans from £3.50 (cheaper than Camden), old TVs ('guaranteed to work'), box-loads of remote controls (£5 each), old football boots and a large number of secondhand records. Some of the old metal teapots would qualify as antiques at Church Street or Camden; here you can snap them up for £2 or less. New goods include sports gear (cricket bats, goalkeepers' gloves), haberdashery, essential oils, tools, petfoods, telephones, lingerie, towels, hair extensions and toilet seats.

Who knows how long it will last, but at present the ad hoc get-together outside Grafton School attracts more Holloway punters than the relatively orderly Nag's Head affair. Proof positive that authorities mess with markets at their peril.

Nearby cafés and shops

There's a **Percy Ingles** bakery and snack bar on the Holloway Road, midway between Seven Sisters Road and Hercules Street. It sells cakes, sandwiches and pies, and you can eat in. If you're going to investigate the couple of stalls farther south on the Holloway Road, call in at **Judy's Café** (No.249), which has British grills and caff food as well as Southeast Asian specialities—a meal rarely costs more than a fiver. Holloway Road also contains many of the usual chainstores.

Queen's Crescent

Address: Queen's Crescent, between Grafton Road and Malden Road, NW5.

Public transport: ⊖ Chalk Farm; ⇌ Kentish Town, Kentish Town West; buses 24, 46, 134, 135, 168, 214, C2.

Opening hours: Thur 9am–1.30pm; Sat 9am–5pm.

Best time to go: Saturday.

Car parking: try Queen's Crescent south of Malden Road.

Main wares: women's clothes, household goods, plants and flowers, fruit and veg, meat, fish.

Specifics: new and secondhand clothes for women.

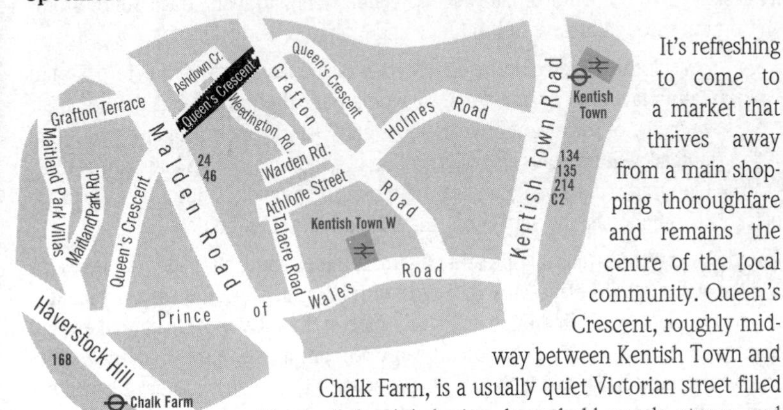

It's refreshing to come to a market that thrives away from a main shopping thoroughfare and remains the centre of the local community. Queen's Crescent, roughly midway between Kentish Town and Chalk Farm, is a usually quiet Victorian street filled with small local bakeries, household goods stores and butchers' shops. But on Thursday mornings and Saturdays, stalls are set up along its northern stretch and scores of people from nearby flats and houses take to the streets to shop, browse and chat.

About 80 traders come here on Saturdays, when the street is barred to traffic. There's a good spread of goods on offer, with all the basics supplied. The scattering of fruit and veg stalls sell the usual bananas, apples, onions and potatoes at fair prices. The two butchers' stalls are more interesting. **J. Simmons** has an old-fashioned barrow full of big joints of gammon, and chickens. He frequently has offal, with lambs' kidneys and hearts selling well. The other trader concentrates on cheese and bacon, selling extra mature farmhouse Cheddar at £2.79 a pound. Two other food stalls are worth noting, one selling a small but glisteningly fresh choice of fish; the other (at the Malden Street end) full of cheap tinned food and cakes, eggs and biscuits.

The market also supplies most essential household items, including disinfectant, toilet rolls, vacuum cleaner spares and chamois leathers. Some shops have stalls on the street to attract custom, among them **Hole in the Wall** (on Ashdown Crescent, just off the main street), a large household goods store selling dustbins, mops and the like.

But though Queen's Crescent also has the usual selection of street market wares—electrical goods, greetings cards, hair accessories, petfood, cheap jewellery, crockery, stationery, duvets, towels, plants and flowers, haberdashery, and even a garden equipment stall with a platoon of garish gnomes—clothes are its forte. Chainstore seconds, new and secondhand garments can all be found here, with women best catered for. Two rails are full of seconds (mostly tops and trousers), selling for £2.99 or £4.99. One trader has a collection of full-length coats in gold lamé—not for the faint-hearted. Another specializes in outsized clothes for women, from size 16 to 36. Unfortunately the selection of big jumpers, track suit bottoms and button-through dresses in lurid lime and orange is hardly alluring.

Few clothes here could be described as fashionable—pastel-hued frocks and suits favoured by middle-aged women are the norm—but there's a fair choice of socks, underwear, shoes and T-shirts (including one stall full of football T-shirts), plus a small selection of children's clothes and men's shirts. One trader does make a valiant attempt to be modish, describing a skimpy black PVC number as 'the very latest, the horniest jacket around'.

Camden's trendiness hasn't spread this far: the tapes and CDs trader (all tapes for £1; two CDs for £5) plays Max Bygraves with impunity. But Queen's Crescent is the sort of place you'll find knots of locals, some of them Cypriots, gathered around to chat about the week's events. You can even join in, and have a political chin-wag with the Socialist Workers Party paper-sellers. The market has been here for a century and a quarter, and happily still seems in its prime.

Nearby cafés and pubs

The **Gossip Stop Café** at 88 Queen's Crescent is appropriately named, clean and modern. It serves all-day breakfasts, sandwiches and pastries. The **Blue Sea Fish Bar** is a traditional chippie on the Crescent. There are three pubs by the market, including the **Sir Robert Peel** at the junction with Malden Road.

Swiss Cottage

Address: The Square, between Avenue Road and Winchester Road, NW3, ✆ (0171) 722 4079.

Public transport: ⊖ Swiss Cottage; ⇌ South Hampstead; buses 13, 31, 46, 82, 113, 268, C11, C12.

Opening hours: Fri–Sun 9am–5pm.

Best time to go: Sunday.

Car parking: try the side streets off Belsize Park, northwest of the market.

Main wares: secondhand clothes, records and tapes, books, jewellery, antiques.

Specifics: look for bargains among the records, tapes and books.

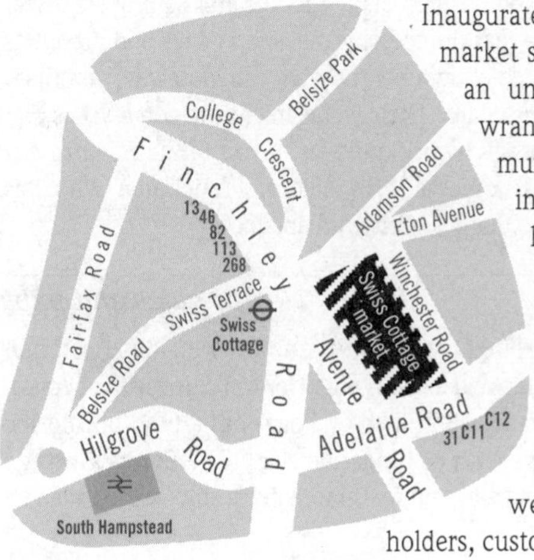

Inaugurated in the 1970s, Swiss Cottage market spent much of its early life facing an uncertain future. Fortunately the wrangles between council, local community and developers were resolved in the 1980s, and the market now has a permanent site on a concrete square away from Swiss Cottage's horrendous traffic, near a community centre.

And there's a feeling of community at the market. By luck or design, it has become pleasingly well balanced in its mixture of stallholders, customers and goods on sale. Over 40 stalls are erected on a Sunday. Many are run by local amateurs, selling bric-a-brac, secondhand books or perhaps (having switched to CDs), their record and tape collections. These are discerning folk, and the quality of their goods is often high; I still treasure my early recording of Etta James, picked up here for £3. The secondhand bookstalls (usually about four of them) contain a fund of classic volumes that befits a market near Hampstead. One trader has a collection of paperbacks and hardbacks from the 1930s to the 1950s (all hardbacks sell for £1); another has literature by women, and dozens of Penguin Classics. A paperback *Madame Bovary* in pristine condition is only £1.50.

Several stalls have a car-booter feel about them, and as many are run by people with a weekday job, they vary greatly from week to week, and are less plentiful on Fridays. You could find anything up to a dozen secondhand clothes stalls here. Most garments are of the sort you'd find at a Home Counties jumble sale: reasonable quality, but rarely groovy. One trader sells all manner of women's clothes at £2 an item. Other secondhand goods include jewellery—a jewellery-repair stall, which also has clocks and basic electrical stuff, sometimes shows up—household goods (old kettles, teapots and the like), and old cutlery (a George VI complete cutlery set was offered for £99). In general, goods are several notches higher in quality than you'd find at the junk markets of Westmoreland Road or Bell Street, but seldom sell at the inflated prices of Portobello.

Along with all this interesting old stuff, the market also provides a fair selection of new goods. The seafood stall has smoked salmon alongside its jellied eels, and there's a fruit and veg trader, a haberdashery stall, and a trader selling electrical goods and tools. Pot plants, underwear, jumpers, jeans, sports bags and greetings cards also crop up. A small batch of traders runs what can loosely be described as crafts stalls. Their wares might include crystals and fossils, patchwork quilts or, if you're lucky, *tarte aux pommes* homemade by a local Frenchman who has entered the market spirit with aplomb.

Nearby cafés and pubs

Cosmo (4–6 Northways Parade, Finchley Road), is an old, well-loved caff and restaurant serving pastas, omelettes and salads, plus Central European specials; **Louis Pâtisserie** (12 Harben Parade, 185 Finchley Road) has a fund of calorific cakes plus daily hot savoury dishes with a Hungarian slant. The **Swiss Cottage** pub (by the tube) is designed like a chalet, but feels more like a ship, surrounded by a tumultuous sea of traffic.

Wembley

Address: Stadium Way, Wembley, Middlesex, ✆ (01895) 812233.

Public transport: ⊖ Wembley Park;
⇌ Wembley Stadium;
buses 83, 92, 182, 223, 224, 297, PR2.

Opening hours: Sun 9am–3pm.

Best time to go: 9am Sunday to avoid the crowds.

Car parking: there's a car park to the west of the market, but to avoid the queues, try around the industrial estate and DIY super stores off Fulton Road and Rutherford Way.

Main wares: clothing, household goods, electrical goods.

Specifics: cheap leather jackets, coats, men's shoes, football strips, hats.

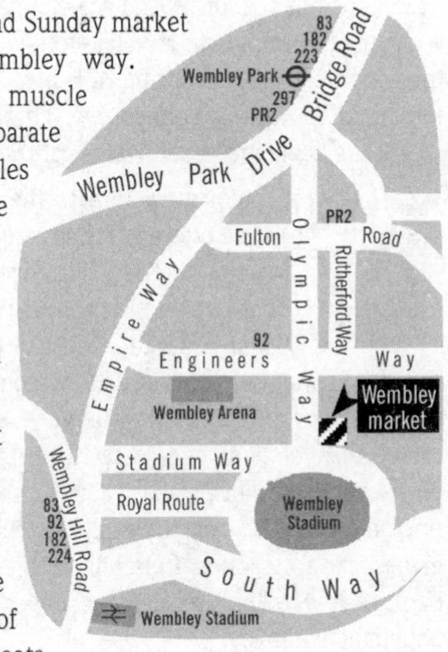

Northwest London's attempt at an East End Sunday market certainly brings the hordes down Wembley way. Coachloads of hefty shoppers shuffle and muscle their way along the wide avenues that separate the acres of stalls. Many have come miles down the M1 from the north; most have come for the cheap clothes and household goods. But anyone who enjoys snuffling around in mounds of old junk will be disappointed; junk there may be, but it is all spanking new.

This is a big market with big stalls—about 450 of them. One of the first you're likely to come across is a newsagent's selling Sunday papers and cigarettes—it's the only one on the market. Then you're among the clothes. Wembley is one of London's best markets for cheap leather coats and jackets. The several large leatherwear stalls have garments in scores of styles, from pink mini-skirts to bulky suede jackets; prices start at £45.

Men, women and children have a vista of clothes to choose from. Womenswear ranges from high-street fashions such as bodies, Lycra leggings, smart suits and woollen skirts to lingerie and nightclub wear. Children's clothes come in swirly patterns, twee frills for toddlers or—fittingly, given the location—as football strips in Premier League team colours (also sold in men's sizes). Men can snap up three polo shirts for £10, new worsted suits for £39.99 (advertised as 'Cheaper than stolen goods, honestly'), or 'work jeans' (i.e. jeans with unknown brand names) for £7.99. One stall has a vast array of trousers, ranging from grey flannels for schoolboys to tent-like togs with 50-inch waists. Jumpers, T-shirts, underwear and socks are made to suit both sexes and most sizes. There's also a couple of discount jeans stalls, selling Pepe and Levi seconds.

Wembley is not primarily a food market. There are only two fruit and veg stalls, but both are large and the traders sell their stocks of mostly standard produce at low prices and with hearty voices: 'No man goes like a mango goes,' yells one lad proffering his most exotic fruit. The bread and cake stall does a good trade in iced doughnuts, and there's also a couple of sweets stalls and a butcher's lorry. Where fast food is concerned, though, the market really comes into its own. As well as the ubiquitous hot dog lorries and jacket potato sellers, there's a Chinese takeaway stall with stir-fries cooked in a wok before your eyes. Some deals are patently aimed at the coach parties: ten spring rolls cost only £1.50 before 11am. You'll also find Indian *seikh kebabs*, cooked over charcoal; hot pancakes; and an outdoor caff, where the beefy market stewards get through gallons of baked beans.

A major attraction to the market are the thousands of household goods offered. These range from electrical gadgets for the kitchen (toasters, kettles, liquidizers), to gnomes, motor mowers, ironing-board covers, keys (cut while you wait) and garden furniture. At many markets you can buy leather handbags, bath towels, toys, rugs, tools, net curtains, duvets, watches, plants and shrubs, country tapes and CDs, net curtains, gold jewellery, videos, haberdashery, dress material, radio-cassette players, and sunglasses. Here, there's more choice of all of these goods, plus several specialist stalls. Tablecloths and napery, car phones, office stationery (including Tippex, cashboxes and reams of paper), amplifiers and speakers, video games, car accessories (from chamois leathers to hub caps and personalized numberplates), wooden furniture, Indian bedspreads, and even AA membership can be bought at Wembley.

A couple of large stalls sell men's shoes at extremely low prices: brogues with leather uppers going for only £10. One stall has a pair of size 14 monstrosities on display. Another highlight is the hat stall. A huge variety of headgear is in stock: Panamas, frilly things for babies, wedding hats and trilbies. A middle-aged woman is trying on a particularly flamboyant model, and her daughter is howling with laughter. The stallholder desperately tries to reassure his customer: 'It looks all right that.'

A market of this size often attracts sideshows, and 'Gipsy Rose Lee' turns up regularly. Her caravan is plastered with notices telling punters of her appearances in the *Western Mail* and at the Royal Welsh Show. She'll read your palm for £3.50. Nearby, a hawker is trying to flog the latest novelty product, the 'power balloon' which, he demonstrates, can be whacked against anything without bursting.

To see all of the market is something of an endurance test. As you walk away from the stalls, leaving Wembley's famous twin towers behind, you might feel like you've played 90 minutes plus extra time in a cup final. In the distance you hear a man at the crockery stall, still trying his darnedest to sell an ugly white china bread bin. 'Tell you what I'll do...'

Nearby cafés

There is nothing worth visiting in the immediate vicinity of Wembley Stadium, so you'd be better off eating at one of the fast food stands in the market. If, however, you've a car and fancy some fabulous, no-frills Punjabi food, head for **Karahi King**, ten minutes' drive away at 213 East Lane, North Wembley.

Willesden

Address: High Road, Willesden, in the grounds of the White Hart pub, by White Hart Lane, NW10.

Public transport: ⊖ Dollis Hill, Neasden; buses 226, 260, 266, 297, 302.

Opening hours: Wed, Sat 9am–5.30pm.

Best time to go: Saturday.

Car parking: Ilex Road just around the corner from the market, has free parking, though is often full; if so, try the side streets to the south of the High Road.

Main wares: household goods, clothing, fresh food.

Specifics: black music, tights and stockings, men's suits.

Willesden's bi-weekly sale is a fine example of a local urban market: compact, well balanced and with a healthy multicultural mix of customers and traders. It is held in the car park of the White Hart, an Irish pub which also contains a club called Biddy Early's. On Saturdays about 40 stalls fill the space.

There are two sizeable fruit and veg stalls. Come at knocking-out time on a Saturday (5pm in summer, earlier in winter) and you might snap up some astonishing bargains (a box of avocadoes for £1, or 3lb of mushrooms for £1.50 for instance). Local Asian women have their weekly haggle with the costermongers at this time—it's all good-natured stuff. A butcher's lorry (selling mostly bacon joints and cheese), and a large stall of biscuits, chocolates, cakes and bread also provide Willesdeners with their victuals.

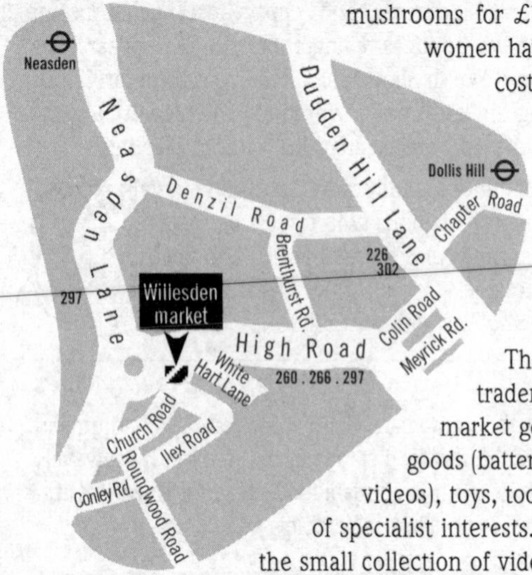

Though this is a small market, its traders supply most of the usual market goods—greetings cards, electrical goods (batteries, watches, blank cassettes and videos), toys, tools—and even cater for a couple of specialist interests. Fans of black music scrutinize the small collection of videos and cassette tapes of reggae bands in concert, or listen to the cool jazz and soul played by a couple of young Afro-Caribbean traders, many of whose LPs and CDs seem to be imports.

The remaining stalls concentrate on clothing. Again, all the basics are present and correct: underwear, T-shirts, tops, fabrics, shirts, shoes and training shoes. But there's also a few intriguing oddities, like the stall with a huge number of tights and stockings laid out neatly in packs; or the hat stall with its straw trilbies for men and colourful felt wedding titfers for women; or the pitch specializing in glittering creations to be worn in Cricklewood nightclubs. In contrast to this flamboyance is the rather sober, old-fashioned stall run by an Asian tailor. His men's suits have waist sizes going from a scrawny 28 inches to a whopping 58 inches. 'Large or small, we serve you all,' says the sign.

Nearby cafés and pubs

The **Hamburger Bar and Café** at 222 Church Road sells run-of-the-mill breakfasts and sandwiches. Otherwise, have a pint of Guinness in the **White Hart**.

East London

Petticoat Lane

Bethnal Green

Address: south side of Bethnal Green Road, from Wilmot Street to Vallance Road, E2.

Public transport: ⊖/⇌ Bethnal Green; buses 8, 106, 253, 309, D6.

Opening hours: Mon–Wed, Fri, Sat 8.30am–5pm; Thur 8.30am–2pm.

Best time to go: Friday and Saturday.

Car parking: try the backstreets north and south of Bethnal Green Road.

Main wares: fruit and vegetables, household goods, women's clothes.

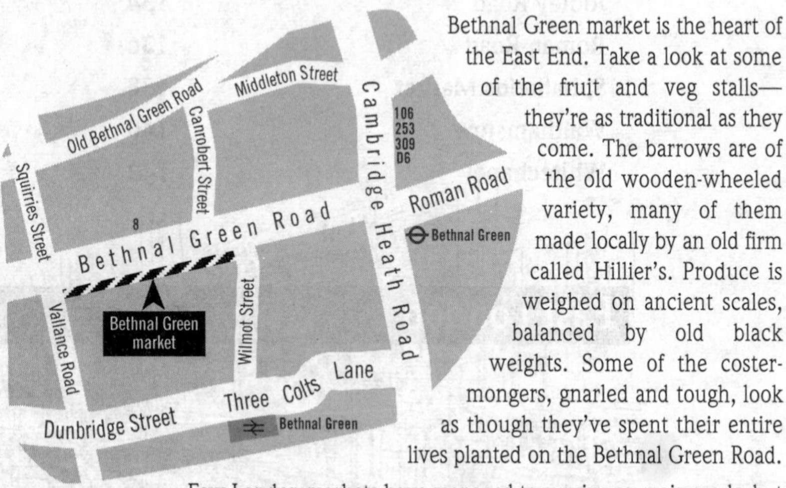

Bethnal Green market is the heart of the East End. Take a look at some of the fruit and veg stalls—they're as traditional as they come. The barrows are of the old wooden-wheeled variety, many of them made locally by an old firm called Hillier's. Produce is weighed on ancient scales, balanced by old black weights. Some of the costermongers, gnarled and tough, look as though they've spent their entire lives planted on the Bethnal Green Road.

Few London markets have managed to survive on main roads, but the stallholders at Bethnal Green soldier on amid the fumes and noise of the A1209. The market has been held here since the early 19th century, and has remained true to its locals, providing clothes, staple foodstuffs and household goods. Henry Mayhew records that 100 costermongers usually attended the market in the 1850s, while Mary Benedetta notes that in 1936 it traded seven days a week, and included furniture and junk stalls. These days it tends to straggle during the week with no more than 20 or so of the 76 pitches taken, but a good enough show is made on Fridays and Saturdays.

Most of the weekly shop can be done here: soap and bin bags at the household goods stall; children's pyjamas and mittens at a clothes pitch; crisps and cheap tins of spaghetti hoops at the cut-price food stall. Among the regulars is a trader selling Afro-

Caribbean produce; as well as yams and plantain, he stocks imported soft drinks and some fresh herbs. There's ample opportunity to buy women's clothing as well, and prices are keen: look out for 'sales rails' where everything costs under a fiver.

Bethnal Green tube station was the site of London's worst civilian disaster of the Second World War. Fearing that the Germans were dropping gas bombs, a crowd of people fled down the steps to shelter in the underground. Someone fell, and over a hundred people were crushed to death. A plaque commemorates the spot. A less sobering local landmark can be found around the corner from the market on Cambridge Heath Road, where the **Bethnal Green Museum of Childhood** houses an enormous collection of dolls and toy trains and cars.

Nearby cafés and shops

There's a fine choice of pie and mash shops in the vicinity: try **G. Kelly's** at 414 Bethnal Green Road, or **S.R. Kelly's** at No.284. At No.332 is **E. Pellicci**, which has traditional caff grub: meat pudding with potatoes and veg, roast beef, etc. In the 1960s, Ronnie Kray, the gang leader, was a regular. Now, Pellicci's is a favourite meeting place for local young artists. A complete alternative can be found ten minutes' walk away at 241–245 Globe Town Road (*see* map, p.136), where **The Cherry Orchard**, a vegetarian café, resides.

While visiting the market, take a look in at **UK International** (348 Bethnal Green Road), a large shop that stocks a fine array of Bangladeshi foods and kitchenware.

Brick Lane (Club Row)

Address: Brick Lane (north of railway bridge), Cygnet Street, Sclater Street, E1; Bacon Street, Cheshire Street, E2.

Public transport: ⊖ Aldgate East, Shoreditch, Bethnal Green;
⊖/⇌ Liverpool Street;
buses 5, 8, 22A, 22B, 26, 35, 43, 47, 48, 67, 78, 149, 243, 243A, B1;
night buses N8, N26, N243.

Opening hours: Sun 6am–1pm.

Best time to go: as early as possible.

Car parking: try the side streets north of Bethnal Green Road; there are parking meters (with free parking on Sundays) on Boundary Street.

Main wares: secondhand goods (from books to furniture), tools, tapes and CDs, leatherwear, tinned food, petfoods.

Specifics: look out for secondhand bargains.

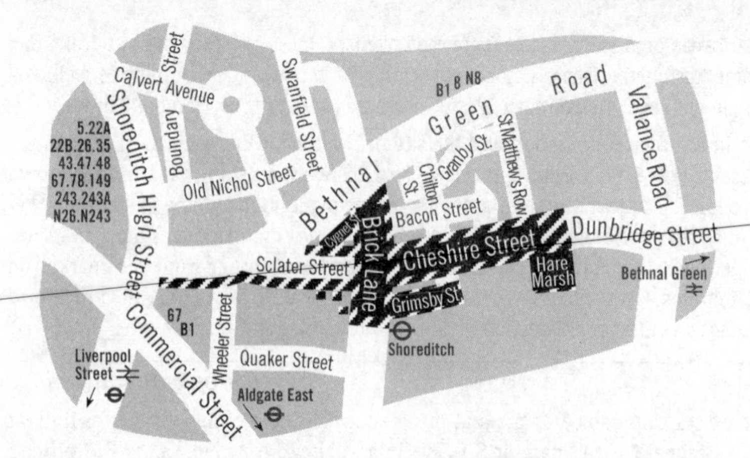

It's 6.40am on a dark Sunday morning and the Happy Inca has already been serving salt beef sandwiches for over an hour. Jewish food sold by a Peruvian: a taste of the multicultural East End. Outside the caff at the junction of Shoreditch High Street and Commercial Road, a forlorn-looking gent stands by a fully extended fishing rod which overhangs the road. He's getting few bites, but his rod marks the beginning of Brick Lane market.

Of all London markets, Brick Lane comes closest to the mayhem of the pre-20th-century marts: lawless, sprawling and splendid; never the same two weeks running, it always attracts thousands of locals (but few tourists) onto the streets.

Trading began here in the 18th century, half a mile from the City of London to escape the taxes imposed by the City authorities. The district has provided a home for a succession of refugees, from Huguenot silk-weavers in the 18th century, through East European Jews fleeing the pogroms of the late 19th century, to the present-day population of Bangladeshis. Unfortunately, the Bangladeshi influence on today's market is small, limited to a few stalls selling leather jackets made locally. The area is periodically embroiled in political strife when racists try to sell newspapers at the market. At the last encounter in 1994, the Anti-Nazi League mustered enough support to drive the British National Party from the streets, and there have been no major conflicts since.

Rooted alongside the rundown Victorian terraces in and around Brick Lane, the market also flourishes on nearby wasteland, in warehouses and under railway arches. As one bit of wasteland is sectioned off for redevelopment, another is taken over by stalls and vans. Until quite recently, one process seemed to cancel out the other, but now the City is encroaching fast and redevelopment gathering pace. The bicycle sale on Granby Street is a thing of the past, and the traders of Chilton Street have disappeared. The next property boom could kill London's best market.

Many locals still know the market as Club Row, but this short stub of a street off the Bethnal Green Road no longer has any stalls on it. Club Row used to be famous for selling birds, ornamental fish and small animals of all kinds. But in 1982 Tower Hamlets Council, under pressure from animal welfare groups, banned the sale of live animals. Hydra-like, Brick Lane accommodated the change and grew in other directions.

The following street-by-street guide should be seen as a snapshot taken one Sunday morning. Though Brick Lane, Cheshire Street and Sclater Street are the heart of the market, half the fun lies in exploring its gloriously frayed edges: the backstreets, lock-ups and cubby-holes where transient traders sell their dodgy wares.

Bethnal Green Road

On Bethnal Green Road, from Shoreditch High Street to Sclater Street, unlicensed traders line up with their backs to an old brick wall and try to sell the contents of someone else's broom cupboard; the poverty is palpable. Competition for pitches is fierce and a first come, first served system applies, so you'll find life here at unearthly times of the morning. One entrepreneur's stock consists only of shirt buttons, two fishing reels and a Harry Belafonte record. Nearby is a pile of car radios and a mountain bike. As if in protest at these mysteriously acquired goods, a burglar alarm whines unceasingly somewhere off Great Eastern Street.

Makeshift clothes lines—lengths of string hung between rusty nails banged into the wall—display crumpled suits and corduroys of uncertain ancestry. Two old men haggle over the price of a broken watch. Surreal combinations of wares are proffered: a septuagenarian woman sells old spectacles and egg whisks. An anxious young man jostles between two traders and opens a grubby case full of pirate porn movies. Yet despite the Dickensian sleaze, the market rarely feels threatening.

Farther along the Bethnal Green Road, the brick wall rises to become a Victorian railway bridge. A few lock-ups are incorporated in its structure. A couple are well-ordered: one contains secondhand books, the other wallpaper. Yet another has an incredible collection of junk, some of it still in Rentacrates, while rusty office furniture fills a fourth.

Sclater Street

Trading takes place on a more legitimate footing in Sclater Street. This used to be the centre of the animal trade; now only a few petfood stalls remain. Electrical goods and tools stalls, selling spanner sets, batteries, pliers, saws and other DIY paraphernalia, dominate the Bethnal Green Road end of the street; further up, it's the stalls selling cheap tins of food and cakes that attract attention. Two old traders are grumbling about the size of the crowd: 'They don't come down here like they used to early morning.'

Sclater Street eventually joins Brick Lane, but before it does so, a large area of wasteland opens to the left, followed by a yard; to the right are two more yards. The one on the left sells old junk and office furniture. The smaller of the two on the right has tools and fuses; the larger has bikes and secondhand junk, ranging from telephones through school text books to old ovens. Tower Hamlets Council has recently tried to beautify the yards with spanking new green gates, decorated with children's pictures and a sign welcoming people to the market. This jars somewhat: Brick Lane is of its essence wayward, lawless even.

The land to the left of Sclater Street incorporates Cygnet Street and a car park. This is where to find the best of the bantering stallholders. **Chabury**, the butcher's, is having a show. 'Cut the bugger in half, mate,' roars the frontman, as his assistant, cleaver held high, takes a lunge at a pork joint. 'Loverley great English pork. You couldn't see less fat on a banana.' Nearby, a frozen-food seller who arrives every week is instructing his audience: 'Today we've got chicken Kiev and chicken cordon bleu, but we'll call them Kevin and Gordon in case you can't get your mouth round the fancy French words. Who'll give me two quid for Kevin, two quid for Gordon?'

Also occupying the car park is a bike seller with scores of good value new and secondhand models; a vacuum cleaner spare parts stall; new hi-fi goods (sold with panache from off a lorry); bread and cakes; coats and jumpers; more tools stalls; and a man selling incense sticks.

Bacon Street

Tucked away behind all this is Bacon Street, a relatively quiet road running parallel to Sclater Street. A few traders occupy one side of the street before it reaches Brick Lane, among them a cake stall and a gloomy lock-up full of cheap new household goods; but Bacon Street is known more for its spivs. Many of these gents look old enough to have sold dodgy ration cards and nylons during the war. Still they huddle together with their fag ash and trilbies, proffering gold rings and watches as hot as the Costa del Sol.

Brick Lane

Brick Lane itself is perhaps the most mundane part of the market. Most of the goods for sale are new clothes: socks, leather jackets and bags, and children's wear.

But there are also a couple of shellfish stands where prawns, jellied eels and whelks are spooned down greedily by traders having an 11am lunch.

The market only occupies the stretch of Brick Lane north of the railway bridge. The southern part is home to most of the Lane's famous Bangladeshi curry houses. After the market ends at 1pm, head this way for lunch. Under the railway bridge is one of the market's most atmospheric lock-ups, a dank, dark Fagin's cave with a cobbled stone floor and grimy brick roof. It contains about 20 stalls full of secondhand and quasi-antique goods: musty books, festering old clothes, printer's blocks, leather suitcases, furniture, old radios and disparate bric-a-brac.

Across the road on Grimsby Street, but still under the railway arches, is a newer, brighter lock-up. At its entrance is a sign: 'You are now passing the Cockney dateline.' Below, a dozen old alarm clocks have been stuck to a board, showing the time in Bethnal Green, Wapping, Stepney and other local districts. Strangely it always seems to be 3pm in the East End. The lock-up also houses a secondhand bookstall (worth checking for bargains), bags, and crazy mixtures of junk: royal jelly capsules might be displayed alongside a three-string guitar and a small teapot from Margate.

Cheshire Street

It's now best to retrace your steps along Brick Lane, past the fruit and veg stall and perhaps an eccentric busker, and turn right up Cheshire Street. This is one of the best stretches of the market. It begins with a couple of stalls selling a huge number of cheap cassettes, including a great choice of R 'n' B. New goods are interspersed with old. Opposite a stall with cheap videos is a man selling old stamps (many Victorian), coins, banknotes and postcards. Nearby, a bric-a-brac stall has the Westwing Senior Tennis cup as its centrepiece. This trophy, won three times by Margo White between 1946 and 1948, could be yours for £3.50. Further up the street are stalls of new tools, spray paints for cars, radios and cassette players, stationery, socks, hats, gloves, jeans, underwear and shoes. Then secondhand goods take over. A bookshop keeps a stall of early Penguins outside; another trader has a collection of 19th-century prints. To the left, at 78–90 Cheshire Street, is a warehouse used as an indoor bric-a-brac market. The highlights here are the antiques stalls specializing in jewellery, war medals, coins, banknotes, Dinky toys, tools and cigarette lighters. A bottle of 1981 Royal Wedding ale, ready to drink at the Decree Absolute celebrations, will set you back £5. There's also a stall full of military paraphernalia including walkie-talkies, burns dressings, searchlights and a German helmet. One trader even sells new fishing tackle—rarely found on London's markets.

Past the warehouse, the market returns to the shabbiness of the Bethnal Green Road. Down Haremarsh, a cobbled prong of a street going down to the railway, disconsolate men stand by small piles of broken electrical goods, battered saucepans and mildewed clothes. This is the East End described by Henry Mayhew, Charles Dickens and Jack London—it still flourishes in 1990s Britain. At this end of Cheshire Street, you might also encounter odd pieces of masonry or fireplaces, liberated from houses in (official or otherwise) architectural salvage operations.

By 1.30pm the market is coming to a close. Only a few would-be traders remain on the streets, cramming discarded clothing and broken hair dryers into shabby shopping baskets. They will be back to try and sell them next week.

Nearby cafés, pubs and shops

If it's too early for jellied eels, walk up to the **Brick Lane Bagel Bake** (open 24 hours at No.159) for a salmon and cream cheese bagel. The **Carpenters Arms** on Cheshire Street is very much a locals' pub, and buzzes with life on a Sunday lunchtime. Non East Enders might feel a little out of place, but it's worth popping in for a surreptitious pint as long as you keep a low profile and don't disturb the regulars. **Nazrul** (130 Brick Lane) is one of the cheapest and best of the curry caffs that have proliferated on the southern stretches of Brick Lane. **The Clifton** (No.126) and **Shampan** (No.79) offer classier food and surroundings, but are also good value. Many of Brick Lane's leatherwear shops are open on Sunday morning; prices are among the lowest in London.

Columbia Road

Address: Columbia Road, from Ravenscroft Street to Barnet Grove, E2.

Public transport: ⊖ Shoreditch, Old Street; buses 8, 26, 48, 55, B1.

Opening hours: Sun 8am–1pm.

Best time to go: busiest in spring.

Car parking: try the side streets north of the Hackney Road.

Main wares: pot plants, shrubs, bulbs, flowers and garden accessories.

Specifics: bulk buys of shrubs; garden ornaments; Christmas trees and evergreens in winter.

The Luftwaffe spared this stretch of Columbia Road during the Blitz, as did the developers in later years. While the surrounding district is covered by stark 1960s flats and houses, the short span of road that entertains the market is flanked by quaint Victorian terraces and diminutive shops—a fitting setting for London's best weekly flower show.

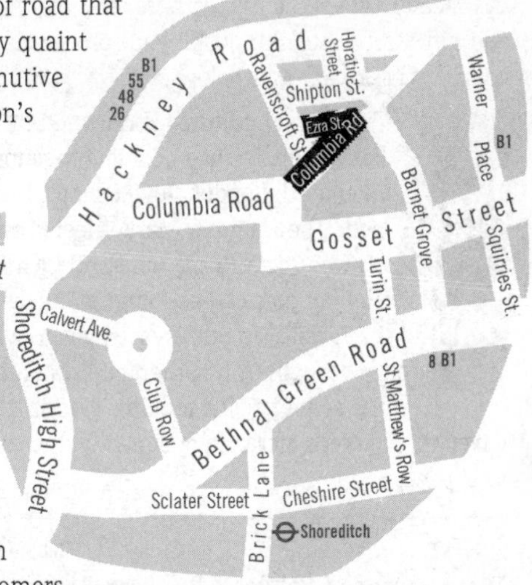

From the start of the market at the junction with Ravenscroft Street, both sides of the narrow road are packed with plants, shrubs, cut flowers, cacti and herbs. Prices are enticingly low, particularly if you're buying in bulk. What's on offer changes with the season, but even in winter there's a scrum of customers jostling for a look at the evergreens. Kangaroo vines, pots of chrysanths, fuchsias, rose bushes, dried flowers, dwarf conifers, various house plants and bundles of twisted willow might be on sale at the 20 or so stalls in autumn. In spring, it can take quarter of an hour to negotiate the hundred yards of the market as a rustling herd of foliage-bearing punters fights through the jungle.

Flower trading started in the 1920s, but there was a large fruit and vegetable market in the neighbourhood during the 19th century. The costermongers were housed in a huge neo-Gothic edifice called Columbia Market. Opened in 1869, the building was financed by a £200,000 donation from the philanthropist Baroness Burdett-Coutts. Resembling St Pancras railway station in its preposterous grandeur, Columbia Market never really took off; the costermongers preferred the streets. By the First World War the building had fallen into disrepair, and in 1958 it was finally demolished to make way for council flats.

During the last decade Columbia Road has undergone some gentrification. Fred Bare, the trendy hat store, has recently opened a branch here, and there are also a few expensive ornament and gift stores. But the poshing-up process isn't complete, so you'll still find a couple of basic caffs (*see* below).

This mix of cultures is reflected in the market. Some traders are East Enders who've been coming here for decades; others seem to hail from bijou north London flower shops. It all helps to generate an exciting tension. The Camden Market feel is especially evident down Ezra Street, off Columbia Road, where old garden tools, garden ornaments and a variety of pots can be found in cubby-holes and alleyways. The backyard of the Royal Oak pub is often given over to collections of interesting pots and wrought-iron garden adornments. Another patch of land has a few stalls selling rustic-looking clothing, bonsai trees and hippyish robes. Given the market's increasing popularity, the trade in 'garden accessories' looks set to expand.

Nearby cafés, pubs and shops

Two stalwarts of Columbia Road are **George's Café** at No.110, with its fry-ups and filled bagels, and **Lees Seafood Shop** at No.134, which provides the London marketgoer's traditional snacks of jellied eels and whelks. On Ezra Street, you'll come across the **Jones Dairy Café** where fashionable Islingtonians drink freshly ground coffee. The local traders are more likely to continue through the passageway and drink at the **Nelson's Head** on Horatio Street.

The ornament and gift shops along Columbia Road are open while the market is in progress. In December they sell Christmas decorations.

Hackney Stadium

Address: off Waterden Road, E15.

Public transport: ⇌ Hackney Wick; buses 26, 30, 236, 276, 308, S2.

Opening hours: Sun 6am–3pm.

Best time to go: before midday.

Car parking: along Waterden Road.

Main wares: secondhand goods (particularly video games and computer software), new clothes, electrical and household goods.

Specifics: electrical goods, computer software; look out for secondhand bargains.

The dividing line between a market and a car boot sale is sometimes flimsy. Many see the weekly jamboree around the car park of Hackney's dog track as a car booter, but the event's longevity and the large number of professional traders selling new goods make it feel more like a market.

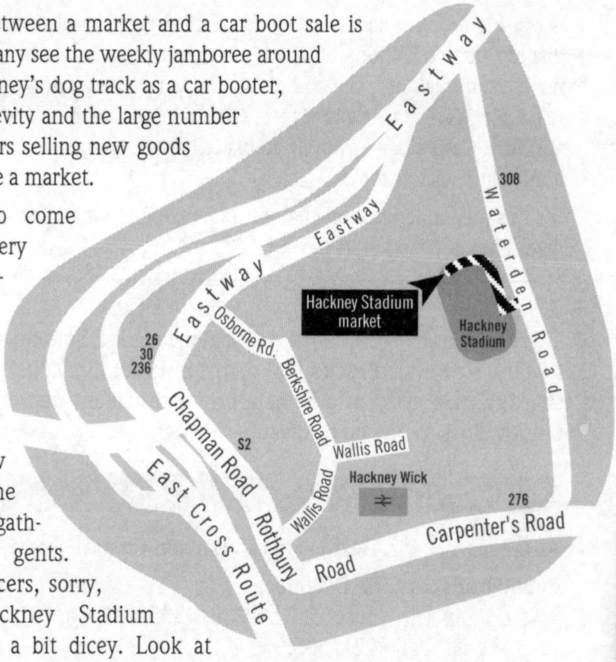

Everyone seems to come here by car, and every Sunday large numbers of vehicles are parked on the roads surrounding the stadium. It's easy to find the entrances: just follow the crowd. At the gates you will see a gathering of muscular gents. These are the bouncers, sorry, the stewards. Hackney Stadium market is like that: a bit dicey. Look at what's on offer at some of the stalls. A naked Cindy doll, a length of piping, and six old hub caps are among one trader's merchandise; pirate software and computer games are major lines; bootleg tapes and videos are not unknown.

The hint of lawlessness brings out the crowds. Thousands of punters and hundreds of traders arrive every week. New goods on sale include a vast array of electrical equipment, from cordless phones and electric ovens to TVs and radio-cassette players; clothing (men's, women's and children's) including jeans, leather jackets and work clothes (boiler suits for £3); haberdashery; discounted seeds, crockery, towels and bed sheets; carpets; stationery; leather bags and purses; DIY materials; petfood; cosmetics; and (a nice touch of irony, this) security floodlights. You might even be lucky enough to discover a local Afro-Caribbean woman who occasionally comes here to sell her West Indian coconut bread.

The secondhand goods are of an even greater variety: 'warehouse-returned phones, sold as seen, no refunds', water pumps for fish aquaria, old dishwashers and washing machines ('with three months' guarantee'), LPs, golf clubs, spectacle frames, Black & Decker power tools, furniture, old shoes, fishing rods, vacuum cleaners, quite a few old books of varying quality, musty piles of clothing, rails of jackets. I even spotted a rather taciturn chap selling his old wedding photos. But it is the high-tech secondhand goods that attract most attention: satellite dishes, vast collections of disks, computer programs with and without manuals, though only the odd bit of hardware. There's also a good trade in Asian film music tapes and videos. One stall is devoted to all things African and Afro-Caribbean—from homemade herbal potions sold in old squash bottles to reggae records.

It's this preponderance of amateur traders, out to grab a few bob on a Sunday, that gives Hackney market its flavour.

Nearby cafés

There are a couple of fast food stands at the market, but otherwise not much in the locality. However, **Frocks** (95 Lauriston Road, E9, ✆ 0181 986 3161), only a short car ride away, is a homely British restaurant that does a superb Sunday brunch. Book to be sure of a seat.

Hoxton Street

Address: Hoxton Street, N1, from Crondall Street to Ivy Street.

Public transport: ⊖ Old Street;
buses 5, 22A, 22B, 43, 55, 67, 76, 141, 149, 243, 243A, 271, 505.

Opening hours: Mon–Sat 9am–5pm.

Best time to go: Saturday.

Car parking: there are often spaces on Pitfield Street which runs parallel to Hoxton Street to the west. Park near the junction with Crondall Street then walk down it to the start of the market.

Main wares: clothes, household goods, fruit and veg.

Specifics: cheap clothing (Saturday).

Forget the north London postcode—Hoxton is part of the East End. From Monday to Thursday the district seems bleak and unpromising. Several shops have closed down; dismal postwar council flats spread out to the west (though most of the main street is Victorian); and the market is desultory, with only a few fruit and veg traders and perhaps a chap selling household goods. On Fridays a few more traders turn up, and there's usually a large stall full of cheap tinned and packaged food. On Saturdays, though, the market, and the entire area, comes to life.

There's been a market here for donkey's years; it goes back at least to Tudor times, when Hoxton was a country village. Though the district lies less than a mile north of the City of London, the City authorities didn't invoke their charter to ban the market, as it had little effect on their trade.

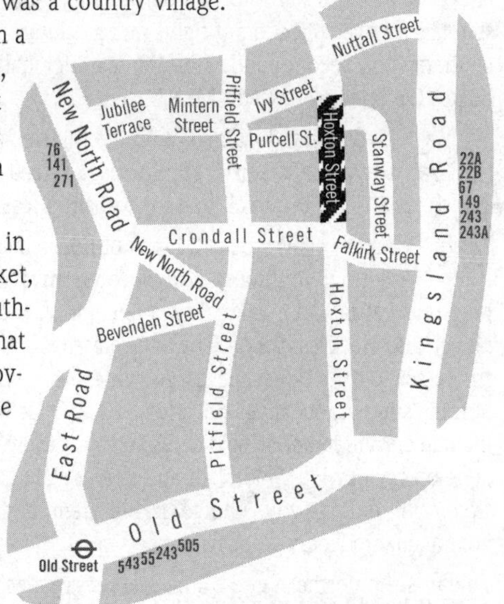

Until 1820, trading took place in what is still called Hoxton Market, just off Boot Street to the southwest of Hoxton Street. But by that time, the district had been covered by workers' housing and the market had become so popular that it outgrew the site. After a spell on Pitfield Street it moved to Hoxton Street in 1840. The original site has been deserted and awaiting development for years.

Hoxton became a centre for working-class entertainment, and in the 19th century there were several music halls and theatres along the main street. But away from the brash jollity of the market, Hoxton was a desperate place. Local resident A.S. Jasper wrote about his childhood here in the early years of this century. He lived with his family of seven in a two-room hovel. Life was full of petty theft, infant mortality, pub brawls and mother scraping a living by selling homemade clothes at the market. Sunday tea was a pint of winkles and some watercress.

It's still possible to buy winkles and watercress at Hoxton Street market, but only on Saturday. **Ron & Son** supplies the seafood (along with pickles, whelks, jellied eels, prawns, kippers, smoked haddock, cockles and mussels) while the **Swinton** family, who run a traditional fruit and veg stall, are 'noted for watercress'. The other food sellers at the Saturday market include a scattering of fruit and veg costermongers (prices are average), a woman selling eggs, a vendor of cheap tinned food, a biscuit seller, and a butcher who sells joints from his van.

But most of the 50 or more Saturday traders deal in clothes, and you won't find many places cheaper. Near the southern end of the street, a big crowd of women are grappling for secondhand (or are they new?) clothes tipped out of bin bags. One of the stallholders stands on a stool, to make sure her stock isn't pilfered. Another stall has a huge collection of tights and stockings. Unattractively screwed up, most of them look secondhand. Nearby, a trader has all his wares in old cardboard boxes. On one is scrawled: 'M&S boxers £1'.

Secondhand raincoats and children's clothes, new shoes, lingerie, women's skirts and dresses (sized 14–30), and more chainstore seconds are all sold for bargain prices.

Other stalls stock all kinds of household goods from Parazone to suntan lotion; you'll also find petfood, duvet sets (a single for £5), cosmetics, greetings cards, net curtains, toys, jewellery, records and CDs (mostly Irish and blues), and electrical goods. The Saturday market is big enough to attract likely lads trying to flog the latest 'bargains'. One has a stock of tacky pottery 'as seen in Sunday supplement magazines for £19.95'. He'll take a fiver. Further highlights include curtain material, sold at 50p a yard ('ay ay, it's all cheap today, the guvnor's gone on holiday'); a good plant and flower stall; and a photography stall where the trader will enlarge your photos, frame them, and show you his picture of the ex-boxing champ Henry Cooper.

Towards the northern end of the market are a couple of stalls selling car-boot-sale stuff: old clothes, radios, crockery, and even an exercise bike. Just past the last stall is **Terry's New and Secondhand Yard**. Furniture is displayed outside, along with fridges and general secondhand household goods.

There's little traffic on Hoxton Street, as it's not a major thoroughfare and only local shops have their premises here. This adds to the tightly-knit feel of the place—though everyone will tell you 'It's not what it was.' On a fine Saturday, groups of old Hoxtonians stand between the stalls, chewing over their memories. But though there's plenty of cheery shouting, it's impossible to get sentimental about chirpy cockneys here. There were no good old days, and the present is almost as bad. Locals are streetwise and tough; the market has been on the decline for years; and, all too obviously, money is tight.

Nearby cafés and pubs

There are several basic cafés along Hoxton Street. **F. Cooke's** pie and mash shop at No.150 even does a vegetarian pie for 95p. Otherwise, call in at **Anderson's**, an old-fashioned bakery which serves hot soup and pies to take away. The pubs on Hoxton Street are very much for locals and can seem intimidating; in the 1960s, Hoxton was part of the Kray gang's manor. If you're spending some time in the area, it's worth discovering what's on at **Hoxton Hall** (130 Hoxton Street, © 0171 739 5431), the last surviving music hall on the street.

Kingsland Waste

Address: Kingsland Road, between Middleton Road and Forest Road, E8.

Public transport: ⇌ Dalston Kingsland;
buses 22A, 22B, 30, 38, 56, 67, 76, 149, 243, 243A, 277.

Opening hours: Sat 9am–5pm.

Car parking: try the backstreets to the south of Middleton Road.

Main wares: secondhand clothes, bric-a-brac, tools and electrical goods.

Specifics: tools, hardware.

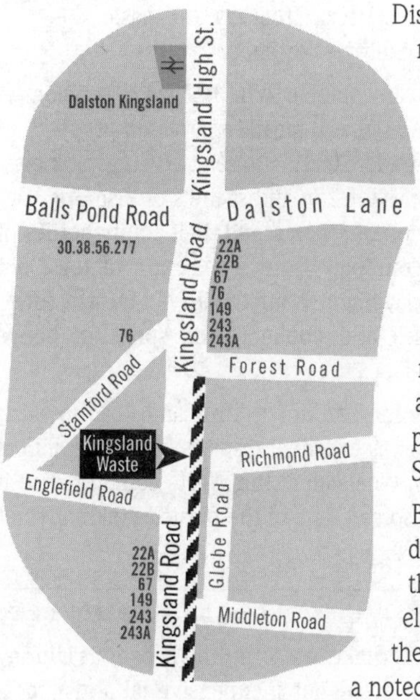

Disrepute works wonders to bolster a market's popularity. Perhaps it's the air of immorality, the feeling you might be dealing with fences, the enticement of sharing in the booty by getting an outrageous bargain.

Whatever it is, Kingsland Waste seems to thrive on it. You might have trouble tracing the history of some of the articles up for grabs, but the wide pavements and cobbled street that run alongside the A10 Kingsland Road are packed with stalls and customers every Saturday.

Both new and secondhand goods are on display, sometimes jumbled together on the same stall. Tools and hardware, plus electrical and mechanical components, are the market's strengths. The Waste has been a noted supplier of artisans, DIYers and bodgers since the market was first held in the mid-19th century. Now you can find anything from door knockers and plumbing pipes to toilet seats and plungers. Some of the tools are of high quality, others are shoddy. A few seem archaic: not much interest was being taken in two great scythes going for £4 each.

But even if you've no DIY talent, there's plenty to rifle through among the three long lines of stalls. You never know what's coming up next. There must be a score of traders selling secondhand hi-fis, car radios, televisions, cameras, video machines and Walkmans—from unblemished consumer durables (but who knows whether they work?) to hollow shells; from the faintly suspect to the downright dodgy. Some of these characters look as though they've stepped straight out of Arthur Daley's lock-up.

New and secondhand clothes get more than a look-in. Old boots and shoes, newly polished, sell for between £5 and £8. You'll also find leather belts, children's coats, jumpers, bundles of shirts, trousers and jackets, even long-johns—many at bargain prices.

Food takes second place here: you'd be better taking the ten-minute walk to Ridley Road (*see* p.134) for your fresh provisions. However, there are some fruit and veg stalls and a couple of popular pitches selling tinned goods, cakes and sweets at very low prices. Whether all the food is within its sell-by date is another matter. Crockery and basic household goods also attract locals out for their weekly shop.

Only Brick Lane and Westmoreland Road can compete with the bizarre conglomeration of junk displayed at some stalls. Beneath a tarpaulin propped up with a couple of old skis, one trader is trying to sell two fluffy pink pigs. Another flogs used video tapes for 25p and sachets of Bisto for 10p. Yet another boasts a selection of secondhand, half-empty bottles of perfume. You can take your pick from a selection of toys, old records and tapes. The pavement is lined with old fridges, furniture, washing machines and cookers—the spoils of house clearances.

A brisk walk from the market, down Kingsland Road towards the City, is the **Geffrye Museum**, which has excellent displays of house interiors from various periods in England's history. One stall at the Waste could provide it with a choice exhibit—a secondhand bedspread, one of the pleated pink polyester horrors much favoured by £10-a-night B&Bs.

Nearby cafés

This is a good area for Turkish food, be it for takeaways (try the kebabs at **Uludag Barbecue**, 398a Kingsland Road), or a lavish but inexpensive sit-down meal (**Istanbul Iskembecisi**—*see* p.135).

For traditional grub or a cup of tea, make a pilgrimage to **F. Cooke & Sons**' pie and mash shop (*see* p.135), or try **Faulkner's Fish Restaurant** (424–426 Kingsland Road).

Petticoat Lane

Address:	Middlesex Street, Goulston Street, New Goulston Street, Toynbee Street, Wentworth Street, Bell Lane, Cobb Street, Leyden Street, Strype Street, Old Castle Street, Cutler Street, E1.
Public transport:	⊖ Aldgate, Aldgate East; ⊖/⇌ Liverpool Street; buses 5, 8, 15, 22A, 22B, 25, 26, 35, 40, 42, 43, 47, 48, 67, 78, 100, 149, 243A, 253, B1, D1, D11.
Opening hours:	Sun 9am–2pm; **Wentworth Street** Mon–Fri 10am–2.30pm; Sun 9am–2pm.
Best time to go:	9am on Sunday, before the crowds get too bad.
Car parking:	possible spaces on the side streets north of Middlesex Street; otherwise try the side streets south of the Whitechapel Road.
Main wares:	new clothes, souvenirs, household goods, electrical goods.
Specifics:	leather jackets; old gold jewellery in Goulston Street.

We will survey the suburbs and make forth our salleys,
Down Petticoat Lane and up the smock alleys.

When the playwright Ben Jonson was writing in 1616, Petticoat Lane had already gained a reputation for clothing. Today, it is London's most famous market. Tens of thousands of Londoners and tourists swarm through these streets every Sunday, but sadly the Lane has become tarnished by its success, losing some of its verve and much of its variety along the way.

In the early 16th century, Whitechapel was known for its piggeries, but by Jonson's time it had become a desirable area. 'Some gentlemen of the court,' observed John Stow in the 1590s, 'built their houses here for the air.' Perhaps it was this gentrification, as much as the link with clothing, that caused Hog Lane to be renamed Petticoat Lane around the start of the 1600s. But the clean air and aristocratic inhabitants didn't last. The plague of 1665 hit the East End badly. The wealthy householders fled, leaving Whitechapel to successive waves of immigrants and refugees: French Protestant Huguenots, East European Jews and, most recently, Bengalis.

Jews have been associated with the market from its inception. Thousands arrived from Central and Eastern Europe in the 18th and 19th centuries. Many entered the rag trade, selling old clothes and hats. Sunday became the main day for trading; the area was—and still is—

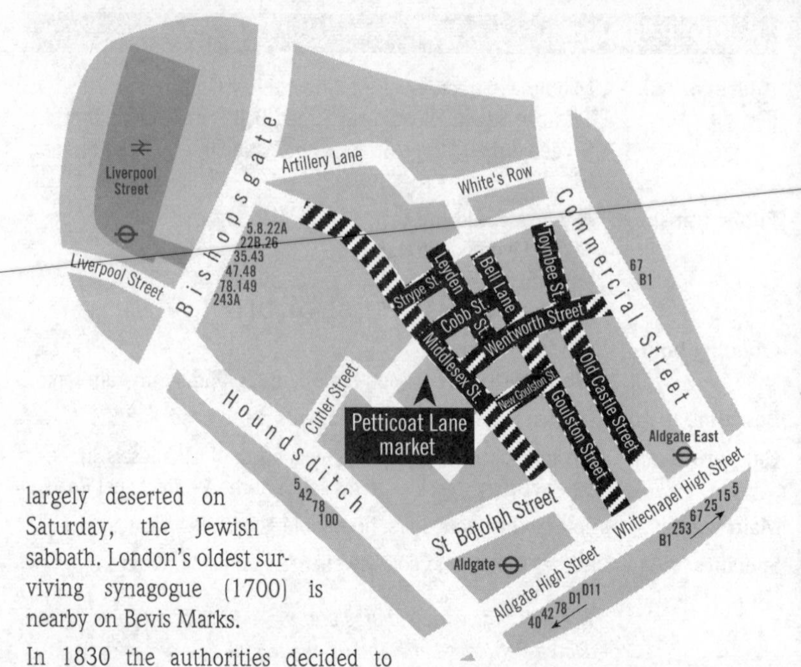

largely deserted on Saturday, the Jewish sabbath. London's oldest surviving synagogue (1700) is nearby on Bevis Marks.

In 1830 the authorities decided to change the name of the market's central artery to Middlesex Street. Few traders or customers took any notice. Street atlases and council documents use the new name, but everyone else still calls the road and its market Petticoat Lane.

By the 1850s, huge clothes auctions were being held every week at Goulston and Wentworth Streets. Henry Mayhew tells of two to three miles of old clothes up for sale, calling it 'a vista of multi-coloured dinginess'. As with many of London's markets at this time, Petticoat Lane was unlicensed. As late as the 1900s, hucksters used to fight each other for the best pitches, resulting in mayhem first thing in the morning. The opponents of Sunday trading tried to abolish the market but eventually, in 1928, Stepney Borough Council stepped in and licensed the traders.

In 1936, Mary Benedetta remarked that '80% of [Petticoat Lane's] wares are said to be genuine.' In those days there were nearly 200 pitches, and Cobb Street, Leydon Street and Strype Street had stalls full of kosher chickens. The place was a haven for eccentrics. Benedetta tells of 'Old Heyday, with his silver hair, rosy cheeks and gentle, courtly manners', who sold rubber stamps and spectacles, and who spent harvest time selling his wares around Norfolk villages; and the foot clinic where customers sat on a table in front of the crowds 'having their corns cured for a few pence'. William Addison, writing in 1953, describes the patter of Mike Stern, president of the Stepney Street Traders' Association. Dressed in Lord Mayor's garb, Stern would declaim in Shakespearean tones: 'Oh, when I am dead and forgotten as I shall be, and sleep in dull, cold marble with...[waiting for the crowd to take notice] these lovely utility towels, ten bob a pair, ten bob a pair.'

Though there are more stalls now, the characters have gone; their oddball descendants are more likely to grace Brick Lane, half a mile to the north. But Petticoat Lane still has a great deal of life. Best come early, while the streets are passable. At 8.30am the stallholders are still cranking up for the day's business. They clear their throats and practise calling across the street to each other: 'Oh-only £7.99, come on!'

Interestingly, Mary Benedetta's book contains a photo of Indian traders selling clothes on the Lane 60 years ago. But it wasn't until the 1970s that large numbers of Bangladeshis moved in to the area. Young Asian men, probably London-born and certainly well-cockneyfied, now run several of the garment stalls. Jewish clothes traders are still in evidence, but most now live in comfortable suburbs and only visit the East End on Sundays. The closure in 1996 of London's most famous Jewish restaurant, Blooms, on Whitechapel High Street, is further evidence of the Diaspora away from the East End.

Nearly all the clothes are new. Petticoat Lane attracts businesses that buy stock from huge discount wholesalers to sell on a stall. Underwear, socks, shirts, mock-fur coats, towels, duvets, blouses, jeans, dresses and shoes: dozens of stalls duplicate these wares on both Middlesex Street and Goulston Street. There are also scores of traders selling leather handbags, purses and jackets. Many of these will have been made locally by Bangladeshi workers. Prices are much lower than in West End shops, but higher than in the Brick Lane leather emporia. If you're after a leather jacket, the best place to look is in the covered section of the market in a concrete car park off Goulston Street. Here dozens of traders compete with each other. The choice is large, with jackets hanging up to the ceiling. Most stalls in the covered section have a similar stock, but if you're lucky you might spot a trader who sells a unique collection of sequin-strewn tops and dresses.

Among the clothes on Middlesex, Wentworth and Goulston streets are occasional stalls selling tourist rubbish—Union Jack hats and busby-wearing dolls. You'll also come across the odd cockney shyster trying to flog the latest wonder product. It's always worth joining the small knot of people around these operators, just to listen to the outrageous spiel as they eulogize their vegetable peelers, glass cutters and window cleaners. Cheap CDs, low-quality hi-fi, trashy jewellery, electronic watches, hairbrushes, holograms, toys, crockery, tablemats and poor quality pottery can also be found on these busy streets. Connoisseurs of kitsch could have a field-day; others might find themselves examining the wares for longer than they'd like, as the crowds make the going slow.

To escape from the worst of the throng, turn off Middlesex Street into tiny Strype Street. Pass more leather jacket stalls, then turn right into Leydon Street. There are yet more leather jackets, but prices are often a few pounds lower than on the main thoroughfares. On Leydon Street you're also likely to encounter a few secondhand or shop-soiled clothes, including tweed jackets that look as though they've been through a flood.

Cobb Street and Bell Lane are also quieter neighbourhoods at the edge of the market. Again, clothes predominate, though there are a few stalls selling shoes and fabrics. On Wentworth Street, close to the junction with Bell Lane, are a couple of fruit and veg traders. Along with a few clothes stalls on this road, these also trade from Monday to Friday. But fresh produce stalls are in a tiny minority—food comes second to fashion at Petticoat Lane.

There's a change on New Goulston Street. Here, the remnants of the Cutler Street gold and coin market congregate. In the early 1980s, about 40 stalls were packed into Cutler Street, about four minutes' walk from Petticoat Lane, until redevelopment forced them to move here. Only a handful of dealers are left, selling old silver and gold jewellery. As you inspect their stock, try to get them to talk about the old days. There's a rich fund of stories to be told about Petticoat Lane.

Nearby cafés

If you're after a traditional snack, visit one of the two **Tubby Isaac's** stalls (on the Bishopsgate side of Middlesex Street, or the Aldgate end of Goulston Street). This old firm has been providing East Enders with shellfish and jellied eels for donkey's years. Also there's the **Kossoff Bakery** (91 Middlesex Street) for fresh bagels.

Queen's Market

Address: off the junction of Green Street and Queen's Road, E13.

Public transport: ⊖ Upton Park;
buses 58, 104, 238, 330.

Opening hours: Mon, Tue, Thur–Sat 9am–5pm; Wed 9am–1pm.

Best time to go: Saturdays.

Car parking: try the side streets off Plashet Grove or Green Street.

Main wares: clothing, fruit and vegetables, household goods.

Specifics: Asian and Caribbean foodstuffs.

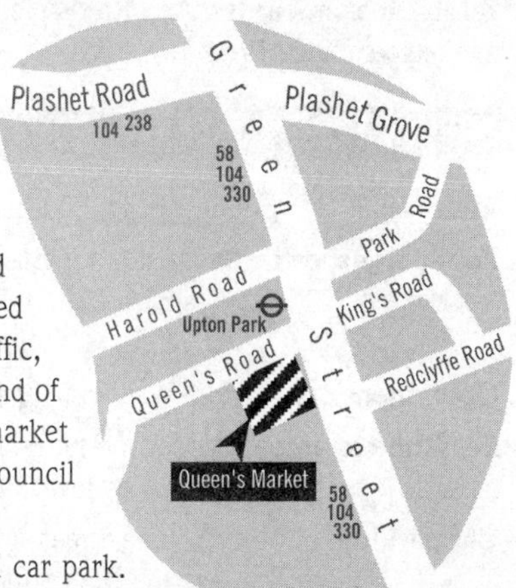

The parish of West Ham dates back to the Middle Ages, when a weekly mart was held there. Today's Queen's Market, however, goes back only about a century, to the time when traders set up stall on Green Street to cater for the inhabitants of the newly built terraced houses. In the 1900s, the market was turfed off the main street to ease the flow of traffic, and transferred to Queen's Road. At the end of the 1960s, Newham Council built a market square off the road; ten years later the council decided to put a roof on top.

The result is rather like an underground car park. But the market is thriving, providing multi-racial Upton Park with a fine blend of foodstuffs, household goods, fabrics, electrical equipment and clothing. Over a hundred stalls set up regularly in the square; more businesses occupy permanent shops around the perimeter.

The local Afro-Caribbean and Asian communities do their shopping here, so the market has an exciting variety of fruit, vegetables, spices, meat and fish. As well as radishes, cabbages, boiled beetroot and oranges, you'll find mangoes, peppers and pomegranates, or even soursop, guavas and green coconuts. One fish stall might have cod, whiting and hake, while its neighbour sells jackfish, snappers and cuttlefish. A smoked ham hangs over the counter at **Goodalls the Butchers**, while a sheep's head takes pride of place at the nearby halal meat store.

A couple of stalls sell beautifully embroidered clothes as worn by Asian children; smart kurtas and flowing saris are also on display. A few yards away, an Afro-Caribbean store stocks a bewildering array of hair accessories including long black wigs. Walk to one side of the square and you'll hear lovers' rock thumping out of the reggae shop; across the way it's bhangra that blares from the Asian food emporium; in the middle is cacophony. Queen's is cooking.

Nearby cafés

There are four cheap cafés worth investigating around the market's perimeter. The **Crisp 'n' Crusty Bakery** has a few bolted-down plastic chairs where customers can sit and eat hot pasties, pies or soup. **May's Kitchen** is a caff of the old school with a menu of breakfast fry-ups, liver and onions, and pea and ham soup. The **Kashmir** restaurant and takeaway provides inexpensive Asian cooking, from seikh kebabs to brain curries. And **Roy's** pie and mash shop has served cheap nosh to marketgoers since 1968.

Ridley Road

Address:	Ridley Road, off Kingsland High Street, E8.
Public transport:	⥈ Dalston Kingsland; buses 22A, 22B, 30, 38, 56, 67, 76, 149, 236, 243, 243A, 277.
Opening hours:	Mon–Wed 9am–3pm; Thur 9am–12 noon; Fri, Sat 9am–5pm.
Best time to go:	Saturday mornings, before the crowds; Friday mornings for stalls run by Jewish traders.
Car parking:	try St Jude Street or other residential side streets to the west of Kingsland High Street.
Main wares:	fresh food, clothing, household goods, records, tapes and CDs, fabrics, haberdashery.
Specifics:	fish, Afro-Caribbean foodstuffs, Turkish foods, fresh herbs, fruit and vegetables, reggae and calypso records.

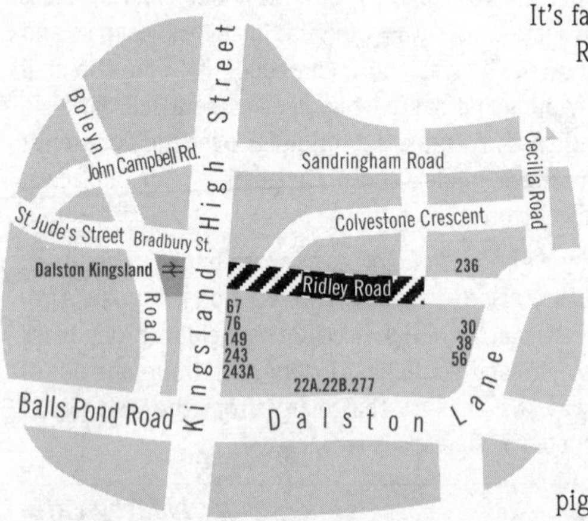

It's faster if you dance along Ridley Road on a Friday or Saturday, propelled by the bone-resonating thuds of the record stalls that give this market its rhythm. Turks, Jews, Asians, cockneys, Africans and Afro-Caribbeans—East Londoners all—join the throng pushing past shanty-town shacks, lock-up shops and old wooden barrows.

The food is similarly diverse: pigs' tails, ox cheeks, cows' noses (labelled 'pomo') and sheep's heads are displayed with aplomb from the butchers' shops. A long-pronged fork is on hand to help customers rifle through the goats' tripe. At one meat emporium, garotted chickens, complete with combs, hang from the awnings over the pavement. The passers-by brush them aside like troublesome fringes.

At **Milly's** tiny **salmon stall** (closed for the Saturday sabbath), old Jewish friendships are renewed, petty grumbles are warmly exchanged, and condolences offered with slivers of fish. The 24-hour **Ridley Bagel Bakery** will provide further ingredients for a snack.

Despite the recent building of Dalston Cross Shopping Centre nearby, the market is thriving. It began in the 1880s, and during the early years of this century was started each morning by a policeman with a whistle. The market expanded to its present size (about 180 stalls) in the 1920s. As with Brixton, Ridley Road has benefited enormously from the influx of immigrants. Paradoxically, they have helped to retain the feel of a traditional East End market—full of zip and bustle. There's nothing like a trip here to buck you up.

Such is the cosmopolitan mix of the place, you might find Turks selling African food, Asians selling West Indian food and cockneys selling Asian produce. The market is excellent for fresh fish (from tilapia and jackfish to scallops and lobster), and has strong lines in fruit, vegetables, fabrics and lace, with traders earnestly vying with each other for custom. 'Who's gotta bit o' money for Rodney,' roars one seasoned costermonger with a laugh that makes Sid James sound like Charles Hawtrey.

At the other end of the market from Kingsland High Street, the atmosphere becomes more Caribbean, helped along by joss-sticks from the 'freedom fragrance' stall. Hot red-pepper sauce, black-eye beans, yams and plantain are all up for grabs. An African stall sells Nigerian-brewed Guinness; another has land snails the size of a man's fist. At the wig stall, a couple of spirited black women try on hair extensions. Nearby, Harry at his record shack takes note and plays some thundering calypso. Hips start swaying, hands clapping... Who needs Notting Hill Carnival?

Nearby cafés and shops

F. Cooke & Sons, opposite the market at 41 Kingsland High Street, is London's most famous pie and mash shop. If you don't fancy the pie, mash, jellied or stewed eels or even a cup of tea, just pop your head in to admire the magnificent tiled and mirrored interior.

One of London's largest shops for Turkish food can be found at the end of Ridley Road on the corner of Cecilia Road and Dalston Lane. **Istanbul Iskembecisi**, at 9 Stoke Newington Road, is among the best of the many Turkish restaurants in the area.

Roman Road

Address: Globe Town, west of Usk Street off Roman Road, E2; Roman Road, from St Stephen's Road to Parnell Road, E2; Roman Square, off St Stephen's Road and Roman Road, E2, ✆ (0181) 980 1881.

Public transport: ⊖ Bethnal Green, then bus 8; buses 277, 309, D6, S2.

Opening hours: **Globe Town** Mon–Sat 8.30–4pm; **Roman Road** Tue, Thur, Sat 8.30am–5.30pm; **Roman Square** Tue, Thur, Fri (antiques), Sat 8am–5pm.

Best time to go: Thursdays or Saturdays.

Car parking: try the backstreets to the south of Roman Road (turn off Roman Road along Grove Road: it is pedestrianized after St Stephen's Road).

Main wares: clothing, household goods, fruit and veg.

Specifics: cheap clothing (underwear, socks, woollens, women's and men's wear, shirts, jackets, babies' and children's wear), fabrics, plants and bulbs, crockery, haberdashery, kitchen-ware, bathroomware, cosmetics, wallpaper, cut flowers.

Roman Road is the East End of pie and mash, boxing clubs and street barrows. There are three markets along its length. **Globe Town** has occupied an austere, purpose-built square off the road since 1961. Only a dozen or so stalls trade at this six-days-a-week market, which provides the local housing estate with essentials such as household goods (from crockery to light bulbs), fruit and vegetables. There's also a fish stall.

Roman Road market proper couldn't be more different. The street is lined by modest Victorian buildings rather than municipal blocks, and the 150-year-old market is one of the East End's largest weekday knees-ups. Even on a Tuesday there are over 150 stalls along the quarter mile of pedestrianized street. One of the first sounds you'll hear if you walk from the western end is old Bill Brown's cry of 'Rock hard Canaries'. He is not, as you might suppose, selling song-birds with rigor mortis, but a barrow-load of tomatoes. There's a helpful note attached to his stall: 'These Canaries are clean, not touched by everyone's hands as in supermarkets.'

Fabrics, haberdashery, women's clothes and shoes are plentiful, and prices are keen. You might pass a throng crowded around a furtive man pulling new clothes out of a box and selling them for a pittance as fast as he can. Ask no questions as to their origins. Secondhand clothes and 'cabbages' (new clothes made from off-cuts) are piled on barrows and rifled by industrious, sturdy women used to getting elbow room. One of the most startling stalls sells sensationally glitzy fashions: gold lamé leggings, bright red bodies and slinky numbers studded with enough sequins to attire a country and western convention.

Food is of secondary importance, but there's a large egg stall and a few fruit and veg traders with wooden barrows full of root crops, including freshly boiled beetroot in season. One stall has West Indian produce (very few of the traders come from the Asian or black communities); another has a brightly coloured array of old-fashioned sweets.

Harmer's Indoor Shopping Centre, halfway down the street, is really a continuation of the market, with stalls selling much the same goods. Two exceptions are the joke shop, with its range of delights for school-aged pranksters, and **Finger Prince**, which sells nail extensions—useful weapons in the fight for bargains at Roman Road's clothes stalls.

If you approach Roman Road market from the west, one of the first things you'll notice is the area's third market, **Roman Square**. This is a new, privately run affair aiming to cadge a few customers off the main street. It is held in a courtyard, bordered by a 1980s building complex of three-storey structures designed to blend in with their Victorian surroundings. Lock-ups full of new furniture (wooden dressers and three-piece suites) and women's clothes (mostly jackets) occupy the ground floor of some of the buildings. The courtyard has space for about 40 stalls. New clothes (leggings, tops, jeans, children's clothes), household ornaments, pot plants, jewellery and household goods can be had here on Tuesdays, Thursdays and Saturdays. A small antiques market occupies the yard on Fridays.

Nearby cafés and shops

Eels and mash at **G.F. Kelly** (526 and 600 Roman Road) is the costermongers' choice for lunch. The No.526 branch also does smashing plum pies. At 591 Roman Road, in the thick of the market, is a shop worth examining. **Ashby's** is an English delicatessen, selling such homely comestibles as sticky toffee pudding, steamed syrup pudding, spotted dick and portions of sausage, mash and onion gravy to take away.

Spitalfields Market

Address: Commercial Street (between Lamb Street and Brushfield Street), E1, ✆ (0171) 247 6590.

Public transport: ⊖/⇌ Liverpool Street; buses 5, 8, 22A, 22B, 26, 35, 43, 47, 48, 67, 78, 149, 243A, B1.

Opening hours: Mon–Fri, Sun 11.30am–3.30pm.

Best time to go: Sunday.

Car parking: car parks in Lamb Street and Steward Street.

Main wares: organic foods, crafts, bric-a-brac, antiques.

Specifics: organic fruit, vegetables and bread.

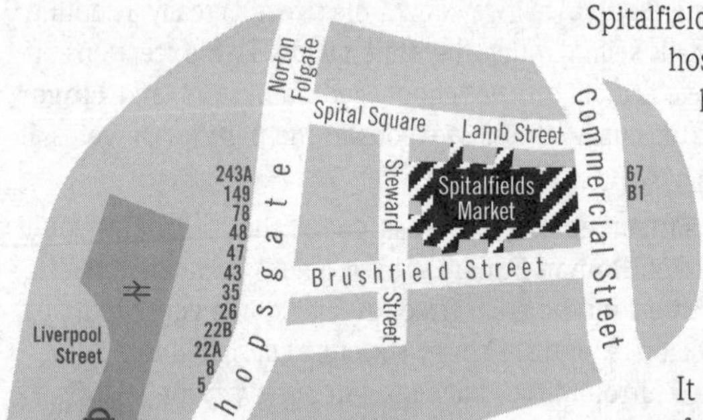

Spitalfields takes its name from the hospital fields that once belonged to the priory and hospice of St Mary. Trading began in 1682, when a local silk-thrower, John Balch, was granted a charter to hold a market in Spital Square. It prospered and grew into one of London's main wholesale fruit and vegetable markets. The present warehouse-like buildings were completed in 1893, five years after Spitalfields gained notoriety for the Jack the Ripper murders. The premises were extended in the 1930s to include a flower market, and the site now covers five acres.

In 1991, the wholesale market moved to more spacious premises in Hackney

Wick. Its old buildings now contain a small sports complex, a party venue inside a marquee, several shops and cafés around the perimeter and, last but not least, a new retail market.

Four years into its life, the new market is still trying to find its feet, so it's worth phoning first to check opening times.

Few traders turn up early in the week; by far the best time to go is on a Sunday, when about 30 crafts stalls and a dozen or so bric-a-brac traders make an appearance, as well as some 15 organic food sellers. It's difficult to predict which stalls will be at the organic market, but **Stepping Stones Farm**, a local city farm, usually has a stall selling its own-made relishes and pickles. It also brings along some lambs and goats to entertain the children. There might also be organic herbs and spices; a couple of bread and cake stalls with up to 20 varieties of bread including olive focaccia, Welsh tea bread and walnut bread; organic wines; and up to four fruit and veg pitches. The largest of these is **Global Organics**, with its impressive variety of produce: alfalfa, grapes, kiwi fruit, salsify and mouli, as well as the more mundane root vegetables.

At the crafts market you might find silk-screen prints, sinewy glass ornaments, silk clothes, rugs, harlequin hats, wrought-iron candlesticks, chunky knitwear, hand-made jewellery, and hand-painted plant pots. If you're lucky, the trader selling customized male underwear will make an appearance—gape in wonder at the size of the posing pouches. Among the regulars is a large stall selling cards and T-shirts emblazoned with feminist and left-wing slogans.

As with most crafts markets, some of the stalls sell twee rubbish: cute animals painted on stone, for instance. Thankfully these are in a minority. Several stalls sell goods that are actually useful—well-made wooden toys, underwear of unbleached cotton, handloom bedspreads woven by the Bengal Women's Union, natural buttons made from coconuts and seashells—and even some of the purely ornamental wares have an aesthetic appeal.

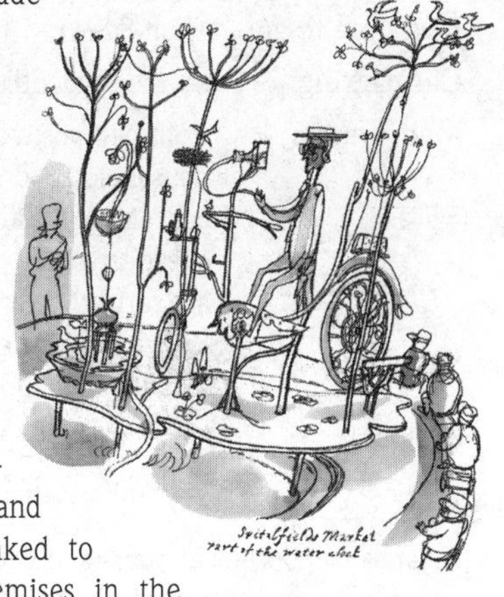
Spitalfields Market
part of the water clock

There's quite an assortment of bric-a-brac on show: one stall is littered with second-hand junk that would look more at home on Brick Lane, while others stock decent LPs, old stamps and postcards, and a pile of second-hand books including many Penguin Classics and volumes of poetry. Another bookstall, linked to **Bookworm**, a shop with permanent premises in the building, sells both new and secondhand titles, including marvellous magazines from the 1940s and 1950s such as *Practical Wireless*, with its pictures of pipe-smoking men and smiling housewifes gazing lovingly at Bakelite.

With any luck, Spitalfields' Sunday market, sandwiched as it is between Petticoat Lane and Brick Lane, will become another great venue for a Sunday outing. I hope the organic traders will prosper. Small-scale producers who bring their foodstuffs to market have almost died out in Britain, but if these pioneers concentrate on providing high-quality foods and unusual varieties of produce that are ignored by the factory farms, they might be able to survive alongside the ubiquitous supermarket chains.

Nearby cafés and shops

Around the perimeter of the market are various wooden stalls selling fast food from around the world: Thai noodles, pasta, satay, nachos. There are tables and benches outside. **Leigh's Farm Shop**, just outside the market, sells organic meats and wines, plus its own-baked pies.

Walthamstow

Address: Walthamstow High Street, E17.

Public transport: ⊖/⇌ Walthamstow Central; ⇌ Walthamstow Queens Road, St James Street Walthamstow; buses 2, 20, 34, 48, 58, 69, 97, 97A, 212, 215, 230, 251, 257, 275, 505, 551, W11, W12, W15.

Opening hours: Mon–Sat 8am–6pm.

Best time to go: Thur–Sat.

Car parking: try the residential side streets to the north of the High Street.

Main wares: clothing (mostly new), fruit and vegetables, bread and cakes, household goods, fabrics, petfood, toys, cheap tinned and packet foods, kitchenware, cosmetics, lace, electrical goods, cheap jewellery, handbags, bedclothes, cassettes and CDs, fish, dried flowers, cushions, lace doylies, leather gloves, Hoover spares, leather belts, tablecloths, fresh flowers, secondhand pulp fiction, tools, hats.

Specifics: haberdashery, petfood, cheese, sausages, outsized men's trousers, football strips.

Fanatical supporters of Spurs and Chas 'n' Dave, yet living in E17 and fond of pie and mash, the people of Walthamstow are uncertain about their geographic identity. Are they north or east Londoners? What is certain is the esteem they hold for their market, claimed to be England's longest (at half a mile), and busy throughout the week.

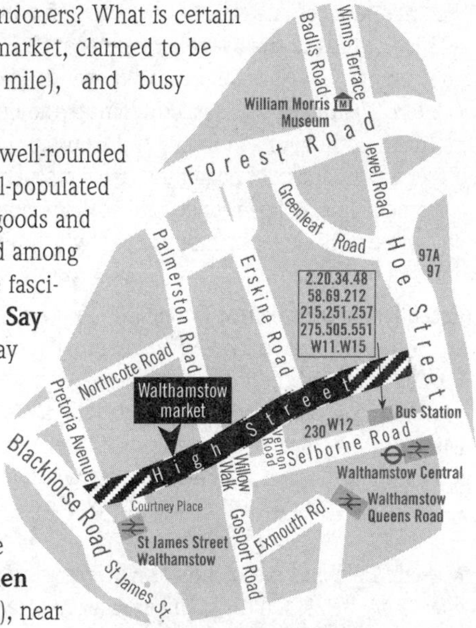

The High Street is really a series of well-rounded local markets serving this well-populated region. Fruit and veg, household goods and cheap clothes are liberally scattered among the 448 pitches, but several more fascinating stalls are worth seeking out. **Say Cheese**, a caravan about halfway down the market, has a good stock of British cheeses; **Joshua Hills'** sausage stall nearby displays about 20 varieties of banger. Gaze in awe at the voluminous grey flannel garments at the **Trousers for Big and Small Men** stall (waist sizes from 30in to 54in), near the junction with Vernon Road.

Competition has led to low prices among the fruit and veg sellers. You might snap up 2lb of mushrooms for as little as £1. Take a look at **Billy Grubb's** stall towards the western end of the market; pineapples and nuts are laid out pretty as a picture. Though there's a dearth of Asian and black traders, there is a stall full of South Asian vegetables, plus a couple of Afro-Caribbean food stalls where, along with yams and plantain, you might find more unusual produce such as sorrel (not the green-leafed plant, but a type of hibiscus whose pink flowerheads are used to flavour a traditional Caribbean Christmas drink). There's also a takeaway stall selling Caribbean fast food: spicy dumplings, Jamaican patties and Guinness punch.

But even if you don't intend buying, it's worth strolling along Walthamstow market for the spectacle. See traders near the Chequers pub take a surreptitious sip from their pints behind their stalls; drool at the shellfish on **H. Clare's** old whelk barrow (est. 1890), also near the Chequers; hear news of Tottenham Hotspur's latest game by the football-kit stall ('Blimey, you don't often see the West Ham strip in these parts,' comments a passer-by); join the knees-up by the large music stall playing Chas 'n' Dave's singalong favourites; and call at the indoor mini-market at No.146–148 to peruse pot-pipes at the Rastafarian stall, or have your palm read by **Christine the Psychic**.

Victorian terraces line much of the street, but there's a jumble of other styles, from 1930s flat-tops to the spanking new shopping centre. The market started in the 1880s when the High Street was known as Marsh Street. In his autobiography *A Hoxton Childhood*, A.S. Jasper describes the market in the early 1920s, when his mother sold homemade frocks and trousers to get enough money for Christmas presents. And today, though the market prospers, the same cannot be said for all its customers: knots of pensioners and hard-up mothers delve for bargains at a stall full of dented tins of food; more rummage through a pile of secondhand clothes dumped on a barrow.

Recently Waltham Forest Council, eager for its share of tourism, has worked hard at promoting the market, even making the extravagant claim that it is now Europe's longest (note longest, not biggest—and Portobello Road could dispute Walthamstow's claim even to be London's longest). The **William Morris Museum** (in Lloyd Park, Forest Road, to the north of the market) is the only other attraction to this area. But even on its own, the market shouldn't be missed.

Nearby cafés and pubs

Manze's pie and mash shop at No.76 has been serving Walthamstow's market-goers since 1929. On the menu are meat pie, mash and eels, with fruit pies for pud. At No.151 is **Duncolm's**, a more modern pie and mash shop which also sells jacket potatoes and salads. Just opposite the turning for Vernon Road is **Rossi's of London** (though its sign has an 's' missing, anglicizing the name to Rosi's)—a 1950s caff and ice-cream parlour. For alcoholic refreshment, or just a sit-down half way along the market, try the **Chequers** pub, favoured by the stallholders.

Whitechapel

Address: Whitechapel Road, between Vallance Road and Cambridge Heath Road, E1.

Public transport: ⊖ Whitechapel; buses 25, 106, 253.

Opening hours: Mon–Wed, Fri, Sat 8.30am–5.30pm; Thur 8.30am–2pm.

Best time to go: Saturday.

Car parking: difficult; try the parking meters to the north of Whitechapel Road.

Main wares: clothing, fruit and vegetables, electrical goods, cheap jewellery, shoes.

Specifics: Asian fruit and vegetables, secondhand records, curtain material.

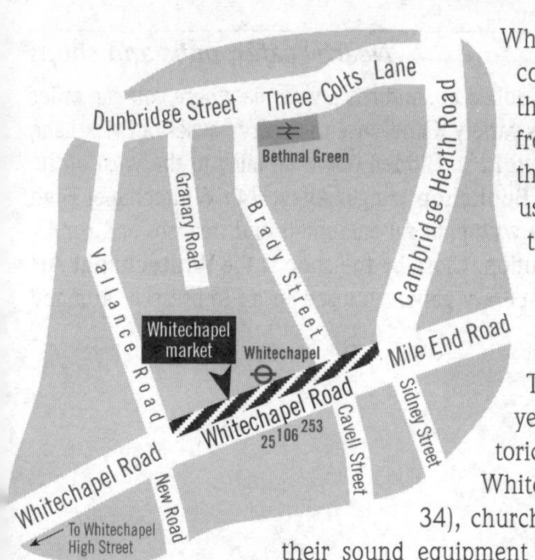

Whitechapel Road is so wide you could have a chariot race down the middle of it. This isn't so far from what used to happen: until the mid-19th century, drovers used to steer their livestock along this stretch of road on the way to Smithfield, and one of London's main hay markets was held here until 1920.

The road is now busy and grey, yet there are some fascinating historical nuggets to be found. At the Whitechapel Bell Foundry (No.32–34), churches have been kitted out with their sound equipment since the 15th century. The Trinity House almshouses (at Trinity Green, about 100 yards from the eastern end of the market) were built in 1695 for old seafarers and their widows. More recent history was made at the Blind Beggar pub in 1966, when Ronnie Kray of the notorious Kray brothers gang walked in and gunned down George Cornell from the rival Richardson gang.

The market takes place on Whitechapel Road's wide northern pavement. It has accommodated traders from the local Bangladeshi population better than most in the district. A couple of stalls stock good-quality Asian fruit and vegetables: okra, herbs, beans and several varieties of mangoes. Other traders sell the colourful, smart tunics and frilly dresses favoured by Bangladeshi parents for their young children. A couple of stalls display tunics and saris for adults. And among the electrical goods you can find the fancily decorated clocks popular among South Asian families.

A few stalls concentrate on secondhand goods: records, tapes and CDs; newly polished boots; overcoats that look a mite shabby. But most traders sell new, everyday items—socks, underwear, cheap jewellery, shoes, cut flowers, fruit and veg, fish, baby clothes, kitchenware, biscuits and sweets—that help to divert shoppers away from the new supermarket at the Cambridge Heath Road end of the market. There are enough stalls and enough variety to make a healthy number of East Enders shop here.

The **Blind Beggar** pub has been dolled up, and has a veranda where you can order pub food of the lasagne and chips variety. Otherwise the curry houses of Brick Lane are only a short walk away (*see* p.120). Hidden down an alley to the west of the market is the **Freedom Press Bookshop** (Angel Alley, 84b Whitechapel High Street), a tiny place well-stocked with political pamphlets and treatises and run by bookish folk awaiting the revolution. Close by the shop is the **Whitechapel Art Gallery**, an innovative contemporary gallery housed in an impressive arts and crafts building.

Southeast London

Bermondsey (New Caledonian)

Address: Bermondsey Square, SE1, ✆ (0171) 351 5353.

Public transport: ⊖ Borough;
⊖/⥂ London Bridge;
buses 1, 21, 35, 40, 42, 78, 133, 188, 199, P3
night buses N1, N21, N70.

Opening hours: Fri 3.30am–2pm, starts closing midday.

Best time to go: as early as possible.

Car parking: there's usually space in the side streets away from the square, but don't leave valuables in your car.

Main wares: antiques.

Specifics: paintings, ornaments, jewellery—anything collectable; expect low prices, but no 'finds'.

Dawn on Long Lane. A paltry procession of grey-faced commuters, in cars and on foot, head for the City and the early shift. No sign of life there. There's a gale blowing, and it begins to pour with rain. Then you notice a few figures darting in and out of a Victorian warehouse. As you approach, more people emerge. These are no commuters: they look wide awake. Many have been here for hours, buying and selling at London's biggest wholesale antiques market.

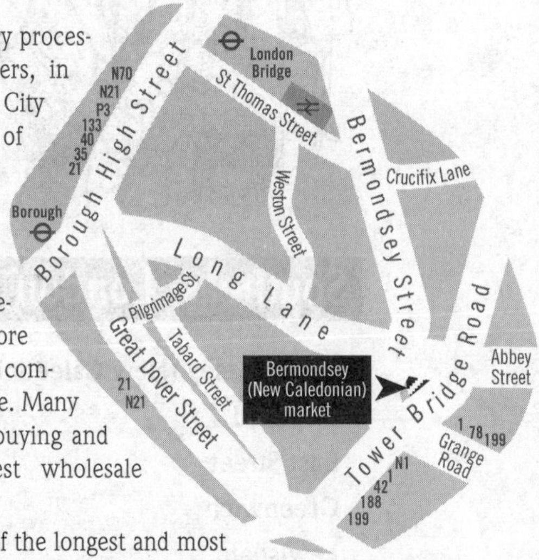

This weekly event has one of the longest and most fascinating histories of all London markets. Its lineage can be traced back to the Middle Ages, when a Friday market was held near Smithfield on the site of the annual Bartholomew Fair (immortalized by Ben Jonson in the play of the same name). Traders used to vie for the custom of farmers who had brought their livestock to market at Smithfield. When the livestock market was moved to Copenhagen Fields near Caledonian Road in 1855, the pitchers, who by then dealt mainly in old clothes, followed. The Friday market grew tremendously in the first decades of this century, fuelled by the new fashion for collecting antiques, which the traders had begun to stock. In the 1920s and 1930s, the 'Cally', as it became known, reached its zenith, filling the square-mile site and attracting more than 2500 stalls and crowds of up to 100,000.

The Second World War closed down this magnificent spectacle. When the conflict was over, the traders were refused permission to return. In 1949, 13,500 people signed a petition demanding the market's reopening. The Court of Common Council rejected the petition, and in the following year the present site in war-damaged, working-class Bermondsey was found. All that remains of the old Cally are three huge pubs, the central clocktower, and a few street names such as Pedlars Walk and Market Road. Although the New Caledonian attracts over 250 stalls each week, dealers from all over southern England plus a fair few from the Continent, the huge crowds and cockney 'silver kings' of the 1930s have gone.

The traders of Bermondsey market proper occupy two patches of land by Bermondsey Square, where their treasures are exposed to the weather.

Most articles up for sale date from the period 1850 to 1950; the majority are English. Several paintings go on display each week, most by obscure artists in styles veering from pastoral to Cubism. Other traders specialize in farmyard animals, writing cases, carriage clocks, silverware, workmen's tools, binoculars, golfing equipment, perfume bottles or old walking sticks. Some stalls are well-ordered, others not, but there is little that seems worthless. You won't find the piles of junk you get at Brick Lane or Westmoreland Road, but nor will you uncover giveaway bargains.

This said, there's plenty to engross even the most eccentric of enthusiasts. Why not start a collection with a croquet mallet, a Victorian urine-testing kit, a rabbit's foot, an ancient trombone and a cumbrous 19th-century diver's helmet straight out of a Jules Verne novel? One stall sports a framed sepia photo of Lady Archer's Garden Party, held at Devonshire Lodge in 1924. Some of the traders seem equally bizarre, wearing battered top hats or ancient fur coats while pouring a cup of tea from their Thermos.

The warehouse at the junction of Long Lane and Bermondsey Street contains the first of several privately-run indoor sales that surround the main market. This one, confusingly, is named **Bermondsey Antiques Market**. The half dozen or so stalls outside are just a prelude to the scores that fill every cranny of the ramshackle building. Antiquarian books (mostly Victorian), wooden carpenter's tools (beautifully worn), silverware, jewellery, pocket watches, prints, ornaments—the variety is stupefying. Some stalls are well-ordered, others higgledy-piggledy, but most stock is in good repair, and everything seems to have a price tag: this is no junk market. One stall has a faintly unhealthy display of Nazi photographs; another has a fascinating collection of Victorian mechanical devices (early phonographs, a tweeting bird in a cage). Upstairs, a coffee shop does a good trade in early morning caffeine.

Bermondsey Indoor Antiques Market, another small private enterprise at 116 Tower Bridge Road, has about a dozen stalls selling a mixture of silverware, ornaments and trinkets.

It's worth exploring the area around Bermondsey Square, as much of it is given over to the antiques trade. You're likely to encounter dealers, hunched over the back of a Volvo estate, haggling over the price of an *objet d'art*; or you might see a van drawing up and being emptied of Victorian armchairs. Bermondsey Street, a rather dingy old road to the north of the square, has warehouses full of antiques, especially furniture. A stone's throw along Tower Bridge Road, southwest of the antiques trading, is a smaller general market. Up to a dozen stalls are set up on the wide pavement outside the oldest pie and mash shop in London (Manze's at 87 Tower Bridge Road). Fruit, vegetables, household goods, sweets and eggs can be bought here.

Over the years, more and more tourists have discovered Bermondsey market, but before 9am, few of them are simply sightseers. Knowledgeable American, German, Japanese and French collectors come to scrutinize the goods, perhaps realizing that many of the articles bought and sold here will reappear at Portobello Road or Camden Passage at a higher price. Every downward lurch the pound takes brings fresh waves from abroad. A bureau de change at the indoor market does some brisk early morning trading.

As 9am approaches, the pace at the antiques market gets less frenetic as late risers come to browse along the stalls. Some visitors might wander around the square—not an ugly place, with some Victorian buildings as well as a few grim modern flats. In the Middle Ages Bermondsey Abbey stood just off the present square on Bermondsey Street, next to St Mary Magdalen church. Behind its late Georgian 'Gothick' façade, the present church is mostly 17th-century. On the Tower Bridge Road, the long line of commuters in their cars seem oblivious to what they are missing.

Next to the indoor market, at 241 Long Lane, is an intriguing shop that also opens early. It sells all manner of antique scientific instruments: bottles of tinctures and acids, telescopes, weighing machines and barometers.

For liquid refreshment, try **The Hand and Marigold** pub, at the corner of Cluny Place and Bermondsey Street, which opens at 7am on Fridays. Early morning fried breakfasts, including black pudding and bubble and squeak, can be had at the **Rose Dining Room** (210 Bermondsey Street). Otherwise, there's a van in the square dispensing mugs of tea and filling the market with the enticing smell of fried bacon.

Deptford

Address: Deptford High Street, from Deptford Broadway to the railway bridge, SE8; Douglas Way, from Deptford High Street to Idonia Street, SE8; Douglas Square, off Douglas Way, SE8.

Public transport: ⇌ Deptford; buses 47, 53, 177, 188, 199, 225, X53.

Opening hours: Wed, Fri 8.30am–5pm; Sat 8.30am–6pm.

Best time to go: Saturday.

Car parking: the side streets south of Deptford Broadway usually have free spaces.

Main wares: **Deptford High Street** fresh food, household goods, clothing, bathroom goods, eggs, greetings cards, perfumes and cosmetics, lingerie, jeans, gold jewellery, books, stockings and socks, shoes, watches, hair accessories, net curtains, cut flowers;
Douglas Way secondhand clothing and records, bric-a-brac.

Specifics: fabrics, children's clothes, haberdashery; look out for secondhand bargains.

'You'd better watch it mate, they'll have your guts for garters down there.' This welcome to Deptford market, by a cheery trader who spotted my notebook and took me for a spy from the authorities, shows how the district is perceived from both within and without. To many north Londoners, Deptford symbolizes the untamed south: wild and forbidding. Even locals would term it rough and ready, with the emphasis on the rough. But times are changing. The borough recently received £37 million as part of the City Challenge scheme, and some of its buildings have already been spruced up. Though you'll find nothing of Greenwich's gentility here, Deptford flourishes on a Saturday, when it is home to one corker of a market.

Starting at the Deptford Broadway end of the High Street, the first thing you'll notice is a huge anchor, a reminder of the district's maritime connections. The market crowds surround it, gathered in front of a trader selling knives for all he's worth: 'You know they retail for £14.95 at a certain shop, but I'm not allowed to tell you the name of the shop...Asda [uttered with the largest stage whisper in Deptford]. Eeyaa, I'll tell you what I'll do, while the guvnor's on holiday. (We always have a sale when he goes missing. Don't tell him when you see him next week.) I'm not going to charge you £8 or £6. Not even going to charge you £5. *Three pounds to clear.*'

Prices are low throughout the market's 250 or so stalls. Along the High Street are dozens of clothes pitches, going from piles of garments on a barrow, all for £1.50, to women's glitzy nightclub wear. A CD and tape stall has some chart albums selling for about half the price you'd pay in a shop, as well as the usual country and western, and 'hits of the 1960s' compilations for £2.99. It also has a small collection of video games.

Few stalls are run by Afro-Caribbean traders, even though many customers come from that community. But even the old costermongers whose families have run a stall for decades now sell okra and fresh ginger, and perhaps a few yams, alongside their cabbages. It's the same story with the High Street's butchers; though many are long-established, they now sell cows' feet and goat meat.

A hundred yards or so up the High Street is the **Anchor Arcade**. This small private market shelters about 15 stalls selling a collection of clothes, net curtains, settees, haberdashery, cosmetics, and Afro hair accessories, plus **Tubby's Café**, which serves fry-ups and sarnies. Most of the stalls are run by stalwart Afro-Caribbean women. There's another small indoor mart, the **Deptford Shopping Arcade**, further up the street. A stall here, named **Electric Avenue** after the Brixton street and the Eddie Grant song, has a fair collection of electrical goods. There is also a good fresh fish stall.

Some stalls have spread onto Giffin Street, where new public toilets have recently been built. Opposite Giffin Street is the market's other main thoroughfare, **Douglas Way**. Lewisham Council maintains that this is a completely separate market, but it keeps the same hours as Deptford High Street. Douglas Way traders sell fruit and veg and new clothes, household goods, fabrics, plants, leather bags, petfood and electrical goods, but the most interesting section is on Douglas Square, a small patch of land on your right as you walk from the High Street. Here, about 40 stalls display a wild variety of junk, from old records to lengths of electric flex and piles of old clothing. You may even come across secondhand spotlights or bathroom scales. One trader's wares consist solely of old cameras and mobile-phone batteries.

Deptford High Street market has existed for over a century, but has often had to battle with the street's shopkeepers for its existence. One such battle to save the market from being cleared off the road was won in the 1950s, by Bill Gallagher, chairman of the Deptford Street Traders' Association. Mr Gallagher ran his stall for 70 years, dying in November 1994 at the age of 84.

Deptford's resurgence has led to one unwelcome development: Sainsbury's is planning to build a superstore in nearby New Cross. The market has a fight on its hands but, at present, the area is flourishing. On a Saturday afternoon, Deptford is an exciting place to be.

Nearby shops and cafés

Wellbeloved Butchers, just across Deptford Broadway from the High Street on Tanner's Hill, is a smashing old-fashioned butcher's shop, established in 1829, which specializes in hot baked pies. Deptford has two pie and mash shops on the High Street north of the market. **Manze's** at No.204 is the most attractive. The **Hale's Gallery Café** (70 Deptford High Street) is decidedly upmarket for the area, with Tuscan bean soup and vegetarian pizzas. The **Chadon** (at No.2) serves Nigerian, Caribbean and European dishes. Just past the northern end of the market, **Eunice's Tropical Food Shop** stocks a wider range of African provisions than you'll find on the stalls. If you want a respite from the market crowds, Thomas Archer's **St Paul's Church**, a famous Baroque structure completed in 1730, is two minutes' walk to the north.

East Street

Address: East Street, from Walworth Road to Dawes Street, SE17.

Public transport: ⊖/⇌ Elephant and Castle; buses 1, 12, 21, 35, 40, 42, 45, 53, 63, 68, 68A, 171, 172, 176, 188, 199, P3, P5, X53, X68.

Opening hours: Tue–Sat 9am–5pm; Sun 8am–2pm.

Best time to go: Sundays.

Car parking: try the side streets on the other side of the Walworth Road.

Main wares: clothing, household goods, fruit and vegetables, flowers and plants (Sunday only).

Specifics: net curtains, haberdashery, shellfish, cut flowers, electrical goods, suitcases, foam rubber, women's hats, petfoods, spectacles, carpets, crockery, cheap dried herbs.

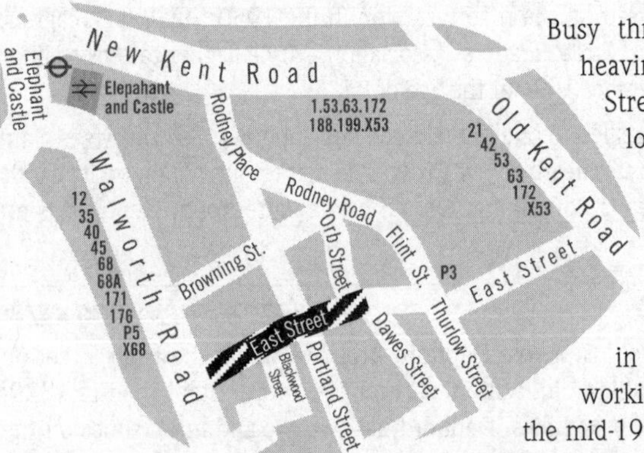

Busy through the week and heaving on Sundays, East Street—known to the locals as 'the Lanes'—is where southeast Londoners come for a knees-up. Like its neighbour Westmoreland Road, the street is in the heart of a huge working-class district built in the mid-19th century. Until 1880, traders set up their stalls on the main Walworth Road, but traffic and the laying of tram-rails forced them off. Nine years after the market moved to its present site, Charlie Chaplin was born at a house on East Street. Right up to 1939, one of the market's busiest times was Saturday night, when women poured in after collecting their husbands' wages, and trading went on to 11pm.

East Street traders guard their licences jealously, and several stalls have passed down the generations. Only on Wednesdays can casuals get a look in. As a result, there are few black stallholders, despite the fact that many market customers are Afro-Caribbean. Even the stall selling West Indian fruit, veg and breads is run by an old white costermonger.

There's a good spread of merchandise among the 250 or more stalls. Fruit and veg traders tend to occupy the Walworth Road end. But though there's enough of them to keep prices low, food is only a sideline at East Street. As with most London markets that have been long-established on a Sunday, several stalls are run by Jewish traders; many of them deal in fabrics, mostly for curtains or upholstery, but there's also one who sells suit material.

Few shops would turn up the chance to cash in on crowds like these, so most of the small businesses that line East Street are open on Sunday. There are several discount stores stocked with the type of goods more often sold in markets, but also a good helping of butchers, including Mitchells of East Street which supplies Arment's pie and mash shop (*see* 'Westmoreland Road', p.167) with its pies.

On Sundays, Blackwood Street, halfway along East Street, becomes south London's answer to Columbia Road flower market. About a dozen big stalls sell cut flowers, bulbs and shrubs, while gypsy women proffer their sprigs of heather at the junction with East Street.

At Portland Street there's a minor hiatus, as this is the only thoroughfare where cars are allowed to cross East Street on Sundays. As you shuffle along with the crowd, look out for the stall full of bikinis (even in winter), another selling cheese, bacon and kippers, and the long-established trader who sells nothing but rock-salt foot cream. There are two whelk stalls where traders come for a breather. At one, a couple of lads are discussing last night's boxing match down the Old Kent Road. On Sundays the market ends at Dawes Street, which has about half a dozen stalls on it, including one selling 'cabbages': cheap clothes made from off-cut material.

The only thing missing from East Street is a secondhand and junk section, but Westmoreland Road is only 10 minutes' walk away. Taken together, these two markets make for an exhilarating Sunday treat.

Nearby cafés and pubs

Marie's Snack Bar and Café (84 East Street) has salads, sandwiches, fry-ups and beans on toast. There are several pubs along East Street; try the **George IV** or the **Royal Albert.** *See also* 'Westmoreland Road', p.167.

Greenwich

Address: off College Approach, Stockwell Street, Greenwich Church Street, Thames Street and Greenwich High Road, SE10, ✆ (0181) 858 6376 (Greenwich Tourist Office); *see individual markets for details.*

Public transport: ⇌ Greenwich; buses 177, 180, 188, 199, 286, 386.

Opening hours: *see individual markets for details.*

Best time to go: Sunday.

Car parking: very difficult—most of the roadside parking is for residents only; try the area off Thames Street, or the meters on streets off Greenwich High Road.

Main wares: secondhand goods, crafts, clothes, books, antiques.

Specifics: prints, books, old jackets and dresses; organic food (Sat only); look for secondhand bargains at the flea market (Sun only).

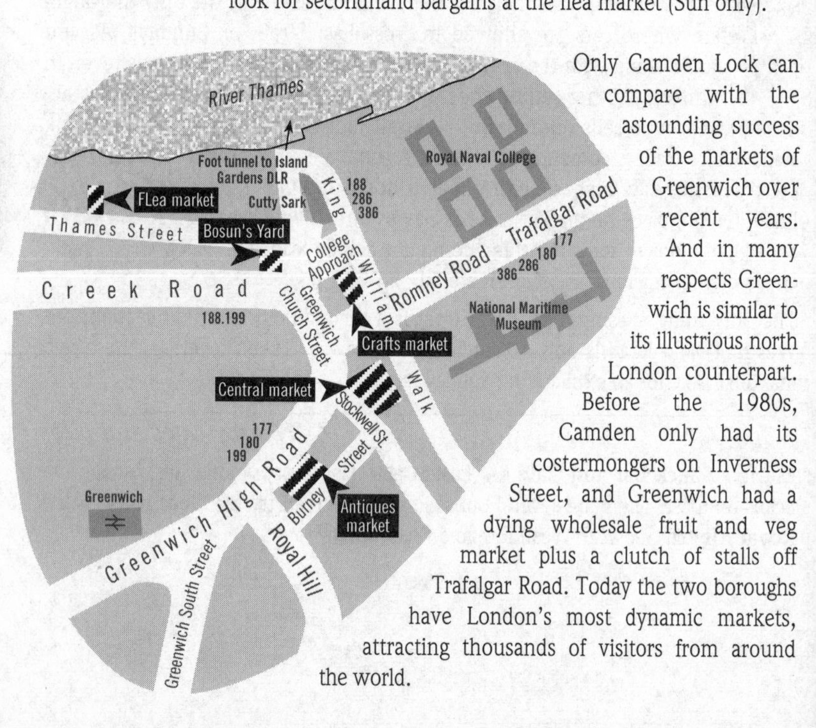

Only Camden Lock can compare with the astounding success of the markets of Greenwich over recent years. And in many respects Greenwich is similar to its illustrious north London counterpart. Before the 1980s, Camden only had its costermongers on Inverness Street, and Greenwich had a dying wholesale fruit and veg market plus a clutch of stalls off Trafalgar Road. Today the two boroughs have London's most dynamic markets, attracting thousands of visitors from around the world.

The major difference is that while flocks of tourists are attracted to Camden simply by the market, Greenwich has some of London's most famous sights. England's greatest architects of the 17th and 18th centuries—Inigo Jones, Christopher Wren, John Vanbrugh and Nicholas Hawksmoor—all contributed to the banquet of classical and Baroque buildings to be found here. The *Cutty Sark*, the sleek 1869 tea clipper, also draws crowds to the riverside.

Though many of Greenwich's markets are held on Saturday—the small new organic food market is only held on that day—the area truly comes to life on Sunday. None of the main markets listed below is geared to providing locals with shopping basics; for these you'd best travel to the markets at Woolwich (*see* p.169) or Deptford (*see* p.149) or, failing that, to the few stalls that trade on Colomb, Earlswood and Tyler Streets, off Trafalgar Road, from Monday to Saturday.

Central Market

Stockwell Street, opposite the Hotel Ibis, SE10, © (0181) 766 6844. Central Market open Sat, Sun 9am–5pm (organic food market Sat only); Village Market open Fri, Sat 10am–5pm, Sun 10am–6pm.

Of all Greenwich's markets, the Central most nearly resembles Camden's shindig, both in the goods sold and its setting. Sited on a largish patch of land off Stockwell Street are scores of outside stalls, a dozen or so lock-ups and a couple of old buildings filled with yet more stalls. Far more activity takes place on Sundays than Saturdays.

A few of the traders with stalls facing Stockwell Street deal in books (new hardbacks at half price; tatty old hardbacks for £1; Penguin Classics in good condition for £2). They are positioned in front of the **Book Gallery**, a two-storey business containing old comics, books and prints. The remaining stalls in this section are strewn with old jewellery, crockery, footstools, copper saucepans, and glassware; a few of the pretensions to be found at the Crafts Market are stripped away here (where stalls cost less to rent), and you might find some genuine craftsworkers selling their wares at

Greenwich market

fair prices: mirrors with distressed pine frames painted in Mediterranean greens, for instance. Behind the Book Gallery, other street traders might tip out a pile of clothes and sell 'anything for £1', or gather together a collection of old tools and traffic warning lights. There is also a building containing **La Cantina**, a fast food shack dealing in kebabs, crêpes and Texan burgers.

To the left of the Book Gallery (looking down from the Stockwell Road) is the **Village Market**, housed in a large two-storey building. It has about 40 partitions for stalls downstairs; upstairs are about 10 more, and a crêperie café. Books were once the main commodity sold here, but now the ground floor is given over to mawkish framed pictures of teddy bears, new mirrors with pine frames and huge Havana cigars. Pay £10 and you can have a tarot card reading. Upstairs (on Sundays) are books (hardbacks all £1), film posters, rare tapes and records, plus a fine collection of old comics and magazines, including copies of *New Statesman* and *Punch* from the 1950s, and back issues of *Fortean Times* which cover a spectrum of weird happenings.

Grouped behind the Village Market are lock-ups and open-air stalls where traders sell secondhand goods. There's usually a couple of stalls packed with old and new stocks of records, tapes and CDs, with all types of music. Rails of old leather, suede, denim and sheepskin jackets are lined up nearby. Prices are high if, to you, 'second-hand' means 'worn and fraying'. If, however, it means 'vintage cool', you'll be queuing to pay £26 for a Levi denim jacket, or £20 for a decrepit leather coat in an original 1960s design.

Furniture and other booty from house clearances accounts for much of the stock in the lock-ups; the more expensive stuff—ornaments, clocks, dressing tables, candlesticks, paintings and the like—is kept under cover, while inky school desks and an elderly standard lamp soak up the showers outside. A few traders sit themselves down round a dilapidated table and open a Thermos of tea. On Sundays, a large shed at the rear of the site is unlocked and traders in furniture and collectables (including old musical instruments) set up stall. To its right, one of the lock-ups has been taken over by some Thai noodle sellers.

There's a second storey above a couple of the lock-ups. Trudge up the fire escape and you'll find a few stalls selling more secondhand clothes, plus collectables: Victorian bottles and military and police equipment, from a woman police superintendent's uniform to a firefighter's helmet.

There's less than half Sunday's number of stalls on Saturday, but one reason for coming to the Central at the start of the weekend is to visit the small **organic food market**. This is held to the left of the Village Market (looking from Stockwell Street). Only about half a dozen traders turn up each Saturday, including the butcher from Longwood Farm, who also visits Portobello Road each Thursday (*see* p.64) and Spitalfields on Sunday (*see* p.138) with his range of organic meats, cheeses, butter and sheep's yoghurts. Next to him, a bread stall has an enticing collection of organic loaves including bara brith (Welsh tea bread, £1.50), olive and onion focaccia (£1.60) and buttermilk and honey soda bread (£1.20). An organic fruit and veg stall sells the full range of common produce, from watercress, carrots and celery, to avocado, kiwi fruit and lemons. It also has dried organic herbs and spices, vegetable juices, and olive oils. A run-of-the-mill fish van (oysters, mussels, trout, cod, bloaters) and a less-than-organic burger van and jacket potato stand complete the picture.

If you go back onto Stockwell Street and cross the railway line, there's a small patch of land (almost opposite St Alphege's church) that contains a batch of fast food stalls known as the **Fountain Food Court**. Here you can stoke up on curry, doughnuts, burgers, Thai noodles or cappuccino. Chairs are placed outside on the unattractive concrete courtyard.

Crafts market

College Approach, with entrances on Turpin Lane (off Greenwich Church Street) and Durnford Street, © (0171) 240 7405. Open Sat, Sun 9am–5pm.

If the Central Market is Camden, this is Covent Garden. Slap in the centre of Greenwich, the crafts market occupies the site of a former fruit and veg mart that fizzled out in the 1980s. The cobbled paving has been retained, but a new translucent corrugated roof keeps the rain off traders. The little alleyways surrounding the market were once the home of greengrocers; now they are crammed with gift shops. Around the perimeter of the trading area are more shops of the same ilk, plus a café and a pub.

Up to 150 stalls are jammed into the small central space; more pitches are taken on Sundays than Saturdays. Here you can buy customized plaster of Paris sports figures, from **Rugger Buggers et al**; mounted butterflies and spiders (a beefy-looking spider from Peru, mounted and framed, costs £25); designer jewellery; artefacts from Asia, the Middle East and Africa; wacky candlesticks; a variety of wooden goods, some useful (an egg-timer, a bowl), some not. Framed sporting prints from *Punch* are sold for upwards of £11 compared to the £5 charged at the Central Market.

Tourists and locals mingle among the stalls, but the place has a rather contrived air. Over the exit of the old market buildings, built in 1831, is the inscription 'A false balance is an abomination to the Lord, but a just weight is his delight.' Outside, a new sign bears the disingenuous inscription 'Greenwich Market, since 1737'.

Antiques market

Off Greenwich High Road, between junctions with Stockwell Street and Royal Hill, SE10. Open Sat, Sun 9am–5pm.

The antiques market only goes off at half cock on a Saturday, but on Sundays all the 50 or so pitches are usually taken. Trading takes place on a patch of tarmac off the busy Greenwich High Road. Some of the old jewellery or 19th-century prints (sold at lower prices than you'd find in the crafts market) might be described as antique. More of the goods would be in the 'collectable' category: Oxo tins, brassware, door-knockers, comics, old wood-carving tools. Others still fall into the secondhand or junk genre: rolling pins, oil cans, furniture, books, fishing nets.

On Sundays there are also secondhand clothes stalls: leather jackets, hats, mock-fur coats. Some of these garments might look as though they've come straight from a jumble sale or charity shop, but a price tag of £25 for a jacket isn't uncommon. Crafts traders also take pitches here on Sundays, selling hats, handbags, hand-painted crockery and the like. Right by this market is the **Studio Bar** where you can pick up a burger, or a more unusual snack such as a chilli nan, or have a drink.

Bosun's Yard

59 Greenwich Church Street, SE10, © (0181) 858 5995. Open in summer daily 10am–5pm; in winter Sat, Sun 10am–5pm.

Located a mast's length from the *Cutty Sark* and the riverbank, you might expect Bosun's Yard to be a tourist market, and so it is. Such are the crowds on summer Sundays that a one-way system for browsers has been instituted. Punters shuffle down the narrow walkways in unison, perusing the 35 or so craft stalls on the hoof; there is no time for dalliance. Here you might find handmade cards, chess and backgammon sets, African and Indonesian jewellery, artefacts and spears (including a collection of phallic fertility symbols made from bone), horrible framed 'Bless This House' notices, pottery, alpaca jumpers, and novelty goods such as a glass model of an egg in the act of being broken. Prices are predictably high. At the entrance to the building is a sandwich bar and a fantastic crêperie.

Flea market

Thames Street, SE10. Open Sun 7.30am–3.30pm.

Walking down Thames Street, away from Bosun's Yard and all the tourist kerfuffle, you soon realize that Greenwich has a large working-class population. Austere blocks of council flats deter casual sightseers; only those in the know continue along the street for a couple of hundred yards to reach a disused warehouse that holds the weekly flea market.

A fruit, vegetable and flower stall outside the entrance is a misleading introduction, as there is no fresh produce or food inside. Virtually everything for sale within is secondhand. Suits, shirts and coats fetch a lower price here than elsewhere in Greenwich, with a tweed jacket in good condition going for about £5. Old books are also cheap, though you'll probably have to root about in cardboard boxes to find anything worth reading.

The warehouse is in a dilapidated state, with a roof that lets in light and rain. There's a faintly maritime feel to the place. Most traders have converted large steel containers, once used by cargo ships, into lock-up stalls. Few seem to be full-time vendors; many simply want to flog the contents of their loft, or perhaps get a few pounds for an old record and tape collection. Some of the containers do, however, hold a more specialized range of goods: crockery, glassware, car headlights, books, record players, well-used toys. The market continues outside at the back of the warehouse, in a yard that leads to the river. Here you can get a good view of Canary Wharf, before walking back to Thames Street and having a drink at the Thames freehouse.

Nearby cafés and pubs

One place in Greenwich that has avoided much touristification is **Goddard's Ye Old Pie House** (the name is an exception) at 45 Greenwich Church Street. Along with traditional minced beef pie and mash, this caff has a range of other pies and pasties. Vegetarians should head for **Escape** (141–143 Greenwich South Street), a meat-free café with generous portions. The **Ton Won Mein** noodle house at 49 Greenwich Church Street, ✆ (0181) 898 1668 (open all week, 11am–11pm), is very good and extremely popular. Most dishes are less than £4.50.

The **Royal Hill Tea Shop** on Royal Hill serves a wide variety of teas and coffees, with an array of cakes, and is open all day. An excellent formal French/English Sunday lunch can be had at the **Spread Eagle** (1–2 Stockwell Street). The **Trafalgar Tavern**, part of the Royal Naval College, overlooks the river and serves reasonable bar food and a good pint. The **Richard I**, next door to the Royal Hill Tea Shop, has a nice garden to the rear, with good barbecues.

Lewisham

Address: Lewisham High Street, SE13.

Public transport: ⇌ Lewisham; buses 21, 36, 47, 54, 75, 89, 108, 122, 136, 180, 181, 185, 199, 208, 225, 261, 273, 278, 284, 380, 484, P4.

Opening hours: 9am–5.30pm Mon–Sat; craft market 7am–2pm Mon.

Best time to go: Saturday.

Car parking: there are parking meters along Albion Way to the east of the High Street.

Main wares: fruit and vegetables, flowers, fish, haberdashery, clothing.

Specifics: cheap fruit and veg, fish.

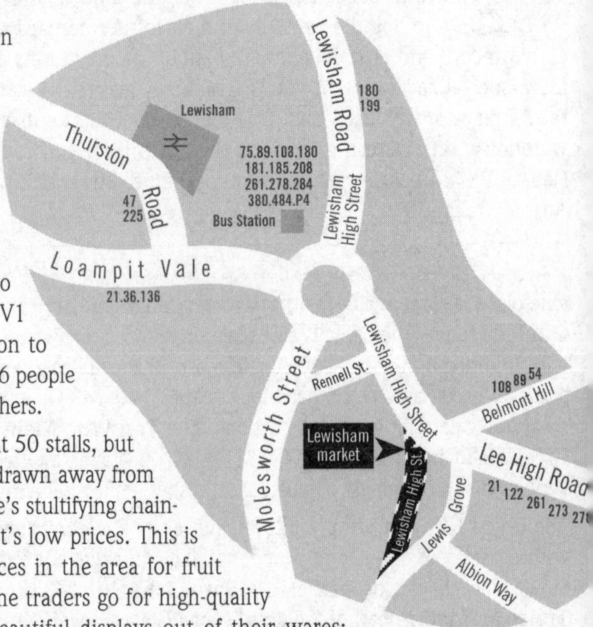

The pedestrianization of Lewisham High Street seems to have been going on for years, but the market continues to flourish amid the rubble. It has had to do so before. In 1944, a V1 rocket fell directly on to the market, killing 56 people and wounding 99 others.

There are only about 50 stalls, but many shoppers are drawn away from the Riverdale Centre's stultifying chainstores by the market's low prices. This is one of the best places in the area for fruit and vegetables. Some traders go for high-quality produce, making beautiful displays out of their wares; others prefer the 'pile 'em high, sell 'em cheap' approach, flogging 3lb of plum tomatoes for 50p, or seedless grapes at 2lb for £1. A few sell more specialist produce: artichokes, Chinese leaves, chicory and frisée lettuce. Some specialize in Afro-Caribbean foodstuffs: yams, green bananas, okra, bottles of sarsaparilla, tins of gunga peas and the unambiguously named 'cock soup'.

As with many markets that attract Afro-Caribbean shoppers, there's a very good fish stall. **F. Davis**, who has traded here for years, sells a wide variety of swimming creatures: king fish, live eels, scallops, whitebait, sardines, calamari, red mullet, kippers and cooked roe. The remainder of the stalls supply locals with everyday merchandise: children's clothes, cheap cakes, cut flowers, haberdashery and greetings cards. About half the stalls currently stand on the High Street's wide eastern pavement; the rest are farther up on the west side, away from the traffic. It's likely the market will continue to be shifted about until the work is finished, when the stalls will occupy the pedestrianized street. Some traders already seem to be getting used to having the street free of traffic; I found one ancient wooden barrow standing deserted in the middle of the street with nought but a cup of tea resting on it.

Nearby cafés and shops

Something Fishy on the High Street by the market is the enticingly-named caff that attracts many locals. As well as fish and chips, and eels, pie and mash, it also has a choice of fried breakfasts, and ice-creams. A short walk south of the market along Lewisham High Street will take you to the new **Turkish Food Centre** at No.227–229, which contains a butcher's, with Turkish sausages and plenty of offal, a baker's selling freshly made round bread, and general stores stocked with pulses and olive oils. Try one of the *baklavas* (sweet pastries).

Lower Marsh

Address: Lower Marsh, from Westminster Bridge Road to Baylis Road, SE1.

Public transport: ⊖/⇌ Waterloo;
⊖ Lambeth North;
buses 1, 12, 53, 68, 76, 109, 168, 171, 171A, 176, 188, X53, X68.

Opening hours: Mon–Fri 10.30am–2.30pm.

Best time to go: Friday lunchtime.

Car parking: difficult; there are some parking meters in the area, or an (expensive) car park 10 minutes' walk away on Library Street.

Main wares: fruit and vegetables, household goods, clothes, electrical goods, haberdashery, bric-a-brac.

Specifics: classical CDs.

Two old women once took me around this part of south London showing me cheap places to eat. Almost as an aside, they started talking of the New Cut market of their youth. I was enthralled. The market they described was not only a meeting place and shopping centre; it was free entertainment that lasted until midnight on Saturdays.

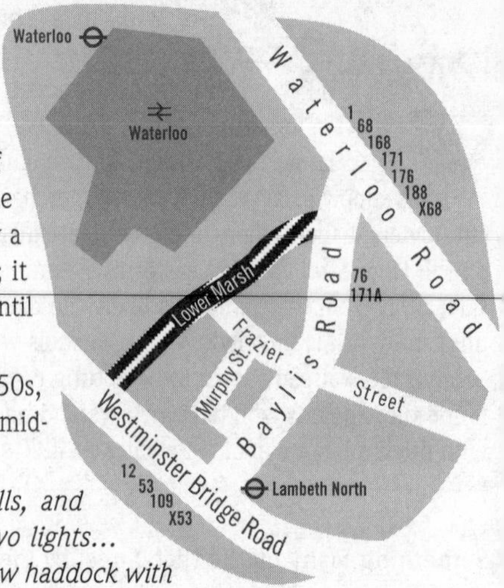

Henry Mayhew, writing in the 1850s, gives a vivid portrayal of the mid-Victorian atmosphere of the place:

> *There are hundreds of stalls, and every stall has its one or two lights... One man shows off his yellow haddock with a candle stuck in a bundle of firewood; his neighbour makes a candlestick of a huge turnip, and the tallow gutters over its sides... Then the tumult of the thousand different cries of the eager dealers...is almost bewildering... 'Come and look at 'em! here's toasters!' bellows one with a Yarmouth bloater stuck on a toasting fork... A little further on stands the clean family, begging; the father with his head down as if in shame, and a box of lucifers held forth in his hand... Then is heard the sharp snap of the percussion-cap from the crowd of lads firing at the target for nuts; and the moment afterwards, you see a black man half-clad in white, and shivering in the cold with tracts in his hand, or else you hear the sounds of music from 'Frazier's Circus', on the other side of the road, and the man outside the door of the penny concert, beseeching you to 'Be in time—be in time!' as Mr Somebody is just about to sing his favourite song of the Knife Grinder. Such, indeed, is the riot, the struggle, and the scramble for a living, that the confusion and uproar of the New-Cut on Saturday night have a bewildering and saddening effect upon the thoughtful mind.*

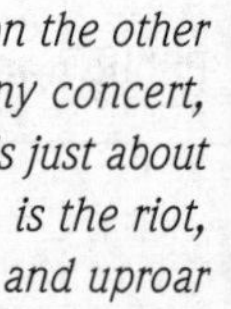

Sadly, the market today is a husk of its former self. It has become a lunchtime affair catering mainly to local office workers, and is now based only on Lower Marsh. Since the Greater London Council was abolished, the supply of customers from County Hall has dried up and the market has contracted further. Mid-week, there can be as few as 30 stalls trading at lunchtime, though more come on Fridays.

A couple of stalls sell secondhand bric-a-brac (including brassware, old tapes and pulp fiction), but otherwise most goods are new. Office workers come to peruse the audio and computer equipment, stock up on underwear, buy a good luck card and flowers for colleagues moving jobs, or browse through the excellent collection of classical CDs at the stall linked to Gramex, which has a shop on the street. But the area also contains much council housing, and the market provides locals with cheap tins of food, fruit and veg, inexpensive clothing and a variety of household goods—from umbrellas and can openers to bedlinen and alarm clocks.

Nearby cafés and shops

Masters Superfish, five minutes' walk away at 191 Waterloo Road, has some of the best fish and chips in London. On Lower Marsh, **Barbarellas** (No.141) is a café serving sandwiches and jacket potatoes. For a more exotic repast, try **Benkei** (at No.19), a Japanese café with a range of low-priced set lunches.

Lower Marsh has several interesting small shops. One of the best is the **Far Eastern Supermarket** (No.120), which sells Chinese crockery, steamers, woks and the like.

Peckham

Address: Choumert Road, between Rye Lane and Choumert Grove, SE15;
Rye Lane indoor market, 48 Rye Lane, SE15, ✆ (0171) 639 2463;
Angora indoor market, Rye Lane (opposite No.98), SE15.

Public transport: ⇌ Peckham Rye;
buses 12, 37, 63, 78, 312, P3, P12, P13.

Opening hours: Mon–Sat 9am–5pm.

Best time to go: Saturday.

Car parking: spaces along Bournemouth Road (to the east of Rye Lane), but you first need to buy a voucher for 60p from shops on Rye Lane displaying the appropriate sign.

Main wares: Afro-Caribbean foodstuffs, clothing, household goods, petfoods.

Specifics: Afro-Caribbean fruit and veg, meat, fish, Afro hair accessories.

Although Peckham has become the butt of Bacardi jokes and been mythologized by the TV show *Only Fools and Horses*, it is not really a stark urban wasteland seething with shysters, wide boys and Robin Reliants. Although there's plenty of urban deprivation if you look for it, Rye Lane on Saturdays is a cheerful, buzzing place, with two indoor markets, an outdoor market on Choumert Road, and side streets dotted with stalls. Rye Lane itself is not overwhelmed by chainstores, but has a fine variety of shops, including halal butchers, Afro haircare stores, and fishmongers stocked with a wide variety of seafood.

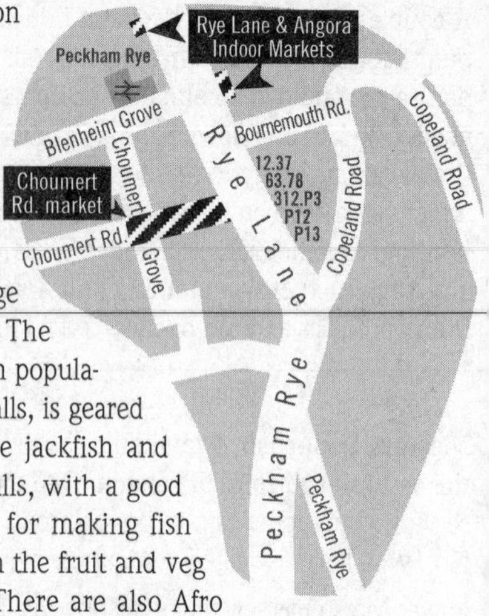

Peckham is a multi-racial area with large Afro-Caribbean and Asian communities. The markets reflect the district's cosmopolitan population. **Choumert Road**, with about 30 stalls, is geared towards Caribbean foodstuffs. There are jackfish and snappers on the two well-stocked fish stalls, with a good supply of salmon heads and fish bones for making fish soup; mangoes, coriander and plantain on the fruit and veg stalls; and reggae on the record stalls. There are also Afro haircare stalls and a trader selling the sort of felt hats well loved by West Indian women of a certain age. The lock-up shops along the street are really part of the market, with many of their goods displayed outside. Several of the businesses, especially the butchers', are run by Asians, but more often than not their customers are Afro-Caribbean.

Back along Rye Lane, the **Angora indoor market** is held in a long, narrow building. Inside it is bright and quite modern, with about 50 traders cramped between partitions off the central walkways. There's a wide variety of goods and services: Afro hair accessories, clothes (mostly women's and children's), toys, secondhand televisions, a key-cutter and engraver, jewellery, reggae and soul records, dried flowers, wool, a printing and photocopying service and a health food stall. In one booth, a manicurist gently tends to shoppers' fingernails; in another, full of interesting leather clothes, women eye up the lace and leather bodices.

The main **Rye Lane indoor market**, sometimes called the Bargain Centre, is across the road to the north. Traders moved here from the old Rye Lane street market in 1931. It was bombed in the war but soon rebuilt, and now has an old-fashioned, murky feel, like the arcades of Brixton or the great indoor market halls of northern England. Most of the 85 or so businesses occupy permanent structures within the old iron hall.

The butchers at **Terry's Meat Market** 'knock out' at the end of the day on Saturday. A crowd of people wait eagerly for cheap chops and joints. The neighbouring businesses are a unisex hair salon, a haberdashery stall and a trader selling bedding. In one corner of the building, an old-established pet stall sells birds, small furry animals and all manner of petfoods. Nearby, a group of young Afro-Caribbean butchers are chopping up meat. A sign at the shop proclaims 'We sell whole goat.'

There's a complete change at the far end of this avenue, where **Steptoe & Sons** has its premises. Piles of old books, records and tapes vie for space with disparate pieces of furniture and non-specific junk. Video games, greetings cards and perfumes can also be bought in the indoor market. Before you go, don't miss a look at **Brenda's** toiletries stall with its row of wigs and hair extensions hanging like scalps from the ceiling.

Nearby cafés

At the back of the Angora indoor market is the **Angora Café**, with a menu of fry-ups and sandwiches. The **Star** at 30–32 Peckham Rye, the southern continuation of Rye Lane, has traditional caff food, roasts and fabulous British puds.

Riverside Walk

Address: Riverside Walk, in front of the National Film Theatre, SE1.

Public transport: ⊖/⇌ Waterloo;
buses 1, 4, 26, 45, 63, 68, 76, 77, 149, 168, 171, 171A, 172, 176, 188, 501, 505, 521, D1, P11, X68.

Opening hours: Sat, Sun, and occasionally in the week, 12 noon–7pm (earlier in winter).

Car parking: at weekends there might be spaces on the side streets south of Stamford Street; there's a big NCP car park on Stamford Street.

Main wares: books, prints.

Specifics: secondhand play texts, old editions of guide books, prints of English architecture.

The Riverside Walk book market is a hardy animal. Even in the depths of winter its long trestle tables are set up under Waterloo Bridge. The concrete surrounds of the South Bank and the wind off the river are mellowed by the quiet bookishness of the customers. You may even find yourself serenaded by virtuoso buskers, fiddling for their passage through music college.

Hardbacks and paperbacks, both fiction and non-fiction, are displayed on eight rows of tables. Quality is high, both in content and condition—there's precious little pulp fiction, and even the oldest books are generally in fine fettle. Secondhand paperback novels cost upwards of £1.50.

Virago and Women's Press are well represented, and most of the classics of English literature can usually be found. You might also discover boxloads of science fiction or detective stories.

Both new and secondhand non-fiction is stocked; most new books are remainders, covering subjects from natural history to embroidery, from politics to pets. Classification is sometimes rudimentary: *The History of the Second World War* might be next to *Understanding Your Dog*. But film, art, food and books for children usually have their own sections. As the National Theatre is only a stone's throw away, it's no surprise to see a good collection of secondhand play texts: Beckett, Ayckbourn, T.S. Eliot, Pinter, Brecht and, of course, Shakespeare—all at slightly more than half price. There's also a wide choice of travel guide books that are a year or so out of date; many are sold for less than half price.

The market has a good line in old prints, culled from 19th- or early 20th-century books and magazines. I found an intriguing set of cookery illustrations from the turn of the century, depicting elaborate, colourful constructions coated in aspic. Engravings of historic buildings and landscapes of England are ordered by county. A series of 1950s adverts features vacuous housewives gazing yearningly at the latest labour-saving devices.

It is sometimes difficult to divine who is running stalls here; as often as not, the owners are poring over books alongside their customers. This all adds to the charm of the market, and the pleasure of browsing is enhanced if you're lucky enough to uncover gems such as *Scouting Thrills* by Captain G.B. McKern VC, published in 1925.

Nearby cafés and shops

The **National Film Theatre** restaurant and bar looks out onto the Riverside Walk market. Otherwise, all the amenities of the South Bank are nearby. A short walk eastwards, just back from the river, is Gabriel's Wharf, with its collection of craft shops, restaurants and bars.

Westmoreland Road

Address: Westmoreland Road, from Walworth Road to Queen's Row, SE17.

Public transport: ⊖/⇌ Elephant and Castle;
then buses 12, 35, 40, 45, 68, 68A, 171, 176, X68;
also bus 42.

Opening hours: Tue, Wed, Fri, Sat 9am–4pm; Thur 9am–2pm; Sun 8.30am–1pm.

Best time to go: Sunday morning.

Car parking: try the side streets west of the Walworth Road.

Main wares: secondhand junk, old books, tapes and CDs, clothes (Sun); fruit and veg (rest of week).

Specifics: secondhand clothes, possible antiques bargains.

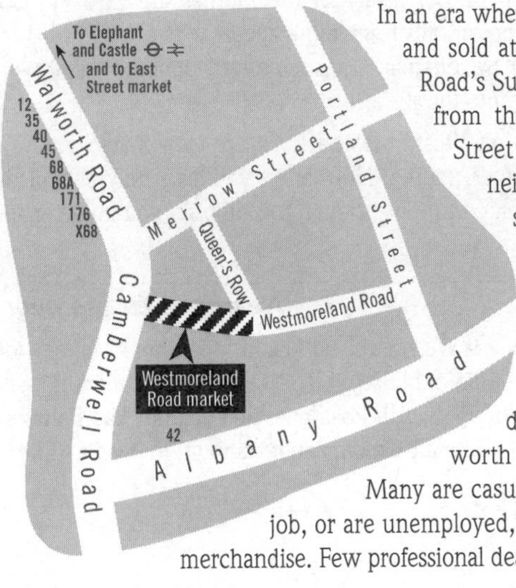

In an era where junk is described as 'heritage' and sold at inflated prices, Westmoreland Road's Sunday market is a joy. It benefits from the crowds visiting nearby East Street (*see* p.152), yet keeps its own neighbourhood atmosphere. This is still a close-knit working-class area. Away from the noise of the Walworth Road, you'll find stallholders who live in the nearby council flats chatting with their friends about the day's takings, and whether it'll be worth paying for a pitch next week. Many are casual traders who have a weekday job, or are unemployed, and have raided their attics for merchandise. Few professional dealers bother to scour the stalls.

During the week the small general market attracts half a dozen traders selling fruit and vegetables and household goods. Over the years it has dwindled, unable to compete with East Street. A couple of fruit and veg dealers and an egg seller also turn up on Sunday, when trade is brisker. They are joined by a shellfish stall, which dispenses cockles to the punters. Otherwise, virtually all the 50-odd Sunday traders sell secondhand goods: tapes, records and CDs, old crockery, a box of toy cars, boots and shoes, books. One stall is full of DIY bits and pieces: nails, screws, washers and the like. There's also a good line in secondhand kitchenware: pots and pans, and old cutlery.

Some traders seem to be selling the contents of their granny's flat; disparate pieces of furniture line the pavements. Other stock has been put in order by eccentric stallholders with a yen for pen nibs, pocket watches, old sewing machines or coins and medals. Some pitches display a glorious madness of junk: a pair of patent leather shoes resting next to tubes of oil paints and a watering can. Others specialize in the exquisitely sordid: a half-used bottle of roll-on deodorant, semi-fresh from an elderly relative's armpit, or bunches of withered flowers pilfered from a neighbour's garden.

The Sunday market is particularly good for cheap secondhand clothes, untainted by the high prices that go with trendiness. A rail of shirts for a pound each; workaday suits for £5. Many of the clothes are wrapped in plastic bags and hung on rails to give the appearance of having been dry-cleaned. Other traders make no such effort, tipping bags of musty garments directly onto the street.

Unlike East Street, most shops on Westmoreland Road are closed on Sundays, though a halal butcher's continues trading. No matter: you'll be fully occupied by the market, for if you're prepared to root through the rubbish, you might snap up a bargain.

Nearby cafés and pubs

Arment's pie and mash shop at 7–9 Westmoreland Road is open from Monday to Saturday, but on Sundays you should either stroll over to East Street market (*see* p.152), or have a pint in one of the Walworth Road pubs and wait for **Las Palmas** (10–12 Westmoreland Road), an authentic Colombian restaurant, to open at 3pm.

Woolwich

Address: Beresford Square, SE18; indoor market off Plumstead Road.

Public transport: ≈ Woolwich Arsenal; buses 51, 53, 96, 99, 122, 161, 177, 178, 180, 244, 272, 291, 380, 386, 422, 469, X53, X72.

Opening hours: Tue, Wed, Fri, Sat 8.30am–5pm; Thur 8.30am–2pm.

Best time to go: Saturday.

Car parking: there are some meters along Woolwich New Road.

Main wares: fruit and vegetables, household goods, clothes, CDs and tapes.

Specifics: fish, cut flowers, low-priced fruit and veg, wool, fabrics.

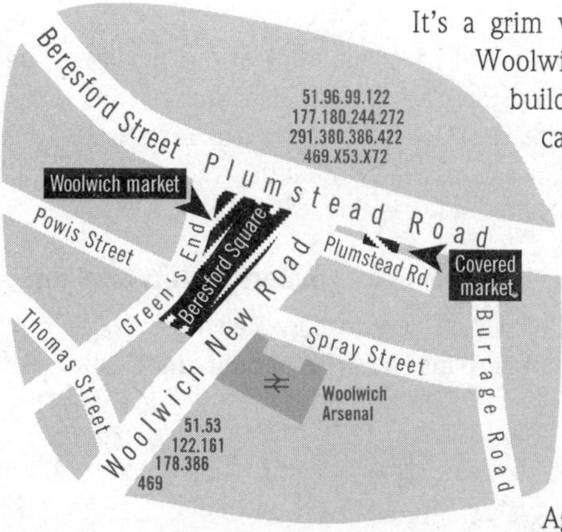

It's a grim walk down Beresford Street to Woolwich's market: featureless grey buildings, no shops, no people, just cars. It doesn't prepare you for the market, a lively, friendly place, and about the nearest you'll get in London to the atmosphere of a market town. This isn't surprising, really, as Woolwich is far enough from central London to have a distinct character and history. There's been a market in the borough since the Middle Ages. Until the 19th century it was held in the High Street and Market Hill (near the river ferry landing stage), but by the 1850s, unofficial stalls were trading on Beresford Square, close to the Royal Arsenal and its thousands of munitions workers.

The square, surrounded mostly by 19th-century buildings, has now been pedestrianized. At its northern end, the Royal Arsenal Gatehouse remains. This impressive structure, built in 1829, is currently being renovated as part of the Woolwich Revival scheme.

Like a small-town market, Beresford Square concentrates on the needs of its locals. There are about 120 pitches in all, selling household goods, clothing for men, women and children, an impressive range of fish, and a good choice of low-priced fruit and veg. Some of the costermongers have their produce beautifully arranged on synthetic grass, vying with the cut-flower stalls in their displays. One has a good range of Asian vegetables: tiny aubergines, okra and chillies. The fabric stalls also seem popular with local Asian women.

There's little reward in exploring the concrete shopping precinct at the western end of the market on Powys Street. It's better to walk along the pedestrianized area to the east, beside the Plumstead Road. Inside a dour 1930s structure, you'll find an indoor market containing 42 lock-ups. The traders sell clothing; drapery (including net curtains); wallpaper, with a big line in lurid 1970s patterns; secondhand books (mainly paperbacks); African staple foods such as cornmeal, yams and black-eye beans; jewellery; hippy pipes and incense sticks; and petfood.

One of the lock-ups has a fund of old 'collectables': cigarette cards, coins, medals and 45rpm records; another sells football shirts and scarves, and a wide range of sporting and military-style trophies.

Long impoverished, Woolwich seems to be coming out of the shadow of its wealthy neighbour Greenwich, and there's a feeling of optimism around the market. However, as is the case at nearby Deptford, there's a blot on the landscape: Sainsbury's has plans to open a Savacentre superstore little over a mile away at Shooters Hill.

Nearby cafés and pubs

Kenroy's pie and mash shop at 5 Woolwich New Road is a newly refurbished café popular among traders. The **Ordnance Arms** and the **Elephant and Castle** pubs are both in Beresford Square.

Dave's vegetable barrow North End road

Southwest London

Brixton

Address:	Electric Avenue, Pope's Road, Brixton Station Road, Electric Lane, SW9, ✆ (0171) 926 2530.
Public transport:	⊖/⇌ Brixton; buses 2, 3, 35, 37, 45, 45A, 109, 118, 133, 159, 196, 250, 345, P4, P5.
Opening hours:	Mon, Tue, Thur–Sat 8am–5.30pm; Wed 8am–1pm.
Best time to go:	good on any day, but busiest on Fridays and Saturdays.
Car parking:	the side streets off Railton Road, ten minutes' walk to the south of the market, have free parking, but it can be difficult to get a space; the multi-storey in Wiltshire Road charges 80p an hour.
Main wares:	African and Caribbean foodstuffs, fruit and vegetables, fabrics, clothing, records, tapes and CDs, secondhand clothing, bric-a-brac, haberdashery, electrical goods.
Specifics:	fish, Afro-Caribbean fruit and vegetables, meat, African fabrics and clothing, black music.

Brixton market is dynamic, tense and vital. People gather simply to watch the entertainment. And by doing so they become part of that entertainment, the parading, cosmopolitan crowd that's as essential to the spirit of the market as the 300 or more stalls and lock-ups that open for business six days a week.

Street trading began in the 1870s along Atlantic Road, and quickly expanded down Electric Avenue to cater for the massive increase in the area's population. The market soon drew customers from all over south London, and became known for its eccentric characters. By 1936, Mary Benedetta, in her own survey of London's street markets, complained that customers at Brixton were a joyless lot, mainly 'serious-minded housewives'. But the stallholders more than made up for it, and she went on to describe folk such as 'Long Dick', who sold a game called hookum for 3d, 'Bertie Bacon', whose streaky never cost more than 8d a pound, and 'Fatty', who sold bargain tinned foods.

Afro-Caribbeans were invited to work in Britain to help solve the country's post-war labour shortage. They began to settle in Brixton in 1948, drawn by the availability of lodging houses within easy reach of central London. There have been problems in the community's assimilation. High unemployment and aggressive policing helped fuel tensions. These reached explosive levels in 1981 and 1985, when riots broke out in the area, and there were further disturbances in 1995. However, it would be wrong to think of Brixton as a ghetto, as blacks and Asians together represent only about 30 per cent of the local population. Though economic problems remain, the local community has worked together in the past decade to ease the tension. In spite of recent events, Brixton market is still a safe place to visit.

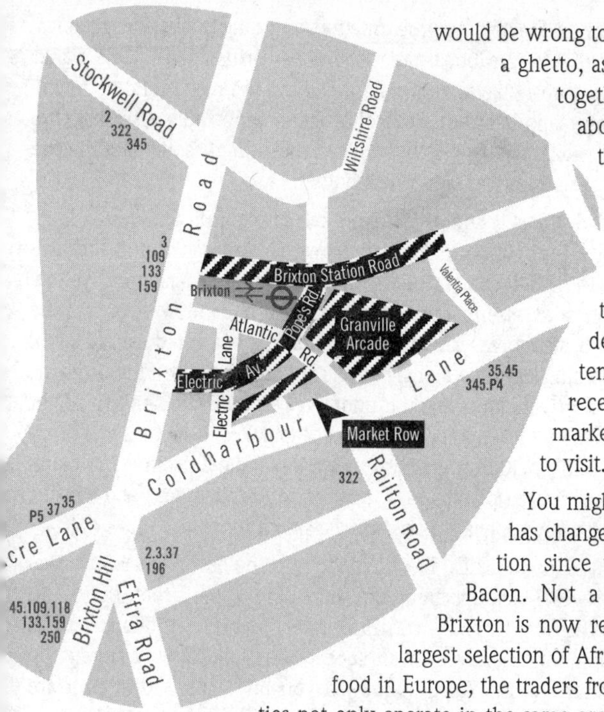

You might think the market has changed out of all recognition since the days of Bertie Bacon. Not a bit of it. Though Brixton is now reputed to have the largest selection of African and Caribbean food in Europe, the traders from these communities not only operate in the same arcades and streets as their 1930s predecessors, they have also kept the jolly, noisy atmosphere and the unashamedly carnivorous feel of the place.

Electric Avenue

Built towards the end of the 1880s, Electric Avenue was one of the first shopping streets to be lit by electricity. The road curves round elegantly, giving a fine view of the late-Victorian housing. But while the market is on, architecture takes second place. Stalls are on the righthand side as you walk up from Brixton Road. They compete for attention with a varied collection of lock-up shops. A crowded pavement separates the two sets of traders. Standard fruit and veg is sold at the first stall. Then come some satiny women's clothes. It's not long before you come across the first stall of African and Caribbean goods, which contains a fine collection of brightly coloured African tops (for only £7.99), plus some jewellery. A nearby stall has a mix of African-made kitchen equipment and foodstuffs: large wooden pestles and mortars are displayed alongside bags of yam flour and contorted black segments of dried fish, kept in plastic bags.

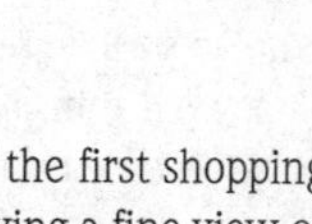

Many of the barrows on Electric Avenue are stocked with fruit and vegetables. There's a good mix of Afro-Caribbean and traditional British stalls. One trader might have plantains, yams, guavas and red-hot chillies; the next could be selling spuds, apples, cabbages and beetroot. Several of the lock-up shops also sell Afro-Caribbean fruit and vegetables, along with spices and tinned foods. Despite the variety and number of stalls, prices aren't rock-bottom.

Music is never far away. Classic soul tracks blare out of one fruit and veg lock-up, while a butcher plays Jimi Hendrix. A small crowd is gathered round the fish-monger's, viewing the milk fish, butter fish, blue runners, snappers, yellow croakers and talapias. Just one such shop with half this variety is more than most British towns can muster; Brixton has nearly a dozen of them. The remaining barrows along Electric Avenue sell the type of goods found at a thriving local market: underwear, shoes (women's in bright red or dazzling white), haberdashery, cheap cakes, biscuits and drinks, electrical stuff (including watches, batteries, radio-cassettes and blank videos), toys, potted plants, bags, fruit and nuts, bedwear and towels, sweets, curtain fabrics, headscarves and hats with fur trim.

Along with Brixton's indoor arcades, Electric Avenue is the best place to buy offal and halal meat. At several lock-ups along the south side of the street, there's an awesome display of carnage. Unbleached tripe—rarely found in Britain and great when simmered for hours in, say, a bean stew—hangs like grey dish-rags on butchers' hooks. It only costs 79p a pound—if you buy 10lb. Cows' feet are plentiful, both fresh and singed, while lungs are 49p a pound. At the back of one lock-up, a gang of butchers are busy chopping oxtails, their heads knocking into a dangling row of pallid, plucked chickens (boilers sell at two for £2.50). Vegetarians who've survived thus far would surely blench at the mysteriously named 'abbadi', sloppy red things in a bowl. It is a mark of how divorced many British meat-eaters have become from the food production process that they would do likewise.

Pope's Road

There's a brief hiatus in the proceedings as Electric Avenue hits Atlantic Road. It was here that the market started in the 1870s, but stalls were banned from Atlantic Road some 70 years ago because of the obstruction to traffic. However, the beat soon picks up again as you cross over Atlantic Road to Pope's Road and hear the thud of reggae coming from a clothes stall. The road curves round a Victorian railway viaduct as trains thunder overhead. The claustrophobic atmosphere at street level is intensified by stalls packing both sides of the narrow thoroughfare. No car could get through here during the market, even if allowed.

There's a couple of traditional fruit, vegetable and salad stalls along the road, plus a brace of florists, but otherwise there's little fresh produce on this stretch of the market. Near one of the railway bridges, a couple of chaps deal in herbal potions and drinks. It's an intriguing stall, decorated by strange cacti leaves hanging from the barrow. Come here for your Jamaican sorrel, dried peppermint leaves (to make tea), and 'constitution bitters'. Opposite is an Afro-Caribbean food stall, mainly stocking tins and jars. A jar of seasoning for jerk chicken shares barrow space with a collection of fizzy drinks imported from Jamaica. Try a can of the banana-flavoured drink.

New clothes account for many of the stalls. Here you can restock your wardrobe with underwear, hats, socks, trainers, jeans, leggings and shirts. One stall has a batch of what look like shop seconds; they're new, but they're crumpled. If you're after a bargain, wait for Brixton Station Road. Further along is a barrow completely overwhelmed by the mass of net curtains piled on it and over it. Look carefully, and you can just make out the head of the stallholder peering from within. At a nearby hair accessories stall, there's the opportunity to stop and have an ear pierced for only £4 including the stud. I see no takers.

Other stalls worth making for are an old barrow full of haberdashery, and another laden down with sunglasses and good-value watches. Toys, electrical bits and bobs (including Walkmans), bedlinen and shoes also pop up on Pope's Road. A couple of traders sell household essentials. One has a good choice of kitchenware, including wooden spoons and sharp knives; the other stocks king-sized Rizla cigarette papers next to the Camay soap—this is Brixton, after all.

Brixton Station Road

The market spread into Brixton Station Road in the 1920s, when stallholders were removed from Atlantic Road. In market terms, it is a road of two halves. The stretch running east from Pope's Road to Valentia Place is full of secondhand goods, both on stalls and in lock-ups under the railway arches. A score of temporary stalls are crammed with good-quality, cheap secondhand clothes and shoes. The garments—dresses, jeans, army-surplus clothing, suits, denim jackets, leather jackets, shirts, overcoats—are hung on rails rather than dumped on tables. Clothes aren't called 'retro' or 'antique' here; they're just secondhand and inexpensive. Lee jeans in reasonable condition cost £3. Among the large stock of suits there's a natty pinstripe two-piece on sale for a measly £5. After I try it on, a stallholder comes to unruffle my coat collar with all the suavity of a Savile Row tailor. Why don't City stockbrokers shop here? Other stalls contain old electrical equipment (including Black & Decker power tools and hi-fis), boots, and a rather bedraggled wig. There's even a wedding dress.

The first lock-up has the sort of stuff you might find in Brick Lane—all manner of junk. Secondhand clothes, old washing machines and cutlery help fill the space. Under the next railway arch are old cassette tapes, shelves of books (some worth perusing, some not—all cheap), a rail of clothes outside for 50p each, and a collection of belts. A sign within reads: 'Pinchers will be nicked. Signed, The Gaffer.' A tinny old stereo outside is playing rock and roll. The third lock-up contains thousands of records organized by type of music: soul, hip-hop, garage. All LPs cost £2 each, 12-inch singles £1, 7-inch singles 50p. Hard-up young bohemians, both black and white, frequent this stretch of the market.

Turning west onto Brixton Station Road from Pope's Road, you'll find mostly new goods. The premises under the arches this side of the junction have been converted into shops and the Max Snack Bar (*see* below). A few of the stalls sell food. One has eggs, another fruit and veg. An Afro-Caribbean trader sells packaged food such as fried chicken mix, escovitch marinade for fish, hot sauce, and tins of pigeon peas. He also has the drinks Jamaican sorrel and Irish moss. This stretch is the site of Brixton's only organic food stall. The produce is mostly British—English apples and potatoes—but there's also some fresh ginger and alfalfa sprouts. Another trader sells cheap tins of food, cans of drink, and sweets.

At one stall there are some quite beautiful African crafts, including long, spindly carvings of women. Next to it, a man is selling all sorts of joss-sticks and pots to stick them in. Then comes a haberdashery stall, followed by traders selling jungle and hardcore bootleg tapes. Household and electrical goods (such as telephone extension wires), shoes, watches, designer jewellery and crystals, polyester skirts, blouses and dresses (many in scarlet or black), and toiletries are also sold along this section of the market. A couple of the clothes stalls are worth scanning. One has tartan trousers for women; another specializes in vibrant hand-knitted woollen hats. The stallholder is busy working on her next creation. There's also a children's-wear stall.

Further hints that gentrification is nibbling at the edges of Brixton can be found at the pot-plant stall, which does a good line in yuccas. But the joyous celebration of Afro-Caribbean culture still holds sway. The sounds of a steel band can be heard at the cassette, CD and video stall (which also stocks African, country, and 1950s music). Near the junction with the Brixton Road, at the end of the market, there's more music: tapes of reggae toasters from live gigs are for sale. As the mega-amplified MC hollers his head off, the three stallholders gyrate in time.

Market Row

Entrances on Atlantic Road, Coldharbour Lane and Electric Lane.

Brixton's two indoor arcades are inseparable from the market. In both Market Row and the Granville Arcade, the music, crowds, aromas and tumult of the street continue indoors. Both halls date from the 1930s and contain permanent kiosks and lock-up shops arranged in avenues. Astonishingly little has changed in the structure of the arcades since they were built. Several lock-ups still have shelving reaching the ceiling, thwarting any attempts at self-service. But on the shelves, the bully beef and tinned carrots of 60 years ago have been replaced by jars of palm oil or tinned callaloo (the green-leafed tops of yams).

Brixton market

The smaller of the two arc-ades, Market Row holds a fine array of household essentials together with fresh and preserved foods. Tea towels cost two for a pound at the discount household goods store, while the haberdashery stall has an abundance of buttons, some of them garishly gaudy. Several businesses sell African fruit and vegetables, and there's also a black haircare salon and a store full of bright material and African costumes.

The pet stall is worth investigation. As well as a wide choice of petfoods, it contains a multi-storeyed collection of fish tanks. Within are both commonplace and exotic species. For £15 you can buy a piranha which, unsurprisingly, has a tank to itself. Out of harm's way, two tanks to the left, is a small talapia. At a nearby stall, the elder brethren of the talapia can be found, moist and fresh, on a fishmonger's slab. Fresh cuttlefish, salted mackerel and salt cod are also sold at this excellent stall. **Blacker Dread**, a record store, graces the Coldharbour Lane entrance to the market. It's good for US and Jamaican imports and, though specializing in black music, also has a Jim Reeves record on display.

Granville Arcade

Entrances on Atlantic Road, Pope's Road and Coldharbour Lane.

Cheerful reggae blasts out of **Crystal Records**, at the Atlantic Road entrance to the Granville Arcade. It helps set the rhythm to the hubbub within. The Granville holds a similar variety of goods to Market Row, but it's bigger. Built in 1937 and painted mostly yellow, it is divided into half a dozen avenues, with lock-ups on either side.

There's a big queue at **Trinder's**, which is divided into a butcher's and a fishmonger's section. The fish are the attraction: customers can hardly keep their eyes off the display of salted mackerel, glisteningly fresh butter fish, salmon heads, crabs and raw king prawns. A couple of lads weave through the queue, full of vim and singing 'Hoo, wheeee!'

It's worth inspecting all the fish stalls at the Granville —they're among London's best, full of a bi-cultural mix of North Sea and Caribbean species. Atlantic blue crab, silver fish, jackfish, pollock, talapia, mackerel, cod (both fresh and salted) and yellow snapper are just some of the varieties on the slabs. The arcade is also a good place for halal meat, especially offal, sold by Asian Muslims to mostly Afro-Caribbean customers. Goat's tripe, ox lungs (lights), sheep's heads and entire chickens are among the delicacies on display. You'd be hard pushed to find pork, but **Woolgar's Bacon** stall has every conceivable cut of bacon, starting with off-cuts at £1.20 a kilo. Several lock-ups sell tinned provisions and spices along with the fresh produce, and there's also a couple of Caribbean bakeries. Try a freshly made pattie.

Several more of the Granville's businesses cater for the cultural and sartorial tastes of Brixton's Afro-Caribbean locals. **NAP Enterprises** is one of the best places for African-style dresses, with a number of colourful tunics on display. There are also places to buy the raw materials for clothing. At **Vicki's Fashion and Fabric** stall you can choose your material and have it made into a garment. But the biggest choice of materials is at **Nasseri Fabrics**, which has a particularly colourful display. More spiritual concerns are addressed by the **Bible Centre & Gospel Music Centre**, which stocks a range of books, records and cards with a religious theme. Evangelical music is played within.

Try to visit the **Wig Bazaar** on 3rd Avenue, with its staggering variety of glossy black, red, yellow, brown and orange hair extensions, hanging like trophies on show. Prices are in the region of £25. The Granville also contains a black haircare centre, and a couple of boutiques run by young women of Afro-Caribbean orig'n.

But it would be a mistake to think that only Caribbean and British goods are to be had. A couple of the best groceries are run by Africans. **Ghana House** must have more than 10 types of salted and dried fish, some looking as though they've been washed up on a beach. It also sells chewing sticks (resembling the stalks of ice-lollies), bambara beans, powdered okra, tins of mentholated dusting powder, and beautiful wooden eating bowls for only £4.50. Opposite are the premises of the **Uddin Brothers** from Sierra Leone. A scrawled sign above the mass of produce reads: 'We sell fish, frozen cassava leaves, potato leaves, sawa sawa, crain, greens and fufu.' One of the jolly bunch of lads serving wears a colourful Islamic hat.

And goods from North Africa form the bulk of the stock at **Jordashe Enterprises**, also in the Granville Arcade. Here you'll find couscous, *tajines* (pots used for Moroccan stews of the same name), and tins of *f'ul medames* (broad beans with garlic and lemon juice). Next door is a butcher's which continues the theme, selling *merguez* sausages.

It is sometimes easy to forget that the West Indies aren't far from the coast of South America. But the connection is made here, both at **El Pilón Quindiano**, a Colombian café and restaurant selling snacks such as *arepas* (cornmeal buns) and *empanadas* (pasties stuffed with chopped meat, eggs and olives), and a nearby butcher's where the price list is in Spanish.

Back out on the street, the noise seems even louder. A train rumbles over the dark Victorian viaduct, drowning for a moment the thumping of the reggae. And as you walk away from this astonishing market, the syncopated rhythms mingle with a speech of Louis Farrakhan, being played at full volume in a hairdresser's shop.

Nearby cafés

John's Café (53 Brixton Station Road) is popular with young locals. It sells fry-ups and the usual caff fare. **Max Snack Bar & Café** (under a railway arch at 18 Brixton Station Road) has Portuguese *petiscos* (like tapas) such as green soup, boiled salt cod, and fried squid at £2.50. **Grits**, at 1 Brixton Station Road, is a take-away place with a few stools within and a notice declaring: 'Swearing and cursing is offensive, please leave them outside.' It sells uncompromising Afro-Caribbean food, including cow's foot soup, mutton curry, ackee with rice and peas, and jerk chicken, or snacks of fish fritters. The **Jacaranda** (11–13 Brixton Station Road) is probably the most amenable café in Brixton. It's open all day, and there's a constant bustle of young Brixtonians; the food goes from jollof rice with chicken and hot pepper sauce to salads and sandwiches. **Pizzeria Franco** is an immensely popular pizza café in Market Row, with tables set out in the avenue. On a Saturday lunchtime, queues stretch outside its doors. Also in Market Row, **Kim's Café** serves liver and bacon and breakfast fry-ups, while **Café Pushkin** is an altogether trendier coffee spot.

Earl's Court

Address: car park off Seagrave Road, SW6, ✆ (01734) 451799.

Public transport: ⊖ West Brompton; buses 31, 74, 190, C1, C3.

Opening hours: Sun 10am–3pm.

Best time to go: midday.

Car parking: there's a pay-and-display car park next to the market, though you should be able to find free parking on a side street.

Main wares: new clothes, electrical accessories, Arabic goods, bags, tools, watches.

Specifics: children's wear, cheap blank cassettes and video tapes, Islamic prayer mats, falafels, olives.

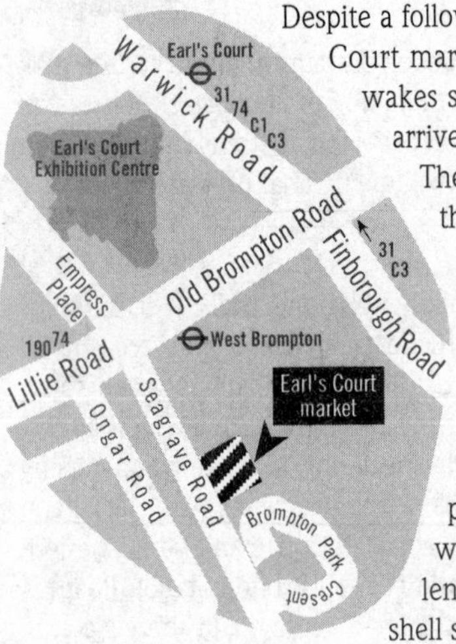

Despite a following among the local Arab community, Earl's Court market has little of the pzzazz of the kasbah. It wakes slowly with a Sunday morning yawn; traders arrive in dribs and drabs, some not until 10.30am. The number of stalls varies through the year, but there are usually about 50 set up in the middle of the vast car park that serves the Earl's Court exhibition centre. During a big exhibition, the market is closed, so it's best to check with the organizers, Hughmark International, a few days beforehand.

Many traders sell clothes. These vary from pastel-shaded nighties and capacious bras wafting in the wind, to checked shirts, full-length coats, jumpers with sequins attached and shell suits in lurid colours. There's a good choice for children. One stall carries a range of clothing from baby-grows to little anoraks; another has frilly, doll-like costumes destined to get ravaged by toddlers; two more specialize in natty little shoes and boots; and another couple have run-of-the-mill dolls, police cars and toy pistols.

Goods common to the newer breed of Sunday markets are plentiful: handbags and suitcases, towels and duvet covers, watches, tools and electrical accessories (including good-value blank videos), rugs, perfumes and curtain material. You'll also come across a few dabblers: part-time traders who buy up job-lots of disparate goods in the hope of making a profit on a Sunday. On one stall is a collection of cod liver oil tablets, Lego sets, condoms and Trivial Pursuit games.

The small band of customers who use this market are mostly local residents. Some of them are Arabs, and the presence of women wearing yashmaks and men in headscarves and robes lends Earl's Court market some colour. A small clutch of stalls has a direct relevance to this community. A falafel stand provides vegetarian fast food, while a nearby trader sells a range of olives, capers, olive oil and nuts. With the sole exception of a burger van (which also has bratwürst and liver and bacon), these are the only food stalls at the market.

But the most fascinating of the Arabic stalls stocks a wide array of Islamic and North African goods: mosque-shaped clocks, Arabic versions of films on video, prayer mats, teach yourself Arabic books, and even compasses to find the direction of Mecca. As a family inspects these wares, the father crouches down and pulls at the hem of his daughter's dress. It has risen a fraction and she is displaying an inch of ankle.

Though it's only worth coming here if you're in the vicinity, Earl's Court is one of those markets where you'll get as much enjoyment from perusing the customers as from scrutinizing the goods on offer.

Nearby pubs

The **Prince of Wales** at the corner of Empress Place and Lillie Road (opposite Seagrave Road) is a Chef & Brewer pub serving Sunday roasts. A couple of doors to the east on Lillie Road is the **Imperial** pub, which opens for fry-up breakfasts from 8am to 10am on Sundays.

Hildreth Street

Address: Hildreth Street, between Balham High Road and Bedford Hill, SW12.

Public transport: ⊖/⇌ Balham; buses 155, 315, 355.

Opening hours: Mon–Wed, Fri, Sat 9.30am–5pm; Thur 9.30am–1pm.

Best time to go: Saturday.

Car parking: there's a free car park off Balham Station Road to the south of the market.

Main wares: fruit and vegetables, flowers, household goods, packet foods.

Specifics: Caribbean fruit and vegetables, Italian packet foods.

Barely 50 yards long, Hildreth Street has been the home to Balham's market since 1903, when traders were swept off Bedford Hill, where they had been operating since about 1900, to make way for trams. Now pedestrianized, it's an odd prong of a road, lined by four-storey gabled red terraces that might seem elegant were it not for the jumble of activity taking place at ground level.

About 18 stalls are constructed on both sides of the road on a Saturday. They complement Hildreth Street's collection of useful small shops—a well-stocked fishmonger's, a halal butcher's, an Afro-Caribbean baker's, a Caribbean food shop, a black music store and a caff. Fresh fruit and vegetables are the main commodities. Prices, though they knock spots off those at local supermarkets, are generally higher than at Brixton or Tooting. About half a dozen stalls specialize in the usual potatoes, cabbages, apples and oranges, perhaps with some Brazil nuts and walnuts in winter. Because of Balham's sizeable Afro-Caribbean community, however, you might also find the odd mango or even some prickly pears. Two black stallholders concentrate on West Indian produce: yams, plantain, green bananas, coconuts, tinned ackee, and bottles of sarsaparilla and pineapple syrup.

Most of the remaining pitches have the type of goods regularly seen at local markets. There's a cut-flower stall; a particularly abundant household-goods pitch with swing bins, brushes and mops as well as the usual toiletries; a greetings-card seller; stalls with eggs, socks and underwear, net curtains; and a dealer with a mix of cushions, rugs, shirts, gloves and umbrellas. More unexpected is the packaged food stall which, along with peanuts, biscuits and sweets, also sells luxury Italian foods, such as olive oil, amaretti and *panettone* sponge cake.

The High Street, once part of the Roman Stane Street which ran from London to Chichester, is now Balham's main shopping thoroughfare. A few independent shops—a halal butcher's here, a discount jeweller's there—find space among the chains.

Balham Continental market, a small indoor concourse occupying a dilapidated building opposite Hildreth Street on Bedford Hill, finally closed in 1995 after more than a decade of decline. But it's still worth popping down Bedford Hill to view the grand and vibrant wall-painting of Hildreth Street market outside the Bedford Hill Gallery at No.50.

Nearby cafés and shops

M&M Bakery (11 Hildreth Street) sells various takeaway snacks, including ackee and saltfish, and Guinness punch. The coco bread is a wondrously fresh white bap, but eating it wrapped around a pattie (as seems the done thing) is rather like consuming a pastry sandwich. Opposite the bakery is **Dot's Café** (open 5.30am to 3.30pm), with fried breakfasts and roasts for lunch.

King's Road Antiques

Address: King's Road, SW3.

Public transport: ⊖ Sloane Square; buses 11, 19, 22, 49, 211, 249, 319, 345.

Opening hours: Mon–Sat 10am–6pm.

Best time to go: Tue–Thur, Fri afternoon, Sat.

Car parking: difficult nearby; try south of the river—Surrey Lane, off Battersea Bridge Road, has free parking and is 20 minutes' walk away.

Main wares: antiques.

Specifics: vintage clothing, theatre and cinema memorabilia, antiquarian books, art nouveau and art deco artefacts.

Chelsea's high street, the King's Road, dates back to the 17th century at least. Despite this, it has no long history of street trading. Until 1830 it was literally the king's road, a private thoroughfare of the monarch. Charles II travelled along it to Hampton Court, and it was George III's favourite road to Kew. Private citizens could only use it with a copper pass stamped 'The King's Private Roads'. Although costermongers did try to set up stalls on the road towards the end of the 19th century, they were forced off their pitches by local shopkeepers and went instead to North End Road (*see* p.194).

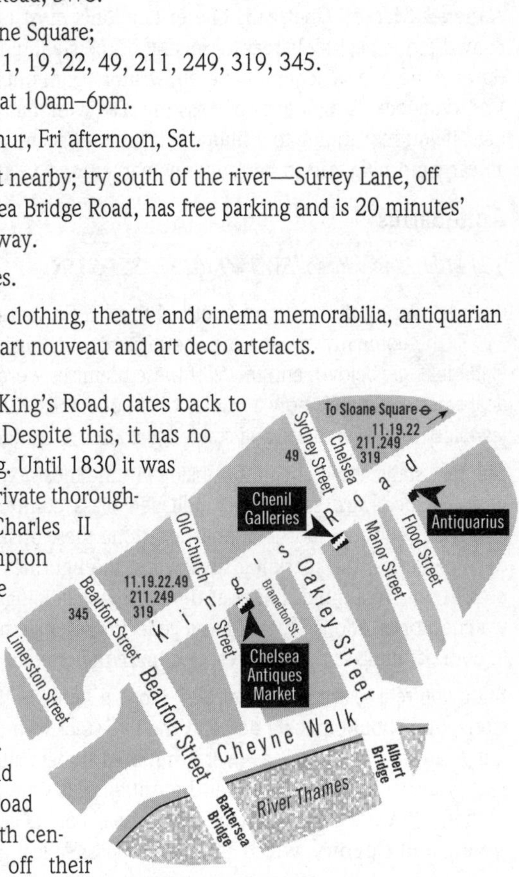

In the 1960s the King's Road gained international fame as the epicentre of swinging London. Dozens of boutiques were set up, mostly along the middle third of the road's two-mile stretch. The Rolling Stones and the Beatles came to be kitted out with psychedelic clobber, and there was a free fashion show as groovy young things paraded up and down the street. The King's Road maintained its position as the headquarters of hipness in the 1970s, when punk gurus Vivienne Westwood and Malcolm McLaren opened a clothes shop called Sex. (The latest manifestation of Ms Westwood's shop, **World's End**, is still at No.430.)

Many of the antiques shops that now litter the King's Road also date from the 1960s, as do two of the indoor antiques markets, Antiquarius and the Chelsea Antiques Market. Chelsea is one of London's most expensive districts, so don't come here expecting bargains. Several of the stallholders accept credit cards and operate the export scheme whereby visitors from outside the EU can claim back VAT on goods. Ask for a form. As is the case with many of London's antiques markets, if you're planning to visit on Friday, better go after lunch, as many traders pay an early morning visit to Bermondsey market (*see* p.146) to replenish their stock.

Antiquarius

131–141 King's Road, SW3, © (0171) 351 5353.

Opened during the antiques boom of the 1960s, Antiquarius quickly thrived. In 1977, the company owning the site expanded its business by opening the Chenil Galleries (*see* below), and in 1989 these premises were refurbished to look a good deal smarter. There's now a display of antique dolls, Russian icons and art nouveau jewellery in the window, and stained glass in the art deco style over the entrance.

The first stalls you'll encounter inside are the most expensive and intimidating. Goods are kept under polished glass counters, like museum exhibits. Even the floor is of polished stone tiles. Briskly peruse the art deco ceramics, the sparkling silverware, the figurines and the oriental pots. If you've a mind, linger at the stalls specializing in vintage wristwatches; or at Adonis, which has a collection of male nudes represented in both paintings and sculptures; or admire the oriental rugs.

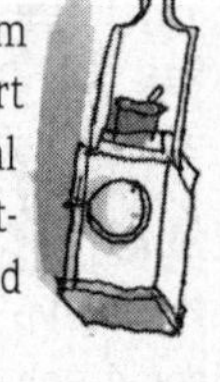

But if you're a seasoned market buff, more at home in the rough and tumble of the street, you should quickly descend the five steps into the main market hall. Here things are more relaxed, as over a hundred traders sit at their stalls, chat with a nearby dealer, or take a break at the Antiquarius Café (fried breakfasts, Brie sandwiches, and pasta al pesto—none of your spag bol in Chelsea). One of the highlights is **King and Country**, which deals in old polished leather, redolent of public school and Empire: bowls sets, shooting sticks, suitcases, boxing gloves and rugby balls. Here you can buy a 1930s picnic set, complete with wicker basket and enamel plates, for £485. Also look out for the antique pipes, some with their bowls intricately carved into faces; or the collection of prints, which goes back to the 17th century.

One trader specializes in Russian icons, but also deals in Russian and Polish military wear including ceremonial swords and daggers; another has a collection of Wedgwood lustre pottery from the 1920s. Yet others have linen baby clothes, or antique toys, or Victorian greetings cards. And do you remember those Noddy and Big Ears alarm clocks from the 1960s? Visit stand E3 to jog your memory.

Chenil Galleries

181–183 King's Road, SW3, © (0171) 351 5353.

Although this is the newest of the King's Road antiques markets, the site is steeped in history. It was the venue for the Chelsea Arts Club between 1891 and 1902, James McNeill Whistler and Walter Sickert being among the founder members. During the 1920s, John Barbirolli conducted concerts here. Antiquarius took over the building in 1987, but its history is recorded on a plaque, and in a fresco on the domed ceiling depicting, among others, the sculptor and designer Eric Gill, and a past member of the Chelsea Arts Club, Augustus John.

Best treat most of the first stalls inside the building as a gallery. There's some fine art deco and art nouveau work, particularly in ceramics, glassware and jewellery. I start off badly, asking the price of an old spoon. Peering disdainfully over his book, the dealer informs me the object was designed by Charles Rennie Mackintosh and costs £700—but for that price you also get a knife and fork thrown in.

Objets d'art, figurines and potential conversation pieces are a forte of the Chenil, but there are also some more everyday items such as old cigarette lighters (including a few enormous flame-throwers) and vintage clocks and watches. One stall is full of old books, but it seems the owner is either a polymath or cares little about what's between the covers; an elderly volume on commercial statistics lies between a biography of Wellington and a treatise on the formation of vegetable mould.

As at Antiquarius, the atmosphere becomes less reverential the further you proceed into the building. There's plenty of silverware and cutlery, old jewellery boxes and china, and even a mechanical bird in a cage. But the most fascinating of the stalls (of which there seem to be about 30) are the three that specialize in vintage clothing. One has a great selection of 1920s flapper dresses; a feathery light number will set you back £350. But a good-quality tweed jacket on the same stall is only £35. The second clothes stall has a couple of rails of garments, mostly post-1960s, plus top hats and handbags, while the third has trays of lace and embroidery, tiny purse-bags and sequinned, between-the-wars party frocks. At the rear of the market, hidden round a corner, is a rather trendy café with chrome chairs, black walls, murals of 1950s cars, milk-shakes, coffees and pastries.

Chelsea Antiques Market

245a–253 King's Road, near junction with Bramerton Street, SW3, © (0171) 352 5689.

There's a general rule on the King's Road: the nearer you get to Sloane Square, the higher the prices you'll pay. Chelsea Antiques Market, the farthest from said square, is the oldest, shabbiest and, to my mind, the best of the three indoor arcades. Here you'll find eccentrics and obsessive collectors with a genuine love of their subject, alongside the more hard-nosed dealers.

Proceed down the tatty old corridor and one of the first of the 20 or so stalls you'll encounter is **Madame Fey Campbell's** (open 1–6pm Mon–Sat)—quite an eye-opener. Madame Campbell's twin pursuits are mohair jumper-selling and clairvoyance. She operates from tiny premises which, along with the jumpers and the mumbo jumbo (parasols, fans; a big hexagon sign with an eye painted on it and the inscription: 'Fey Sutherland Campbell, highland medium seeress'), contains pictures of strapping lads playing bagpipes while sporting the Campbell kilt.

Opposite Madame Campbell's premises is the first of several stalls full of trinkets, decorative objects and glassware. Chess sets, candlesticks and little pottery things can be seen inside, while a silver cigar piercer (£24) is on display in the window. Another trader majors in jewellery, with a good line in cufflinks. There are also touristy trinkets such as little models of Grenadier Guards or London buses. Codswallop like this usually costs about 50p at Piccadilly Circus; here the trinkets are of 14-carat gold and cost £75. Light jangles around the stall, bouncing off polished silver and cut-glass chandeliers. A brass pestle and mortar is one of the few useful things inside.

Fear not, there is better to come. You can almost smell the greasepaint at **Casta-side**, a stall full of playbills, posters and theatre programmes. The dedicated owner, a quiet man (did he once tread the boards?), has filed each playbill by star (including Jonathan Pryce, Dulcie Gray, Frankie Howerd and Larry Grayson), and each programme by author. A copy of the programme for the 1945 production of Noël Coward's *This Happy Breed* at Hammersmith costs £1.50, while a playbill of the 1950s piano wizard Russ Conway, starring at the Birmingham Hippodrome, goes for £10. Don't miss the framed photos of the cast of Billy Petch's *Celebration*, a glittering, end-of-the-pier type show that flaunted the unspeakable fashions of its era (1971). Cineastes don't have to wait long for their turn. The next stall is packed with film posters, photos and postcards. Mugshots of the stars are meticulously ordered and labelled; less well organized are the dusty cardboard boxes crammed with film magazines. American movies are covered best, with photos ranging from Laurel and Hardy to *Thelma and Louise.* An original American poster advertising *Four Weddings and a Funeral* costs £6.50.

Apart from a chap who sells silver snuff boxes, and the stall of original watercolours and old prints (filed under titles such as 'Ladies Portraits', 'Victorian Romantics' and 'Crustacea'), the rest of the market is taken up by **Harrington's** antiquarian bookstore. Occupying three floors, it is particularly good for works on topography and travel; the titles are arranged by country. Other strengths include children's books and general literature, including a first edition of *Lord of the Rings.* One room is full of leather-bound collected works in pretty good condition, which makes the place look like the library of a stately home. But, as with such libraries, one suspects these books are meant more for display than for reading.

Nearby cafés, pubs and shops

The **Chelsea Diner** (98 King's Road) is one of the best budget diners in London. A favourite with students, it is open all day and serves popular international dishes (moussaka, curry, pastas, salads). You can even sit outside on a fine day and people-watch. The **Chelsea Bun Diner**, just north of the King's Road on Limerston Street, is another budget venue open all day. Cosy and with a cosmopolitan clientele, it specializes in huge, American-style breakfasts. The **Coopers Arms** (87 Flood Street, south of the King's Road) is a bar-style pub selling food and Young's beers. There are, of course, a plethora of antiques shops and boutiques along the King's Road, but if you want an expensive treat after parading along its length, visit **Rococo Chocolates** at No.321.

Merton Abbey Mills

Address: Watermill Way (opposite Savacentre), off Merantun Way, SW19; ✆ (0181) 543 9608.

Public transport: ⊖ Colliers Wood; buses 57, 152, 155, 200, 219.

Opening hours: Sat, Sun 10am–5pm.

Best time to go: Sunday.

Car parking: there's a large free car park right by the market, entrance via Watermill Way.

Main wares: crafts, clothing, toys, books, records, sheet music, flowers, jewellery, paintings, fast food.

Specifics: designer and ethnic clothes and jewellery, secondhand books, wooden toys, Indian pastes and pickles.

'Have nothing in your houses that you do not know to be useful, or believe to be beautiful.'

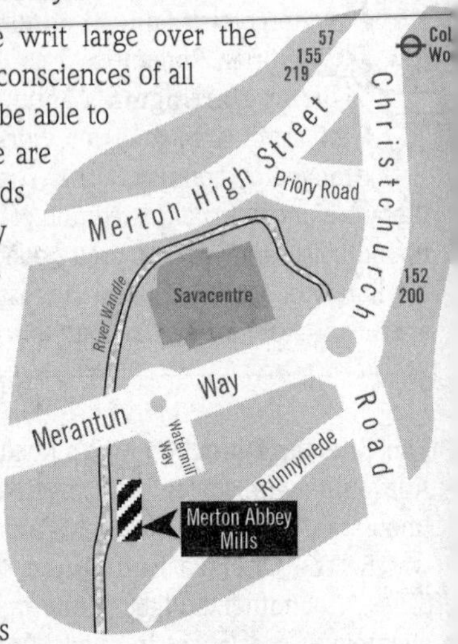

Perhaps William Morris's words should be writ large over the entrance to Merton Abbey Mills, to prod the consciences of all who trade there. Several craftsworkers would be able to walk underneath with head held high; there are some beautiful, practical and worthwhile goods sold here, many of them skilfully made by hand. But, as with all crafts markets, there's also cods-wallop: twee twaddle and hideous knick-knacks sold at ludicrous prices.

William Morris, the 19th-century socialist, poet, designer, and multi-talented craftsworker expanded his arts and crafts business to Merton Abbey in the 1870s. In this southwest London suburb he revived the art of tapestry weaving, experimented in the use of vegetable dyes and continued his wallpaper-designing work. Young workers were recruited to be trained in techniques that had all but died out. All were encouraged to use their creativity.

But though Morris was the major inspiration behind the arts and crafts movement, it was Arthur Liberty who provided more substantial assistance for today's Merton Abbey market. Liberty, a follower of Morris and founder of the famous Regent Street department store, bought this site by the River Wandle in 1904. He used existing buildings and constructed more to house his fabric-printing works. The half dozen or so structures were restored in 1989 and are now occupied by a restaurant, a café, a pub, several crafts shops and, at weekends, an indoor crafts market.

Though the market is held on both days of the weekend, Saturday trading is a small affair, and traders have to be lured to take a pitch with a 'two days for the price of one' deal. On Sundays, dozens more traders arrive and most pitches are taken both indoors and outdoors around the buildings.

It's 9.25am on a Sunday morning and many of the outside stalls are still being constructed. Craftsworkers are later risers than costermongers. A man with a wicker basket full of plant pots staggers by, followed by a woman wheeling a trolley on which a stripped-pine chest of drawers is precariously balanced. Nearby, a couple of lads are hanging their agate wind chimes around a stall. The tinkling sounds like thousands of jostling wine glasses. 'It's the wrong time of day for this,' remarks a trader at the vintage jeans stall, nursing a hangover.

There's more than a passing resemblance to Camden Lock, but everything is a little more manicured. Families from the sedate sitting rooms of Wimbledon account for many of the customers. Quite a crowd arrives on fine Sundays, but you won't get the irksome throngs that bedevil central London crafts markets.

The **1929 Shop**, a former print shop raised slightly above the other buildings, houses several businesses. There's the **Booktree Crafts** shop, which sells handbooks on techniques as diverse as needlecraft and working with paper. Some of the craftsworker's raw materials are also stocked: acrylic paints, brushes and the like. There's also a branch of the **Gourmet Pizza Company**; the **Therapy Room**, offering aromatherapy, massage and counselling; **Carina Prints**, with art reproductions, limited editions (including pictures of famous horse races), engravings and posters; a rather twee lace shop which also sells mobiles, picture frames and pillowcases; and **Charlie's Rock Shop**, with polished fossils, necklaces, shiny pebbles, and the aforementioned wind chimes.

Shortly before 10am, a knot of casual traders gathers round the entrance to the main market hall. The market supervisor then reads out numbers, as if calling a raffle. This is how pitch positions are decided. By now most of the regular traders are putting the finishing touches to their displays. A man surrounded by stripped-pine furniture adjusts a mirror; clothes sellers organize their piles of Andean jumpers, or vibrant-coloured skirts, or T-shirts emblazoned with African designs. One trader specializes in waistcoats, with styles ranging from suede, through bucolic-looking wefts, to vivid prints for children; another has a large collection of cheap CDs.

By 10.30am the stalls are all up and the punters are beginning to arrive. There's plenty for them to peruse at the outside stalls: chunky pottery cups and plates, flat caps and women's headgear (all looking homespun and utterly worthy), candlesticks, thick jumpers and rugged checked shirts. New Age sun and moon symbols are everywhere, on mobiles, ornaments, brooches and earrings. The market also attracts a few young clothes designers who bring their velvet and silk tops, their mini-skirts made from blanket material, and their floppy hats.

Alongside the market hall is a batch of shops that are open through the week. At weekends some place stalls outside. Haberdashery, art deco ceramics, pot plants, garden gnomes and ornaments in wood, pottery, stained-glass and metal are among their wares. One stocks a wide array of records, tapes and CDs: outside, albums are sold for £1, singles for 50p; inside are framed autographed photos of stars. Bonnie Tyler is worth £12, BB King £45, Ringo Starr £90.

A stall near these shops sells door stops in the shape of pigs, metallic money boxes in the shape of General Pershing, and unnervingly lifelike dolls. The stallholder approaches looking concerned. 'You're not nicking our ideas are you? People do, you know.'

Skip past more garden gnomes and you might encounter brightly and wildly painted wooden furniture, smartly upholstered stools (made to order), children's clothes (mostly in tartan) and a large stall full of beautiful but expensive wooden toys, from colourful little rocking chairs to penguins that totter down a slope. There are also a few more designer clothes stalls and a couple of clairvoyants: 'Janet and Avis invite you to come to the caravan.'

Near the eastern limits of the market is another Victorian structure, the **Coles Shop**. Picture framers work within, but part of the building contains **Kenny's Comics**. Secondhand books and annuals are displayed outside this store, while inside is a feast of comics, including editions of *Hotspur* and *Rover* from the 1940s and (not for sale) two editions of *Police News* from 1888 that graphically detail the Whitechapel murders of that year, committed by Jack the Ripper. The Coles Shop also contains the **Abbey Mills Gallery Café**, where coffee, lunches and cream teas are served amid prints, engravings, watercolours and cards. There are several tables outside.

The open-air stalls tend to vary from week to week, but there's always plenty of jewellery (both ethnic and locally designed) and clothing. Jumpers might come from the Himalayas, Ecuador, Peru or Wandsworth. Highlights might include homemade cakes, wooden chess and backgammon sets, embroidered waistcoats from Thailand, homemade salad oils (containing mixtures such as rosemary, garlic and lemon; or chilli, cinnamon and ginger), legitts (small wooden stilts for children), handmade lingerie, Kate Bramwell-Cole's gorgeous ceramic bowls, and Peruvian moccasins, ponchos and mirrors. Apart from the cakes and salad oils, there's not much food on sale, except at the occasional wholefood stall or Indian pickle maker's.

There are four other buildings in this odd little commune near the river. **The Apprentice Shop** now contains a large secondhand bookshop which puts much of its stock outside on fine days. There's a huge number of paperbacks, with authors ranging from Aristophanes to Barbara Taylor Bradford. Most cost around £1.50. Another bookshop also specializes in old sheet music, with thousands of popular and classical scores (a hardback book of Gilbert and Sullivan songs cost £7). **The Colourhouse**, one of London's oldest industrial buildings (dating from 1730), now houses the Colourhouse Theatre, where children's and family shows are staged through the day during summer weekends; ✆ (0181) 641 6880 for details. **The Wheelhouse** contains a watermill and information about the history of the site. There's usually a group of children watching the wheel spin, and then looking at the dials indicating the electricity generated. Occasional demonstrations—of traditional hand-spinning, for example—are also held in the Wheelhouse.

The remaining building holds the **indoor market**. It has space for scores of traders, with stalls neatly arranged in lines. Several sell similar goods to those you might find at Covent Garden or Greenwich, with plenty of jewellery, handmade greetings cards, candlesticks, oil lamps and cutesy pottery. Some natty handmade dungarees for children (£14) might catch your eye, or you might prefer a limited-edition print of photographer Mike Furber's British landscapes.

'Smoker, mate? Like a puff?' murmurs a bloke rather at odds with this genteel setting. He sells various mixtures of herbal tobacco. 'Just like the real thing—but legal.' Nearby is one of my favourite pitches, Mrs Monteiro's Goan food stall. She makes her own pickles, chutneys and pastes without artificial additives, and her vindaloo paste (£3) is the real thing: distinctly spiced and slightly vinegary, rather than the chilli-packed 'bet you can't eat this' slop found in most curry houses. Some of the more interesting stalls of ethnic goods are also inside the hall. One has Native American artefacts, including peace pipes and beads; another displays chunky Kenyan jewellery; a third has handmade recycled Nubian glassware from southern Egypt.

Here you can also have your future told by a tarot-card reader, find out the derivation of your surname, buy a pottery pendant imprinted with runes or a piece of toast turned into a clock, procure a leather punch-bag and boxing gloves, or order a wedding cake. There's a couple of antiques stalls full of old glassware and crockery, but most goods are new. Sadly, a stall of crockery in bright, original designs attracts less interest than a nearby pitch filled with dreary Victoriana.

Yes, it's all rather dignified at Merton Abbey Mills, without Camden's rough edges or Brick Lane's spontaneity. But mass-produced goods are, for once, in a minority here, so there are plenty of diverting wares to look at, even if you don't buy. What's more, the market makes a fine place for a family outing, sited away from busy roads and with plenty for children to enjoy, be it the toys stalls, the theatre, the watermill, or the faggots and mushy peas (*see* below).

Nearby cafés and pubs

Fast food stalls are grouped in a semi-circle at the western end of the market. Mexican tacos, Belgian waffles, hot doughnuts, Filipino or Thai noodles, Indonesian satays and British roasts are at the various pitches, but before midday it is only the egg, bacon and sausage stall that does good business. I usually plump for British food and receive a bending plateful of faggots, mushy peas, creamy mashed potatoes with onions, stuffing and lashings of gravy—all for £2.50. Smashing. Pity, then, that there seems to be nowhere to consume the feast apart from a disused railway sleeper in the car park.

Behind the 1929 Shop (*see* p.189) is the **William Morris** pub, with its patio overlooking the canal-like banks of the little River Wandle—a view only partially marred by the enormous electricity pylon opposite. The pub (open from midday on Sundays) has a choice of real ales, pub grub (steak and Guinness pie, vegetable Kiev), a Thai menu, and chicken nuggets and other stuff deemed fit for kids.

Nine Elms Sunday Market

Address: New Covent Garden Market, Nine Elms Lane, SW8 ✆ (01895) 639912.

Public transport: ⊖/⇌ Vauxhall; ⇌ Battersea Park; then buses 44, 344.

Opening hours: Sun 9am–2pm.

Best time to go: early for the secondhand bargains.

Car parking: free parking on site.

Main wares: clothing, tools, meat, fruit and vegetables, secondhand books, bric-a-brac and junk.

Specifics: look for bargains among the secondhand stalls.

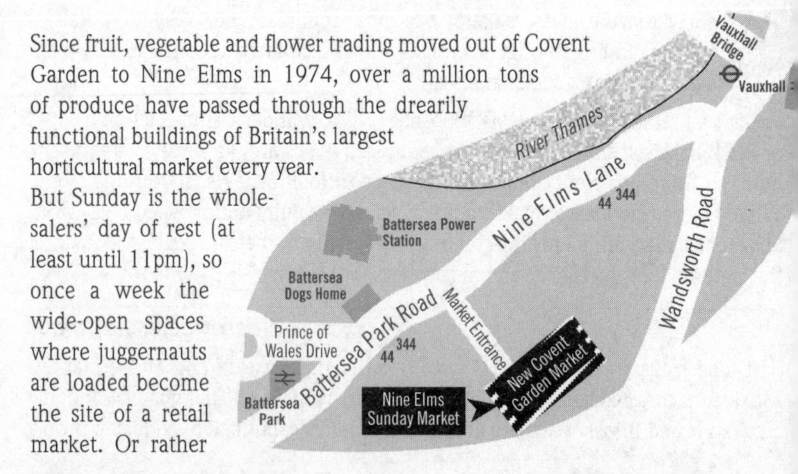

Since fruit, vegetable and flower trading moved out of Covent Garden to Nine Elms in 1974, over a million tons of produce have passed through the drearily functional buildings of Britain's largest horticultural market every year. But Sunday is the wholesalers' day of rest (at least until 11pm), so once a week the wide-open spaces where juggernauts are loaded become the site of a retail market. Or rather two markets. For as well as the dealers selling new goods, there's a car boot sale tacked on each week. Altogether more than 150 traders turn up.

The approach to the market can seem off-putting. Railway sidings, the famous disused Battersea Power Station, and Battersea Dogs Home are near neighbours, and the 68-acre site has been designed to ease the access of immense cabbage-laden lorries, rather than with any aesthetic consideration. Cars are ushered along concrete ramps and thoroughfares to be parked by the main market buildings.

Food plays only a minor role and, despite the location, there's only one fruit and vegetable stall. Here the stallholders tempt customers into buying at least 2lb of produce at a time, bellowing 'any scoop you like for £1'. The selection is fairly unadventurous. A big meat lorry turns up each week, and the butcher also sells in bulk, asking £5 for 4lb of pork chops, for instance. Otherwise, you might find eggs, a stall full of bread and pastries, and the ubiquitous burger van.

Though most of the stalls in the new goods section are typical of Sunday markets—sweatshirts, jumpers, sportswear, cushions, leather jackets, greetings cards, dresses, underwear, bedsheets and duvets, cheap CDs and tapes, car-cleaning stuff, pyjamas, training shoes and electrical goods—there is the occasional oddity. One stallholder has a bewildering variety of goods, stocked higgledy-piggledy: royal jelly and cod liver oil, tools, nails and screws, cassettes and video tapes, cheap oil paints for artists, and plastic dinosaurs.

Another trader worth searching for, if only to admire his stock, sells elaborate sequin-covered Indian women's clothing: a full-length dress costs about £80. A few stalls display children's wear, and you'll also find petfood, leather bags, jewellery, toys, boots and shoes, dried flowers, tools, lace, candles and aromatherapy goods. There are several household-goods pitches, including a particularly well-stocked stall full of unglamorous but useful bits and bobs, such as packs of indigestion tablets, umbrellas, and plastic food bags.

It is the 30 or 40 stalls selling secondhand clobber that hold most interest for the market connoisseur, however. The scope is wide: there's old clothing, scuffed suitcases, curled up shoes, golf balls. Occasionally you might be tempted to make a beautifully pointless purchase, perhaps a pocket diary that got wet in a flood and now has a nasty stain across half the pages—it only costs 10p, and so what if all the days are marked in Portuguese?

There's a mix of genuine part-time car booters and professional traders. One of the former has some fantastic bargains among his boxes of old books: eight Penguin Classic paperbacks in good condition (by Nabokov, Sartre and Somerset Maugham, among others) go for 50p. Of course, stock changes every week, so get ready to encounter anything: a collection of old toilets, army-surplus clothes, vast numbers of records, books, and even a stall full of press photos.

A couple of the shadier professional operators arrive in battered lorries and proceed to sell old televisions or vacuum cleaners from them. Fortunately they also carry generators, so you can test the stock before purchasing it. One trader has the nerve to offer six-month guarantees. Another likely lad is selling arson-proof letter boxes and some new books. His stock includes a pamphlet entitled *How I Cured My Duodenal Ulcer*. He displays it with his cookery books… Perhaps it *is* a cookery book.

As you trudge back towards the car park, loaded with bargains or baloney, just occasionally you'll spot an enormous carrot or a squashed onion lying on the tarmac, to remind you of the other market that takes place here the rest of the week.

Nearby cafés and pubs

Apart from the burger vans at the market, the only chance of food nearby is at **Tony's Café**, inside the market buildings. All the usual breakfast fry-ups are served. If you've a car (and it's best to arrive here in your own transport, as the nearest tube station is a long walk away), head west along Battersea Park Road to the **Legless Ladder** (at No.339), a pub with a clientele as varied as its (very good) food.

North End Road

Address: North End Road, SW6, ✆ (0171) 385 4054.

Public transport: ⊖ Fulham Broadway; buses 11, 14, 28, 74, 190, 211, 295, 391, C4.

Opening hours: *see individual markets for details.*

Best time to go: Saturday, early afternoon.

Car parking: there is pay-and-display parking off North End Road on Racton Road.

Main wares: **General market** fruit and veg, household goods, clothes; **Old Crowther Market** antiques, crafts, secondhand clothes.

Specifics: cheap fruit and vegetables; look for secondhand bargains.

General Market

North End Road (east side), from Walham Grove to Beaufort Mews, SW6. Open Mon, Tue, Thur–Sat 9am–5pm; Wed 9am–12.30pm.

Unlike Chelsea, which has always been associated with the nobs, Fulham was once a working-class area. And—despite gentrification during the 1970s and 1980s—

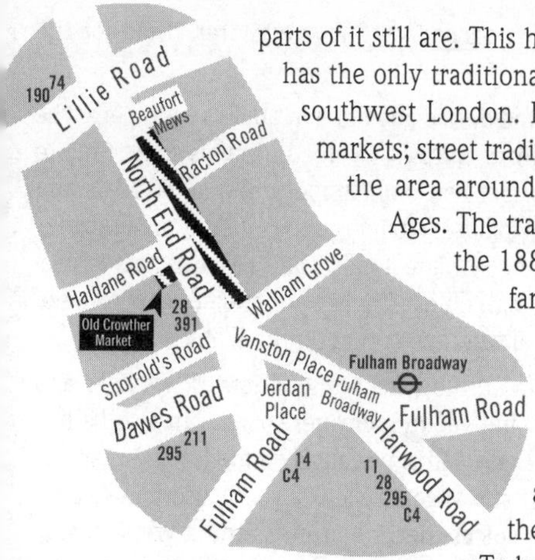

parts of it still are. This helps to explain why North End Road has the only traditional street market north of the river in southwest London. It is probably one of the city's older markets; street trading took place at Walham Green (now the area around Fulham Broadway) in the Middle Ages. The traders moved on to North End Road in the 1880s, spreading northwards almost as far as Hammersmith until 1927, when the council limited them to the area south of Lillie Road.

Well into the 19th century, Fulham was noted for its market gardens, and no doubt these once provided the traders with much of their produce. Today North End Road is still an excellent source of cheap fruit and vegetables, with traders in fresh food taking the lion's share of the 60 or so pitches. The **Seabys**—'pea and potato' sellers, according to the old decorative sign over the stall—are typical. Most of their stock consists of traditional British vegetables, but they have added okra, aubergines and fennel. **Shoey's** stall, farther up the street, specializes in salads (cucumbers, tomatoes and celery), but also has fresh herbs in pots, including basil, chives and parsley. Prices are keen. I snap up some green and red peppers for only 35p a pound, and discover two pounds of tomatoes going for 50p. Another salad stall has a boxful of beetroot, fresh from the boiler and still steaming.

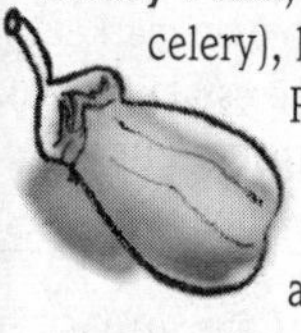

Traders take great pride in their stalls. Much of the produce is beautifully displayed, and at least one costermonger has the sign 'London's finest vegetable stall' hanging from his barrow. Judging by the queue, his customers agree.

For the whole length of the market, pitches are cut into the pavement so that trading doesn't hinder the busy traffic on the road. The space also gives stallholders enough room between the pavement and the road. There are always plenty of shoppers, as local stores complement the market well. One of the best butchers' is **Dickenson's** at No.365, which has wall-to-wall meat inside, and up to a dozen lads getting down to it with cleavers.

A woman emerges from one of North End Road's bakeries with a tray of bread pudding. She takes it to her egg stall (duck eggs £1 for half a dozen) at the southern end of the market and shares out pieces, still hot, with her neighbours. One of them runs a household goods stall full of small, useful things such as corkscrews, candles, sink plungers and washing-up brushes. The second half of his stall is packed with toys; children plead for the miniature Barbie dolls.

Several traders deal in new clothes. One does a good line in appliqué jumpers. The next is overwhelmed by soft furry things and best avoided; it takes some time to realize that these balls of fluff are in fact bedroom slippers. Women's coats and jackets, T-shirts and jeans, underwear, blouses, training shoes, tartan mini-skirts—there's little out of the ordinary. At one stall are T-shirts and baseball hats emblazoned with the crests of London football clubs. Chelsea, of course, gets pride of place, the ground being just around the corner on the Fulham Road.

A brace of stalls specialize in cut flowers, while toiletries, watches and watch repairs, net curtains, and vacuum cleaner spares can also be had along the street. But North End Road is principally a food market, and in addition to the wealth of fruit and vegetable stalls, you'll also find sweets, cakes and biscuits; a trader in spices, herbs and nuts; and a wet-fish stall with a good line in fresh boiled crab.

Old Crowther Market

282 North End Road (Studio One, © (0171) 385 8815). Open Wed–Sun 10am–4.30pm.

One trick in finding some of London's best antiques, crafts and bric-a-brac markets is to plump for the recently opened venues that have yet to become established. You can discount Covent Garden or most of Portobello Road for bargains, but you might just find something at the relatively undiscovered Old Crowther Market, opposite North End Road's general market.

Opened in May 1995, the market occupies the interior, the courtyard, the stables and the area beneath the colonnades of a crumbling but impressive mock-Georgian building, made from two villas built around the 1840s and set off the road. It's all rather like the Stables section of Camden market (*see* p.83), but without the incessant crowds and with a delicious sense of decayed grandeur. On its courtyard is a burger van with chairs outside, and a shop

the Old Crowther Market North End Rd

full of glassware and lamps. There's also a couple of stalls, one with shiny secondhand boots, the other with a collection of oriental artefacts including candlesticks.

Pass down an alley to the left of the building and you reach the **Secret Garden**. This is more of a rear courtyard and is dotted with stalls, disparate pieces of furniture, various garden ornaments and a rusty tangle of old bikes and their constituent parts. If you've a garden and a fork-lift truck handy, it might be worth perusing the stone cherubs; otherwise have a swift look round the stalls (containing, perhaps, a box of old LPs and some rather overpriced and tatty furniture) before making for the stables at the rear.

Inside these rickety premises is a cobbled floor, wooden roofing and about 12 stalls full of bric-a-brac, antiques and junk. Here you can get your old chairs upholstered, or buy old books, glassware, crockery, 78rpm records and a few grimy paintings. There's also some stripped-pine furniture.

Next to explore is the space beneath the colonnades (which were given to Mr Crowther by a Rothschild in the 1920s, I am informed). This is mostly given over to secondhand furniture of varying condition (a tatty old dresser costs £60), and also a collection of bidets (one for £50). In addition, there's a stall selling secondhand shoes and clothes.

Within the basement and ground floor of the house is a piecemeal collection of businesses down staircases and along corridors. It's a case of creeping and peering before entering. One cubby hole in the basement contains an aromatherapy den, full of essential oils, burners, glass candles, herbal apothecaries and an unpleasant cacophony of aromas; another holds oriental plates and venerable tea sets, books, old lamps, and huge ancient wirelesses tuned to the Home Service. Up a floor is a room packed with bric-a-brac and crockery, and another with secondhand jeans (Levi's £16) and leather jackets (£20–£50). The latter business also sells swim- and dancewear, cowboy boots and waistcoats.

The main section of the market is called the **Long Gallery**, up on the next floor of the building. Up to 30 traders operate in this ramshackle yet impressive room. At the far end is **Studio One**, with new paintings for sale and picture-framing undertaken. It's a wonderful setting for a studio, and the paintings bear close inspection. But just as diverting is the young man inside, dressed with excruciating formality in Victorian clothes and carrying a polished walking stick. He is probably an artist.

There are a few out-of-the-ordinary stalls in the Long Gallery, none more so than **Titanic**, which specializes in ocean liner memorabilia, including photos, menus, postcards, medals and paintings. A friendly woman who sells Andean artefacts and rugs chats to me about business. Few customers venture up here, even on a

Saturday. Carved African ornaments, silverware, jewellery, and a collection of old radios and record players also find space in the gallery, and there's a fascinating accumulation of old toys and children's annuals. At the opposite end to the art studio is a comfy-looking café with paintings on the walls, hot and cold snacks, and a laid-back atmosphere. Through the café is a room where Mrs Tina Stewart, clairvoyant and healer, operates. I do not enter her lair.

Nearby cafés and pubs

There's a couple of fish and chip shops along the market stretch of North End Road. Try **Owen & Hill's** at No.348, which is clean and has somewhere to sit. Another option is **Chapel Lafayette** (No.374), a New Orleans-style bar and restaurant, housed in a former church and open all afternoon. Traders drink at the **Jolly Brewer** (No.308), a cosy old pub.

Northcote Road

Address: Northcote Road, SW11, (0181) 871 6384.

Public transport: ⇌ Clapham Junction; buses 35, 37, 77, 219, 319, 337, G1.

Best time to go: Saturday.

Car parking: there's 30-minute waiting on the west side of Northcote Road; otherwise try side streets—a few have free parking, but most have pay-and-display machines.

Main wares: fruit and vegetables, fish, clothes, CDs, cassettes, antiques.

Specifics: flowers and foliage, salad foods, Afro-Caribbean produce.

The semi-gentrified districts of London are a joy. In the 1980s, houses in several areas that had traditionally been home to families of office clerks or factory foremen were snapped up by young professionals. By the time of the collapse in property prices of the 1990s, these districts had a noticeable but not overwhelming cluster of the new arrivals, now in negative-equity limbo.

The result at Northcote Road is a cosmopolitan, stimulating area and its markets reflect this diversity. The general market provides most daily essentials, while the antiques market stocks mantelpiece fillers prized by couples restoring their late-Victorian abodes. The new arrivals support a scattering of alluring luxury food shops, while local people with modest incomes keep the fry-up cafés, charity shops and cheap hardware stores in business.

Such neighbourhoods should be visited quickly, before the next boom turns them into ghettos of thrusting young executives, or the next recession clears out all but the discount stores.

General market

Northcote Road (west side), between Bennerley Road and Battersea Rise, SW11. Open Mon–Sat 9am–5pm.

Northcote Road and its market have a similar ancestry to several other shopping streets in London's suburbs. First came the railway station, in this case Clapham Junction, built in 1863 and now one of the busiest train stations in the world. Then followed the housing: grey-brick Victorian terraces were built all around the Northcote Road area during the 1870s and 1880s. Soon after came the market.

At first traders gathered on Lavender Hill, Falcon Road and St John's Road, as well as Northcote Road. But in 1910 they were evicted from St John's Road (where most of the dull high street chains, plus Arding and Hobbs department store, can now be found), and Northcote Road became the prime site. In recent years the success of the market has been helped not only by the influx of wealthy inhabitants, but also by the proximity of New Covent Garden wholesale market, which moved to Nine Elms in the 1970s. Northcote Road is now a healthy local market, with about 30 traders setting up stall on a Saturday.

The majority of traders here deal in fresh produce. A flower seller takes one of the first pitches at the northern end of the market. As well as the usual blooms, she stocks the dried and fresh foliage used to decorate fashionable Clapham homes. A nearby salad stall also has some upmarket touches, displaying lollo rosso and frisée as well as the traditional bunches of watercress. Vegetable stalls might have aubergines, artichokes or, very occasionally, wild mushrooms, as well as the more usual British crops; fruit stalls could have papaya, figs and coconuts alongside their grapes, apples and oranges. There's a couple of stalls specializing in West Indian produce, to cater for locals of Caribbean origin. Eddoes, soursops, green bananas and yams, together with tins of egg nog and ackee, are displayed at one pitch, while the other also has fresh herbs, plantain and impossibly large avocados—shiny as apples and big as grapefruit. West Indians also like to shop at the halal butcher's on the corner of Cairns Road, and at **Dunbar's** fish stall at the corner of Shelgate Road. Tuna, shark, swordfish, calamari, whitebait, soft roe, crab sticks, fresh boiled crab, cockles, salmon and trout make up the glorious display.

Other stalls sell cut flowers, clothes (including women's glitzy jackets and hippyish dresses), music (with 'any cassette, CD or video £1 only' in one box) and eggs. I'm pleased to see white eggs at this last stall—because of the ludicrous equation of health-giving properties with anything brown, they seem to have almost died out. As I prepare to have a bite to eat, a young child solemnly warns me not to go into one of the cafés: 'I had flies in my bread there.'

Antiques markets

155a Northcote Road, SW11, © (0171) 228 6850, and 70 Chatham Road, SW11, © (0171) 738 2896. Open Mon–Sat 10am–6pm; Sun 12 noon–5pm.

Ten minutes' walk south of the fruit and veg stalls is the main site of the indoor antiques market. It opened in 1986, occupying the ground and first floor of a Victorian terraced shop. In 1994 a smaller annexe was opened farther up the street, at the corner with Chatham Road.

A big advantage here is that you can be reasonably sure that all the stalls will be open, as traders co-operate in running the venture and look after each other's businesses on a rota basis. There's space for about 25 dealers crammed into the small building. To make more room, some pieces are kept outside in fine weather: an old corner cupboard, a child's ironing board, an enamel bread bin. Within are traders specializing in jewellery, glassware and art deco ceramics. Most, however, have a selection of goods, perhaps some silver cutlery, a few murky old paintings, the odd necklace or set of cut-glass drinking vessels, and various pieces of Wedgewood-like crockery.

Old adverts for cars have been mounted and are sold for about £10 by one dealer, while another's stock includes a faded box of pistol caps for children. In one corner is a collection of antique kitchenware. Near the stairs, an Ealing Cinema world is evoked by a box of postcards from the 1940s. Some have saucy seaside scenes on the front, with captions like 'I do wish I could see my little Willy.' Greetings are written on the back of several. In June 1948, Flo from Clapham received a card from Weston-super-Mare: 'The weather is grand. Love, Mrs Reed.'

Upstairs there's more silverware, jewellery and ceramics, plus **Otto's Café** with its menu of sandwiches, jacket potatoes, salads and espresso coffee. A trader tells me that Sundays are almost as busy as Saturdays, but on a Saturday afternoon there are mercifully few punters. More than 50 in here would cause pandemonium.

The new annexe to the market is even smaller. On the ground floor a few pieces of furniture (including a 1930s dining table for £225), some girls' annuals and a couple of linen boxes help fill the place. In the basement are rolling pins (£5–£10), a fine collection of antique fountain pens (a 1925 Waterman costs £225), and a stall called Panorama, where Chris and Vinny sell petrol cigarette lighters and powder compacts dating from the 1920s to the 1960s.

Though a notch above most bric-a-brac, the goods sold at both these sites tend to fall into the category of 'collectables' rather than that of expensive antiques. As one trader told me, 'You might find anything, from £1 to £500.' The polished presentation and hefty prices of Chelsea and parts of Portobello or Camden Passage are absent here, making browsing all the more pleasurable.

Nearby cafés and shops

There are several enticing food shops along Northcote Road. **Salumeria Napoli**, at No.69, is a good local Italian deli with own-made pesto sauces. **Dove's**, the butcher's at No.71 (established in 1889), has a fine stock of game in season and makes game pies to order. At No.64 there's a popular bakery called **Rae Ra El**. Afro-Caribbeans run the place, but as well as West Indian breads they bake focaccia and poppy stollen. **Hamish Johnston's** cheese shop, at No.48, has a range of British and Continental cheeses, plus extra-virgin olive oils and Welsh laver bread. Near the antiques market, at No.135, is the **Grape Shop**, with cases of vintage wines. On Saturdays it has a classy shellfish stall outside, with mouth-watering displays of oysters, lobsters and mussels.

Eating places vary from basic caffs to fashionable Italian venues. The **Northcote Café** (No.74) is open from 6.30am and serves fried breakfasts all day to stallholders. **Osteria Antica Bologna** (No.23) is a cosy Italian restaurant with a modish regional menu. It's open all day on Saturdays. The trendiest and most popular place to hang out at lunchtime is **Buona Sera** (No.22), a reliable and enjoyable restaurant with good pizzas, and tables outside for you to eye up the market crowds.

Tooting

Address: Upper Tooting Road, SW17.

Public transport: ⊖ Tooting Broadway;
buses 44, 57, 77, 127, 133, 155, 219, 264, 270, 280, 355, G1.

Opening hours: Mon, Tue, Thur–Sat 9am–5pm; Wed 9am–1pm.

Best time to go: Fridays and Saturdays.

Car parking: try the side streets to the north of the markets.

Main wares: fruit and vegetables, meat, fish, clothes, household goods, records and tapes, fabrics, furniture.

Specifics: Irish music, Afro-Caribbean foodstuffs, Sri Lankan food, petfoods, babywear.

Tooting remained a small settlement until relatively late in the 19th century. But soon after the London County Council was formed in 1889, it decided to turn the Totterdown area of Tooting into a housing estate. The district became covered in the suburban terraced houses which still provide homes to the customers of Tooting's two markets. These occupy almost adjacent indoor halls, both built in the 1930s off one of the borough's main thoroughfares. They look similar to the indoor arcades found at Brixton (*see* p.172), with fixed, lock-up stalls either side of a corridor, but trading is on a more modest level.

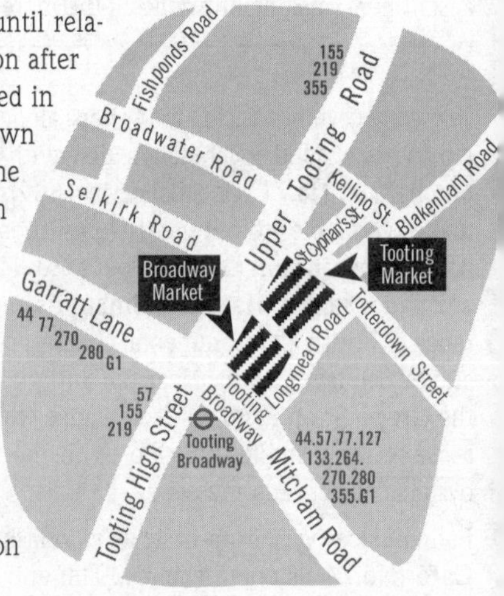

Today, Tooting is an appealing place, a typical London suburb but none the worse for that. You'll rarely find excesses of wealth or poverty, and there's a pleasing mix of communities—Afro-Caribbean, Irish, South Asian and English. Both markets reflect this, and provide a useful range of goods that undercuts the chainstores on Tooting Broadway and Mitcham Road and complements the collection of take-aways, Indian food shops and discount stores on Tooting High Street and the Upper Tooting Road.

Tooting Market

Entrance also on Totterdown Street, SW17.

I always like starting an exploration of Tooting's markets from this building, the farthest from the tube station, though only five minutes' walk away. And I always begin the adventure from Totterdown Street, partly because of the splendid name (would that there were a pub here called the Totterdown), but also to approach the market from a residential street. This makes it seem all the more part of the neighbouring community—a local treat.

Though the structure of the 1930 building is somewhat spare, all corrugated roofing and metal girders, the lock-ups within are colourful and brightly lit. Three of the best food stalls greet you at the Totterdown Street end. **Tony's Greengrocery** has a large stock of traditional root vegetables, oranges and lemons, but also a few green bananas and yams. Opposite, **Cut-Price Fisheries** has a wide choice of piscine creatures also aimed at Afro-Caribbean custom: yellow croakers, fresh tiger prawns and a huge tuna fish. At 5pm on a Saturday, a few local regulars gather by the stall hoping for a bagful of bargains. Next, the large butcher's shop usually has some goat's meat and oxtail (both often used in Caribbean cookery) among its stewing steak and loins of pork. But unlike the halal meat merchants of Brixton and Ridley Road, these butchers—a cheery gang of lads who heave great trolley-loads of carcases in from the street first thing in the morning—steer clear of cows' feet, goats' tripe and sheep's heads.

The 30-odd businesses at Tooting Market provide an exceedingly well-balanced mix of goods. **Grady's petfood** lock-up has its bird cages, dog baskets, budgie food and goldfish bowls piled seven feet high; **Mac's children's-wear** stall has baby clothes, rattles, bottles (and a forthright woman owner who saw off a shoplifter with a roar); there are cut flowers and pot plants, Afro-Caribbean haircare and hairdressers', and a women's-wear trader with a yen for polyester and sequins. Close to the corner of the L-shaped trading floor is a café where you can wolf down a fried breakfast, 'dripping toast' or meat pie while gazing at the wood-veneer walls.

Nearby is **Norman the Curtain King**, and **Express Key-Cutters**, which is also a locksmith's and stocks ironmongery goods. Football scarves, mugs and hats are sold at the stall which also specializes in 'Freedom for Tooting' T-shirts (after the 1970s TV sitcom, *Citizen Smith*), and less savoury garments emblazoned with 'British by birth, English by the grace of God'. Another lock-up will supply much of what you might need to equip a kitchen, including glasses, crockery, cutlery and swing bins.

The Irish music stall is a glorious oddity. As well as a fair collection of tapes of traditional Irish and country music, you'll also find a scattering of mementoes for homesick expats from the Emerald Isle: socks emblazoned with the Guinness logo, and portraits of Irish saints in glistening frames.

Stannards of Tooting stocks a similar array of meat to its neighbour round the corner, while a greetings card stall also has board games, jigsaws and stationery. Opposite, a man is standing on a table trying to sell some frocks. Here is a pro. His patter is ceaseless, and the small crowd of women gathered around never seems to diminish. There's a sizeable haberdashery stall nearby, if you prefer DIY garments.

Further on, a trader sells African and Caribbean foods, including a decent amount of fresh produce—*dasheen*, *cho cho*, breadfruit and sugar cane—plus a few drinks and tinned goods. The remainder of the market is taken up by a furniture lock-up, full of highly polished pieces; a secondhand bookstall dealing mostly in pulp fiction; **Gary's Galleries** with Gary's collection of shiny, cheap ornamental brassware; a trader selling handbags; and another selling women's coats. At the Upper Tooting Road end is a tobacconist (bag a box of snuff for 60p), and a bright and bustling fruit and veg pitch, where the traders sell their surplus off cheap at 5pm on Saturdays.

As you leave Tooting Market and emerge on to the main road, take a look at the building's art deco façade, which makes it seem almost like a cinema. But there's scarcely time to muse, as bellowing fruit and veg traders from both here and the Broadway market spill out onto the pavement, nearly colliding in the middle.

Broadway Market

Entrance also on Longmead Road, SW17.

The Broadway Market, built in 1936, is a little larger and a mite gloomier than its neighbour. It also duplicates several of the stalls of Tooting Market: there's a couple of large fruit and vegetable pitches, a butcher's (selling pheasants, in season), a hairdresser's, a florist's, a café (most adventurous dish: spaghetti bolognese), a fishmonger's and a haberdashery stall.

But many stalls are worth close attention. With luck, the Wickkamaratne family will still be selling their Sinhalese Sri Lankan foods. They started trading in 1995, stocking a variety of canned and bottled goods as well as Ann Wickkamaratne's homemade pickles, sauces, sambals (Sri Lankan relishes) and snacks. I can vouch for her fish patties (40p), packed with fish and full of flavour. Next time I'll try a watalappan (a rich, spicy egg custard).

There's also a better choice of Afro-Caribbean produce at the Broadway, with two well-stocked stalls. At one, the trader grins as I study a bottle of 'Atwood's physical vegetable laxative'. In front of him is a collection of sticks with what look like twirls of liquorice stuck to them. 'They're dried snails,' he explains. At the front of the stall, the seemingly mutant big brothers of these desiccated little lads almost fill a packing case. Land snails from Ghana, with their slimy feet as big as your tongue (from tonsils to tip) are a delicacy I've yet to try.

Dozens of African and Caribbean ingredients are sold here, including bright-red pigs' tails, soursop nectar, tinned ackee, a contorted mass of dried fish, yam flour, four species of hot pepper and eight types of yam. There's also a takeaway stall. Ashamed at my lily-livered refusal to invest in a land snail, I order a snack called *kenkey.* I am given a small package, heavy as a grenade and wrapped in maize leaves. Inside is a glutinous cornmeal paste with a sour lime flavour. Small wonder the woman who serves it is puzzled—'Have you eaten this before?' Fried fish, rice and beans, and fried plantain are some of the more manageable victuals sold here and, for more conservative diners, there's a hot doughnut stall and a shellfish stand at the market.

A few of the clothes stalls also veer from the norm. Keep an eye out for the Indian women's-wear stall and its striking *salwar khamese* robes. Block printing onto fabrics is also undertaken by this business. There are two boutiques run by Afro-Caribbean women and both have a forte in snazzy party clothes. Several other stalls are also aimed at the black women's fashion market. Two sell the beautiful, exuberantly coloured fabrics favoured by African women; another deals in wigs and hair accessories; there are also cosmetics and perfumery stands. But perhaps the most intriguing stall is **Just Nails**, which offers just that: false nails with names such as 'silk wraps', 'French tips' and 'extended wraps'.

Near to the biggest of the two fabrics stalls, **D.N. Fashions** is a black record specialist. Soul, reggae, roots and jungle CDs, records and videos share shelf space with, perturbingly, the BBC recording of the 1981 Royal Wedding. A similarly odd mix of goods is sold at a stall where pasta, eggs, herbs and spices are stocked next to artificial flowers and foliage.

Also worthy of mention at Broadway Market is the large and well-stocked discount stationery stall; a watch and clock vendor's; a wool stall; a hardware lock-up packed with cleaning fluids, vacuum cleaner bits, dustpans and brushes; and Tooting's best petfood store. This is divided into two. Part one contains livestock, including both tropical fish and goldfish (occupying three tiers of tanks), hamsters, several finches and budgerigars. Next door is an abundance of petfoods and accessories, from 'pussy pyramids' (for cats to scratch) and dog baskets, to books such as *Beginning With Snakes* and *Tarantulas and Scorpions.*

Whereas Tooting Market is L-shaped, the Broadway more resembles a Y. The remainder of its space is taken up with a cobbler's, a cheap packaged food lock-up, and traders selling rugs, leather belts, nighties, bags, shoes, towels, duvets, football pendants and strips, lingerie, greetings cards and party goods. There's also a computer games stall and a large shop, the **Wacky Warehouse**, which sells cheap electrical goods, CDs, kitchenware, tools and toys.

Both markets at Tooting have a fine, community feel to them. At 'knocking out' time on a Saturday, it's almost a local custom for a crowd to gather by the fresh produce stands, waiting to pounce on a bargain.

Nearby cafés and pubs

Harrington's pie and mash shop, just across Upper Tooting Road on Selkirk Road, is a peach among pie shops, open since 1916 and with prices among London's cheapest. Tooting is also a great area for South Indian food; two of the best restaurants, both low priced, are **Shree Krishna** (192–194 Upper Tooting Road) and Jaffna House (90 Tooting High Street), a Tamil Sri Lankan café. The **Castle** (38 Tooting High Street) is a large, friendly pub where Young's ales are quaffed in earnest.

Wimbledon Stadium

Address: Wimbledon Stadium car park, Plough Lane, SW17, ✆ (017268) 17809.

Public transport: ⊖ Wimbledon Park;
⇌ Haydons Road;
buses 44, 77, 156, 270.

Opening hours: Sun 9am–2pm.

Car parking: plenty of free parking in the stadium car park.

Main wares: clothing, tools, electrical goods, meat, fruit and vegetables, toys, bread, toiletries, petfoods, car accessories, greetings cards, tapes and CDs, sweets.

Specifics: football strips, women's outsized clothing.

Greyhounds bound around Wimbledon Stadium on weekday evenings; stockcars smash themselves to scrap on Sunday nights; but on Sunday mornings, the stadium car park is given over to equally entertaining—and only slightly less frenetic—activity as over 150 stalls are set up for trading.

As is the case with many of the newer breed of Sunday markets, cheap mass-produced clothing makes up a large slice of the wares sold here each week. Dozens of traders deal in jumpers and women's tops, and you'll have no trouble finding socks, underwear, shirts, women's jackets, skirts, new shoes and children's clothes. A few stalls have leather jackets, but not as many as you'll find at Petticoat Lane (*see* p.129) or Wembley (*see* p.109). Wimbledon does a better line in football strips, with most of the Premiership teams represented; several stalls also sell mugs, scarves and hats emblazoned with team names.

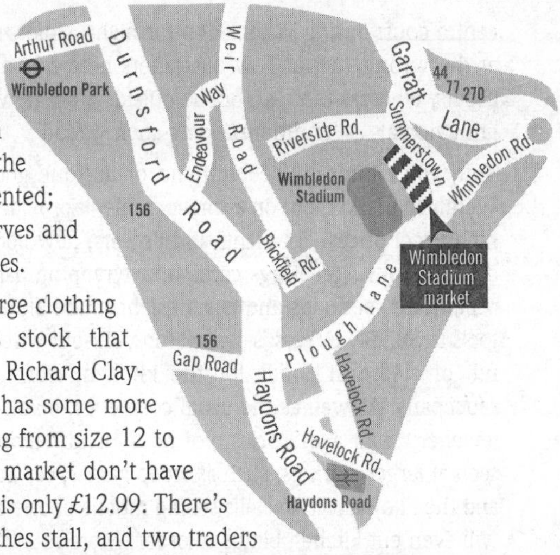

A couple of stalls specialize in large clothing for women. One, sadly, has stock that wouldn't look out of place at a Richard Clayderman concert, but the other has some more modish prints and frocks ranging from size 12 to size 30. Most jeans sold at the market don't have famous labels, but the going rate is only £12.99. There's also a good lingerie and bedclothes stall, and two traders who sell waxed jackets for under £20.

But the clothes stall with the most earnest group of customers sizing up its garments deals in imitation designer menswear. Calvin Klein, Ralph Lauren and Armani (long-sleeved grandad shirts for £15) all have their names displayed on the shirts. 'Guaranteed fakes', a scrawled notice proudly proclaims. Another stall, that must be equally unpopular with large fashion houses, sells fake perfumes. 'I smell like Opium' is one of a dozen or so signs written above the bottles. Each perfume costs about £3—a snip, if you can stand the whiff.

Food forms only a minor part of the market's business. There's a small collection of fast food vendors, with baked potatoes, ice-cream, doughnuts, hamburgers and salt-beef among the attractions. Away from the rest of the stalls is a shellfish stand with the usual crab sticks, winkles, whelks and cockles. If you're shopping for your Sunday lunch, look out for bargains at either of the two meat lorries: one butcher is trying to sell three large joints of Scotch beef for £12. There's a big stall of sweets and two bakery stalls, one with soda bread and bread pudding as well as more mundane loaves, the other full of doughnuts and cakes. Close by, a trader is selling nuts, biscuits, cheese (£2.20 a pound for mature Cheddar) and gruesome-looking sealed plastic packs of cooked meat. At the three large fruit and vegetable stalls, all the traders try to sell in bulk, tying up plastic bags full of produce and flogging them for £1.

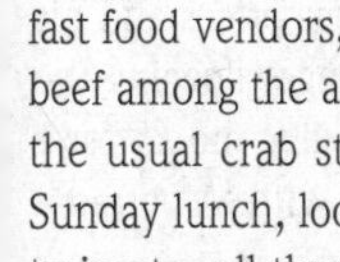

The social gap between punters that come to Wimbledon and those at Merton Abbey Mills (*see* p.187), little over a mile away, is almost as wide as the chasm between local dog-race enthusiasts and the select clique that occupies the centre court during Wimbledon fortnight. Unfortunately, one chap has set up stall at the wrong venue. Few customers here buy his olive oils, pistachio nuts and capers, whereas there's a queue outside a burger van which, no joke, advertises its grim victuals as 'traditional home-cooked food'.

You won't find any secondhand or antique goods at Wimbledon. Rather like Wembley market, but on a smaller scale, it provides high street goods at lower than high street prices. Pot plants and flowers, new books (mostly pulp fiction and children's books), greetings cards and wrapping paper, towels and duvets, garden ornaments, petfoods and curtain fabrics are all up for grabs. Two large stalls sell tools to Sunday DIYers: saws, clamps, chisels, wire brushes and paint sprays. One is full of electrical goods for the kitchen: irons, vacuum cleaners, kettles and saucepans. As well as the usual cosmetics, blank video and cassette tapes, cheap jewellery, hair accessories, pot pourri and handbag stalls, there's also stuff only seen at larger markets, such as video games, car accessories (seats, tow ropes, mats and the like), and two stalls selling mobile-phone carriers and batteries. One trader will even cut kitchen blinds to order. More mundane household goods range from light bulbs and soap to bin bags and bubble bath. The large video stall sells new feature films for £6.99, while children's films and 'pre-viewed' videos go for £4.99. There are two traders in tapes and CDs. One is geared to dance music and has two large speakers belting out chart hits. He also sells empty CD cases and cardboard slips for 45rpm records. The other has plenty of Irish music, but also soul and reggae.

A few traders sell toys: one gigantic stall occupies a juggernaut lorry at the northern end of the market. A crowd gathers as the seller goes through his spiel, with his helpers carrying large robots, Action Men and Tonka trucks out to the buyers. Towards 2pm the action reaches a climax as the toy seller drops his prices and his (amplified) voice has to compete with the lusty roar of a costermonger flogging the last of his produce off cheap. A mad cacophony ensues as 'Who'll give me £5 for a dinosaur? Come next week and it'll be twice the price,' coalesces with 'A pound a bag of peppers.'

As you leave, you might catch a glimpse through the stadium fencing of a sign urging owners to extract as much urine as possible from their greyhounds for chromatography testing. On Sunday mornings, the fun is in watching traders trying to perform the same task on the punters.

Nearby pubs

The **White Lion** and the **Plough** public houses are both opposite the entrance to Wimbledon Stadium on Plough Lane. Alternatively, if you've a car and it's a fine day, take the ten-minute drive westwards for a picnic on Wimbledon Common, a 1100-acre park which includes a restored windmill.

The following markets were too small or too distant from central London to include in the main body of this book. Opening times at the smaller markets might vary from week to week.

Barnet

St Albans Road, High Barnet, Middlesex, © (0181) 449 4092. Open Wed, Sat 9am–3pm.

An outdoor general market of about 40 stalls, with the emphasis on fruit and veg.

Battersea High Street

Battersea High Street, SW11. Open Fri, Sat 9am–4.30pm.

Only half a dozen traders turn up here, but most household essentials can be bought. From about 4pm, the large fruit and vegetable pitch sells off its produce for a pittance.

Bexleyheath

45 The Broadway, Bexleyheath, Kent, © (0181) 303 5455. Open Mon–Sat 9am–5.30pm.

A small general indoor market with about a dozen stalls.

Borough Green

Borough Green BR car park, Borough Green, Kent, © (0836) 284 213. Open end of March–Oct, Sun 9am–2pm.

An open-air general market near the centre of the village.

Other Markets within the M25 Area

Broadway Market

Broadway Market, E8. Open Fri, Sat 9.30am–4.30pm, © (0181) 672 6613.

Only a couple of traders turn up to this street market (held since Victorian times). There's usually a flower seller.

Bromley

Station Road car park, Bromley, Kent. Open Thur 9am–3pm.

A good local general market nearly 800 years old.

Camberwell

Ratcliff's Yard, 346 Camberwell New Road, SE5. Open Mon–Sat 8am–6pm; Sun 10am–3pm.

A dozen traders at outdoor stalls and lock-ups around a yard, plus a few more in an old stable. Goods sold: Caribbean food, bric-a-brac, and secondhand clothes, beds, electric goods and records. Sunday's market is smaller.

Catford Broadway

Catford Broadway, SE6. Open Sat 9am–5.30pm.

About 30 stalls on a pedestrianized street every Saturday. Traders deal in clothes, household goods, flowers and food (including Afro-Caribbean ingredients, and fish).

Chalton Street

Chalton Street, NW1. Open Mon–Fri 12 noon–2pm.

The descendant of the riotous Victorian Brill market now has only 25 or so stalls even on a Friday. Household goods, cheap tinned food and low-priced women's clothes are on offer.

Chatsworth Road

Chatsworth Road, near junction with Rushmore Road, E5. Open Mon–Sat 9am–4pm.

A Victorian market on its last legs; only a couple of stalls are set up on a Saturday.

Chiswick

Essex Place, off Chiswick High Road, W4. Open Mon–Sat 9am–5pm.

A half dozen or so wooden lock-ups, just off the High Road.

Chrisp Street

Chrisp Street, E14. Open Mon–Sat 9.30am–3.30pm, © (0171) 247 3952.

A fair-sized general market, partly of lock-ups, partly of stalls trading under a new awning in a postwar concrete square. Good for children's clothes.

Croydon

Outdoor market, Surrey Street, Croydon, Surrey, © (0181) 686 4433. Open Mon–Sat 8am–5pm.

A well-established street market with over 90 pitches; particularly good for fruit and vegetables.

Indoor market, 68–74 Church Street, Croydon, Surrey, © (0181) 666 0335. Open Mon–Sat 9am–5.30pm.

General indoor market, 70 pitches.

Dartford

Priory Centre car park, Dartford, Kent, © (01322) 343812. Open Thur 8am–4.30pm.

A large general market with about 300 pitches, many of them under a canopy.

High Street, Dartford, Kent, © (01322) 343812. Open Sat 8am–5.30pm.

An open-air general market with about 100 pitches.

Ealing

MGM Cinema car park, Uxbridge Road, Ealing, W5, © (01895) 812233. Open Tue, Sat 9am–4pm.

A general market with about 30 stalls. There's also a small antiques market held inside the local shopping centre on Fridays and Saturdays.

East Ham

East Ham Shopping Hall, Myrtle Road, E6, © (0181) 472 1748. Open Mon–Sat 9am–5pm.

An old-established general indoor market containing about 120 units selling a wide range of goods, from greengrocery to computer games.

Edmonton

Edmonton Green Shopping Centre, South Mall, Edmonton, Middlesex, © (0181) 666 0335. Open Mon–Sat 9am–5.30pm.

A general market with 37 pitches within the shopping centre.

Elephant and Castle

Outside Elephant and Castle Shopping Centre, SE1, (0171) 708 2313. Open Mon–Sat 7am–7pm.

About 30 stalls selling mostly new clothes, but also electrical goods, cosmetics, fish. There's a Nigerian takeaway, and a good secondhand CD pitch.

Enfield

Market Place, Enfield, Middlesex, © (0181) 366 9986. Open Thur, Fri 8.30am–4pm; Sat 8.30am–5pm.

A traditional outdoor general market with 94 pitches.

Epsom

Beside the clocktower, Market Place, Epsom , © (01372) 732342. Open Thur 7am–4pm; Sat 7am–4pm.

A general outdoor market with about 30 stalls in a newly restored charter market place. Best on Saturday.

Erith

Pier Road, Erith, Kent, © (0181) 303 7777. Open Wed, Sat 9am–5pm.

A fair-sized outdoor general market in the town centre.

Feltham

Bedfont Lane, Feltham, Middlesex, © (0171) 739 9900. Open Mon–Sat 9am–6pm.

A recently opened market containing 60 pitches.

Finchley

Tally-Ho Corner, Kingsway, N12 , © (0181) 505 6637. Open Tue, Fri, Sat 9am–4pm; car boot sale Sun 9am–2pm.

A general market attracting about 45 traders during the week. Secondhand goods are sold at the car boot sale on Sunday.

Grove Park

Baring Hall Hotel car-park, Downham Way, SE12. Open Fri 9am–3pm.

A fair-sized general market, with fish and meat stalls as well as fruit and veg.

Harrow

Elmgrove Road, Harrow, Middlesex, © (01562) 777130. Open Thur 9am–4pm.

An outdoor general market with 150 pitches.

Hounslow

Hounslow West tube station car park, Hounslow, Middlesex, © (01895) 639912. Open Sat 9am–4pm.

A general market with about 70 pitches.

Kingston

Charter Market and Apple Market: Market Place, Kingston, Surrey , © (0181) 546 6425. Open Mon–Sat 9am–5pm.

A traditional town-centre market with up to 42 stalls; good for fruit and veg.

Fairfield Market: Surface level of multi-storey car park, Fairfield West, Kingston, Surrey. Open Mon 9am–1pm.

A large general market held on the site of the old cattlemarket (now a car park). Over 200 stalls.

Lambeth Walk

Lambeth Walk shopping precinct (between Black Prince Road and Old Paradise Street), SE11. Open Fri, Sat 9am–5pm.

The street is famous for the song named after it, but the Victorian market scarcely musters four stalls on a Saturday.

London Bridge

Outside London Bridge Underground Station, SE1. Open Sat 10am–4.30pm (a few stalls other days).

A small collection of crafts and souvenir stalls join the flower-seller on a Saturday.

New Addington

Central Parade, New Addington, Surrey, © (01895) 639912. Open Tue, Fri 9am–5pm.

A medium-sized general market.

Penge

Maple Road, Penge, SE20, © (0181) 313 4768. Open Tue, Thur–Sat 9am–5pm; Wed 9am–1pm.

An open-air market with about 25 pitches, just off the High Street.

Rathbone

Off the south side of Barking Road, E16. Open Tues, Thur, Fri, Sat 8am–6pm.

Canning Town's market has most everyday commodities among its two dozen or so stalls. There's fish, meat, fruit and veg, crockery, pots and pans, music cassettes, clothes and a couple of secondhand goods pitches.

Richmond

The Square, Richmond. Open Mon–Sat 9am–5pm.

A small general market occupying permanent lock-up stalls in an alley.

Romford

Open-air: Market Place, Romford, Essex, © (01708) 772373. Open Wed, Fri 8am–5pm; Sat 8am–5.30pm.

A huge open-air market with nearly 300 stalls selling food, clothing and bric-a-brac. Worth the trip out from London.

Indoor: 33 Market Place, Romford, Essex, © (01708) 740492. Open Mon–Sat 9am–5pm.

An indoor general market with about 120 stalls.

South Harrow

Northolt Road, opposite South Harrow tube station, Middlesex, © (0171) 739 9900. Open Mon–Sat 9am–6pm.

About 80 kiosks under cover.

Southall

Car park off High Street, opposite North Road, Southall, Middlesex. Open Tue, Wed, Sat 9am–3pm; Fri 9am–1pm.

The Tuesday poultry market and Wednesday's horse market bring country people and travellers into Southall; there's a junk market on Friday and a general market on Saturdays. For Asian food and clothing, peruse the stalls set up each day outside shops on the Broadway.

Southwark Park Road

Market Place, off Southwark Park Road between Blue Anchor Lane and St James' Road, SE16. Open Mon–Sat 9am–5.30pm.

A dozen or so food and clothes traders gather at this old market, once known as 'The Blue'.

Staines

Market Square, High Street, Staines, Middlesex, © (01734) 451799. Open Wed, Sat 9am–4pm.

An open air, general retail market with about 40 pitches in the town centre.

Stoke Newington

117–119 Stoke Newington High Street, N16, © (0171) 739 9900. Open Mon–Sat 9am–6pm.

A small outdoor market just off the high street.

Stratford Mall

Stratford Shopping Centre, E15. Open Mon–Sat 8am–6pm.

About 30 brightly-lit stalls transform the drab 1960s concourse of Stratford's shopping centre into something more enticing. Fruit and veg, fish, clothing and handbags are among the wares.

Sutton

Tesco car park, corner of St Nicholas Way and Crown Road, Sutton, Surrey, © (0171) 240 7405. Open Tue, Sat 9am–4.40pm.

A smallish general market held outdoors.

Swanley

London Road, Swanley, Kent, © (01734) 451799. Open Wed 9am–5pm.

A busy general market with about 140 pitches.

Uxbridge

Pavilion Shopping Centre, Uxbridge High Street, Middlesex, © (01895) 250993. Open Thur–Sat 9am–5.30pm.

A general market (food, clothing, household goods), with 17 double-pitch stalls, and four single pitch stalls occupying a modern shopping precinct. Best Thursdays.

Watford

Beechen Grove, Watford, Herts, © (01923) 246066. Open Tue, Fri, Sat 7am–6pm.

A large general market with over 160 different stalls in the centre of Watford.

Watney

Watney Market, off the south side of Commercial Road, E1. Open Mon–Sat 9am–5pm.

Up to 40 stalls trade on this concrete pedestrian precinct. Two of the best sell Asian fruit and veg and clothing; you can also buy fish, chickens and eggs, crockery, petfoods, household goods and traditional greengrocery.

Wealdstone

31–35 High Street, Wealdstone, Middlesex, © (0181) 666 0335. Open Mon–Sat 9am–5.30pm.

An indoor market with 36 pitches.

Well Street

Well Street, between Morning Lane and Valentine Road, E9. Open Mon–Sat 9.30am–4pm.

A fine but small local market on a quiet Victorian street. Fruit and vegetables, household goods, clothes and a wealth of East End chat are the attractions.

Wembley

Lancelot Road, Wembley, Middlesex, ✆ (01734) 451799. Open Tue, Thur–Sat 9am–4pm.

A general indoor market near Wembley town centre.

West Drayton

High Street, West Drayton, Middlesex, ✆ (01895) 812233. Open Thur 9am–4pm.

An open-air general market in the town centre.

White City

Ariel Way, off Wood Lane, W12. Open Sun 9am–2pm.

Reclaiming a stark piece of urban wasteland every Sunday, about 20 traders provide locals with breads and pastries, fruit and vegetables, meat, electrical goods, clothing and household goods. A couple of stalls are full of secondhand what-nots.

Wood Green

Wood Green Shopping Centre, High Road, N22, ✆ (0181) 888 6667. Open Mon–Sat 9am–5.30pm.

A small general market within the shopping centre.

The language used on the markets continually changes. Rhyming slang, though still much used in TV situation comedies, is not heard as often as you may think on East End markets. Along with backslang (such as 'reeb' for beer and 'esclop' for police) it was used by traders to confuse outsiders. Most Londoners know what it is to take a butcher's (butcher's hook: look) or when to close their north and south (mouth), so the point is lost. However, several words survive that are used among London's traders. The following is a collection of street market jargon, some of which you may hear, some of which has almost died out, some of which can only be heard in certain districts, notably the East End. As can be seen, there's a strong Yiddish influence, a result of immigration by Jewish cloth traders from Eastern Europe.

bat	price
billig	cheap price
bin	pocket
bunce	profit
burster	good day's trade
carpet	£3
casual	newcomer or occasional trader
clocking	looking
cockle	£10
cow's	50p
demic	damaged, broken
demmer	trader who demonstrates wares (usually vegetable peelers or window cleaning devices)
deuce	£2
edge	crowd gathered round a stall, i.e. 'getting an 'edge (hedge)'
exis	£6
fence	a buyer and seller of stolen goods
fents	remnants of material

fiddle	a fair day's profit
flash	a display of goods
flim	£5
flyer	fast selling line
funt	£1
gaff	open market
ganiff	thief
gelt	money

grafter	speciality seller
grand	£1000
jacks	£5
joint	stall
kipper season	January and February (the low season for markets, when punters can only afford to eat kippers)
kite	cheque
knocking out	selling goods cheap at the end of the day
line	type of goods
monkey	£500
neves	£7
nause	complaint, problem
oncer	£1
packing down/out	setting goods out in a display (the opposite to packing up or packing in)
patter	sales talk
pitch	allotted space on market
pitching	method of selling using sales talk to attract crowd
plunder	goods sold at or below cost to attract custom
poke	money
pony	£25
punter	customer
readies	paper money
ream gear	quality goods
rouf	£4
score	£20
shmatty	poor quality
snides	unserviceable goods
spiel	sales talk
strike	£1
swag	cheaper lines
tilt	stall cover
toby or tobé	formerly a worker who set up a trader's stall; now the name for a market superintendent
ton	£100

Some of the best spiels on London markets can be heard at Brick Lane (on the wasteland off Bacon Street) and Wembley, both on a Sunday; at Church Street (the toy seller), Deptford and Hoxton Street, all on a Saturday; and, for sheer volume, at Charlie and Paul's stall on Berwick Street from Monday to Saturday.

Adburgham, A., *Shops and Shopping 1800–1914* (George Allen & Unwin, 1964).

Benedetta, M., *Street Markets of London* (John Miles, 1936).

Britnell, R.H., *The Commercialisation of English Society 1000–1500* (Cambridge University Press, 1993).

Burke, T., *The Streets of London* (Batsford, 1940).

Cousins, E.F. and Anthony, R., *Pease and Chitty's Laws of Markets and Fairs* (Charles Knight, 1993)

Davis, D., *A History of Shopping* (Routledge & Kegan Paul, 1966).

Drummond, J.C. and Wilbraham, A., *The Englishman's Food* (Pimlico, 1994; first published 1939).

Fisher, F.J., 'The Development of the London Food Market, 1540–1640' in *Economic History Review V*, 1935.

Forshaw, A. and Bergtsröm, T., *The Markets of London* (Penguin, 1983).

Guy, S. (ed.), *The Time Out Shopping and Services Guide* (Time Out, 1995).

Guy, S. (ed.), *The Time Out Eating and Drinking Guide* (Time Out, 1995).

Howse, C., 'A Dying Market' article in the *Sunday Telegraph Magazine* (5 November 1995).

Jasper, A.S., *A Hoxton Childhood* (Centerprise, 1969).

Kershman, A., *The London Market Guide* (Metro, 1994).

Mayhew, H., *London Labour and the London Poor* (1851).

Perlmutter, K., *London Street Markets* (Wildwood House, 1983).

Raven, H. et al, *Off Our Trolleys?: Food Retailing and the Hypermarket Economy* (Institute for Public Policy Research, 1995).

Shore, W.T., *Touring London* (Batsford, 1930).

Stow, J., *The Survey of London* (J.M. Dent, 1912; first published 1598).

Urban and Economic Development Group (URBED), *Vital and Viable Town Centres* (HMSO, 1995).

Weinreb, B. and Hibbert, C., *The London Encyclopedia* (Macmillan, 1983).

Index